Reader's Digest
Pathfinders

Creatures of the Air and Sea

Published by Reader's Digest Children's Books
Reader's Digest Road, Pleasantville, NY, U.S.A. 10570-7000 and
Reader's Digest Children's Publishing Limited, The Ice House
124-126 Walcot Street, Bath UK BA1 5BG

Reader's Digest Children's Books is a trademark and Reader's Digest
is a registered trademark of The Reader's Digest Association, Inc.

Conceived and produced by Weldon Owen Pty Limited
59 Victoria Street, McMahons Point, NSW, 2060, Australia
A member of the Weldon Owen Group of Companies
Sydney • San Francisco • Auckland

© 2003 Weldon Owen Inc.

WELDON OWEN PTY LTD
Chairman: John Owen
Publisher: Sheena Coupe
Creative Director: Sue Burk
Design Concept: John Bull
Editorial Coordinator: Jennifer Losco
Production Manager: Caroline Webber
Production Coordinator: James Blackman
Vice President International Sales: Stuart Laurence

BIRDS
Author: Edward S. Brinkley
Consultants: Kevin J. McGowan, Noble Proctor
Illustrators: Jane Beatson, Dan Cole/Wildlife Art Ltd,
Barry Croucher/Wildlife Art Ltd, Christer Eriksson, Lloyd Foye,
Gino Hasler, Rob Mancini, John Richards, Peter Scott/Wildlife Art Ltd, Chris Stead
© 2000 Weldon Owen Inc.

SHARKS AND OTHER SEA CREATURES
Author: Leighton Taylor
Consultant: Sylvia James
Illustrators: Martin Camm, Marjorie Crosby-Fairall,
Marc Dando/Wildlife Art Ltd, Ray Grinaway, Gino Hasler,
Ian Jackson/Wildlife Art Ltd, Roger Swainston, Chris Turnbull/Wildlife Art Ltd
© 2000 Weldon Owen Inc.

WHALES, DOLPHINS, AND PORPOISES
Author: Bronwyn Sweeney
Consultant: Linda Gibson
Illustrators: Anne Bowman, Christer Eriksson, Ian Jackson/Wildlife Art Ltd,
David Kirshner, Rob Mancini, Peter Scott/Wildlife Art Ltd, Christine Stead,
Kevin Stead, Glen Vause, Laurie Whiddon
© 2002 Weldon Owen Inc.

ISBN 0-7944-0353-0

Color Reproduction by Colourscan Co Pte Ltd
Printed by Imago Productions (F.E) Pte Ltd
Printed in Singapore

10 9 8 7 6 5 4 3 2 1

A WELDON OWEN PRODUCTION

A NOTE TO READERS AND PARENTS
This publication contains the opinions and ideas of its writers and is designed to provide useful information to the reader on the subject matter covered. When engaging in any activities which may be suggested in or relate to the subject of this publication, always exercise caution, and children should always be under adult supervision. Any references in this publication to any products or services do not constitute or imply an endorsement or recommendation. The publisher and the author specifically disclaim any responsibility for any liability, loss or risk (personal, financial or otherwise) which may be claimed or incurred as a consequence, directly or indirectly, of the use and/or application of any of the contents of this publication.

Reader's Digest
Pathfinders

Creatures of the Air and Sea

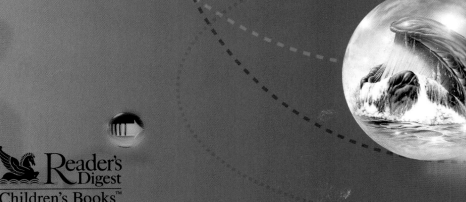

Reader's
Digest
Children's Books™

Pleasantville, New York • Montréal, Québec

Birds

Contents

What Is a Bird? 8

The Way Birds Act 26

Where Birds Live 44

Pick Your Path!

PREPARE FOR TAKEOFF on a flight of discovery through the world of *Birds*. Start at the beginning and learn about the physical characteristics of birds. Or, if you're interested in the colors of birds' feathers, jump right into "Brilliant Plumage" and move through the book from there.

You'll find plenty of other discovery paths to choose from in the special features sections. Read about discoveries by birdwatchers in "Inside Story," or get creative with "Hands On" activities. Delve into words with "Word Builders," or amaze your friends with fascinating facts from "That's Amazing!" You can choose a new path with every reading— READER'S DIGEST PATHFINDERS will take you wherever *you* want to go.

INSIDE STORY
The Champions of Birds

Imagine yourself standing in the middle of a rain forest, in the still darkness of night, recording the sounds of nocturnal birds. Find out how raising goslings won a zoologist a Nobel Prize. Trek through a blizzard and experience the excitement of discovering a rookery of Emperor Penguins. INSIDE STORY introduces you to the men and women who have made studying and protecting birds their life's work. Read these people's stories, and you'll be inspired to observe and care for birds yourself.

HANDS ON
Create and Make

Jump up and down and see how fast you can make your pulse race. Is it as fast as a hummingbird's? Use a plastic milk carton to make a bird feeder. With water and some plaster of paris, start your own collection of bird footprints. HANDS ON features experiments, projects, and creative activities that will teach you more about the world of birds.

Word Builders

What a strange word! What does it mean? Where did it come from? Find out by reading *Word Builders*.

That's Amazing!

Awesome facts, amazing records, fascinating figures— you'll find them all in *That's Amazing!*

Pathfinder

Use the *Pathfinder* section to find your way from one subject to another. It's all up to you.

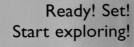

Ready! Set!
Start exploring!

What Is a Bird?

ABOUT SIX BILLION people live on Earth. That's a lot. But did you know that more than 100 billion birds live on our planet as well? Most of these birds can fly, but some can also swim, and others can run faster than a horse. Birds have evolved in amazing ways so that they can survive in different climates and environments all over the world. Turn the page and start to discover what makes birds unique in the animal world.

8

Rufous Motmot
(American rain forests)

Desert Wheatear
(Eurasian deserts)

Goliath Heron
(African waterways)

Plains Wanderer
(Australian grasslands)

Goldcrest
(European woods)

A World of Birds

IMAGINE IF SOME of us were the size of coffee cups and others were taller than houses. That's how it is with birds. The Bee Hummingbird is smaller than a moth, and the Ostrich is taller than a basketball player. In between these extremes are more than 9,000 unique bird species.

When birds began to fly millions of years ago, they settled in different places on all the continents of the world. They adapted to life in various habitats, including deserts, rain forests, grasslands, and even out at sea. In these places they found different kinds of food to eat and made different nests from the materials available. Each species had to adapt to its surroundings, or else face extinction.

The same needs for adapting exist today. The Desert Wheatear, for example, keeps its eggs from getting too hot in the daytime or too cold at night by nesting in burrows left by desert mice or other rodents. The Goldcrest has short, rounded wings—perfect for weaving through the trees in the woods where it lives. The Goliath Heron, on the other hand, lives near water. It has legs like stilts for wading into the water, and a bill the shape of a dagger for spearing fish. The Plains Wanderer seldom flies because it doesn't need to. It has evolved in color and habits so that it can hide from predators among the grass of its homeland. Even brightly colored birds often blend into their surroundings. The Rufous Motmot of South America is almost invisible to predators in its tropical rain-forest habitat.

**Bird Habitats
of the World**

Cities

Woodlands

Rain forests

Grasslands

Mountains

Hot deserts

Polar regions

- An **ornithologist** is a person who studies birds. The word comes from two Greek words, *ornis,* meaning "bird," and *logos,* meaning "word."
- A **habitat** is a place or environment where a particular species of plant, bird, or other animal lives. It comes from the Latin word *habitare,* which means "to live in" or "to inhabit."

- The Ostrich of Africa is as heavy as two adult humans. It can weigh up to 300 pounds (136 kg).
- A newly hatched Bee Hummingbird chick of Cuba weighs about as much as a fingernail clipping. Its weight is less than a tenth of an ounce (2 g).

- In adapting to a habitat, some birds have developed special feather colors. Go to pages 18–19.
- Does the food in a habitat have an effect on the way a bird has adapted? Turn to pages 36–37.
- Some habitats, such as forests, are home to a large variety of bird species. How do so many different species live in a single habitat? See pages 54–57.

AGAINST ALL ODDS

We see birds in the cities and the suburbs, on farmlands and the open plains, in forests, and on the beaches. But some birds live in places where conditions are so tough that even humans find it hard to survive. How do they exist?

KEEPING THEIR COOL

Most shorebirds lay their eggs in a shallow scrape on the ground. But in the desert climate along the Persian Gulf, eggs would roast. The Crab Plovers that live there dig deep holes into sand dunes along the shore and lay their eggs in the holes. The sand is moist and cool, so the eggs are protected from the hot sun.

BUNDLING UP

The thickset Adélie Penguin is well adapted for polar conditions. From a young age, these penguins grow dense, short, furlike feathers that provide protection from icy weather.

FLYING HIGH

Birds survive even in the highest of all mountains, the Himalayas. The Lammergeier has long, broad wings that enable it to glide easily in thin air for hours in search of food.

WHAT A SCOOP!

The Greater Flamingo lives in shallow lakes and coastal regions in America, Africa, and Asia. With its long legs and neck, it is perfectly adapted to its environment. When it feeds, the Flamingo bends forward, turns its head upside down, and drags its hooked bill through the water. It scoops up mud and water containing small shellfish, insects, single-celled animals, and algae in its upper jaw, which is lined with a row of slits. The bird then closes its bill and uses its lower jaw and tongue to pump the muddy water out through the slits. The food particles remain, ready to be eaten.

INSIDE STORY

To the Rescue

In 1951, a team from the American Museum of Natural History went to the islands of Bermuda off the North American coast to search for the Cahow, a bird described in the writings of early European settlers. David Wingate, a 16-year-old Bermudian, joined the searchers. The museum expedition discovered a small and endangered colony of birds. Many ornithologists think this bird is the mysterious Cahow, but they gave it a new name, the Bermuda Petrel. David Wingate was inspired by the search and became a bird specialist. He has made it his life's work to protect and study the rare petrels. Thanks to his devotion to his task, there are now about 200 petrels in the colony.

Fishes with lungs crawl onto land
408–362 million years ago (mya)

Insects take to the air
362–290 mya

Dinosaurs evolve
248–208 mya

First birds evolve
208–144 mya

Homo sapiens evolves
2–0 mya

The Early Birds

YOU WOULDN'T PUT out a bird feeder if you thought it might attract a ferocious dinosaur like *Tyrannosaurus rex*. But every time you pour seed into a feeder, you could be providing a meal for one of its relatives. Scientists believe that the earliest known bird, *Archaeopteryx*, was related to the theropods, the group of dinosaurs that includes *Tyrannosaurus*. The feet of *Tyrannosaurus* and its smaller dinosaur relatives are surprisingly similar to chicken feet.

Scientists are still trying to work out exactly where birds came from. To do this, they compare the fossils of birds that lived millions of years ago with today's birds. *Archaeopteryx* dates from the Jurassic period, 208 to 144 million years ago. Bird fossils have also been discovered from the Cretaceous period—144 to 65 million years ago. These birds were more like the birds we see today. The most famous finds were *Hesperornis* and *Ichthyornis*. *Hesperornis* couldn't fly, but swam underwater after fishes, like a cormorant. *Ichthyornis* was probably a strong flyer. Built like a tern, it probably flew over the water and dived for fishes—just like today's terns.

AN EVOLUTIONARY FLIGHT

Only birds have feathers, and feathers enable most birds to be skilled flyers. No one knows what creature had the first feathers—perhaps some theropod dinosaur. *Archaeopteryx* is the first animal known to have feathers. But over millions of years, a huge variety of birds has evolved.

Following the Past

Charles Darwin (1809–82) was an English naturalist whose theory of natural selection explained how different animal and plant species evolved. He suggested that species with features that helped them to survive within their habitat ate better and reproduced more effectively. For example, in the Galápagos Islands off the coast of South America, he noted many species of finches. He speculated that all the finches came from a single ancestor, and those that had evolved to suit the habitats had survived. So, in an area where there were plenty of seeds, finches with strong seed-cracking bills increased while finches with different bill shapes had to find food elsewhere or face extinction.

Ichthyornis

Archaeopteryx

Reptilian theropod dinosaur

UNEARTHING DELIGHTS

Imagine the thrill for ornithologists in 1861 when the fossils of *Archaeopteryx* were discovered in a limestone quarry in Germany. At first glance scientists might have classified the find as a reptile. After all, the creature's jaw contained strong teeth, and its head and tail looked rather like those of a theropod dinosaur. But, miraculously, the fine silt that covered *Archaeopteryx* showed a complete outline of feathers. Scientists chose the name *Archaeopteryx* because it means "ancient wing."

📖 Word Builders

• **Taxonomy** is a branch of science that gives names to species, and groups closely related species together. The word taxonomy comes from the Greek words *tassein*, which means "to put in order," and *nomia*, meaning "law."

• **Paleo-ornithologists** study ancient birds and use taxonomy in their efforts to piece together evolutionary puzzles. *Paleo* is Greek for "old."

✴ That's Amazing!

The tallest birds ever to have walked on Earth lived in New Zealand. These were enormous birds called Moas. They stood over 10 feet (3 m) tall, higher than a basketball hoop. Humans hunted the Moas to extinction. The last known species died out before 1800.

📑 Pathfinder

• To find out about the modern relatives of the ancient flightless birds, go to pages 22–23.

• Ancient birds such as *Hesperornis* had bills like modern birds, but they also had teeth like reptiles. The birds we see today don't have teeth—or do they? Turn to page 24 to find out.

Snow Goose

FISHING THROUGH TIME

Hesperornis was a flightless, fish-eating bird that lived over 100 million years ago, during the Cretaceous period. It was nearly 5 feet (1.5 m) tall and had teeth like *Archaeopteryx*. Its fossil was discovered in 1870 in Kansas in the U.S.A.

PLAINS STALKER

The Terror-Bird is appropriately named. It stood over 9 feet (2.7 m) tall, and it stalked the grasslands of South America. Its head was as large as that of a present-day horse.

A PIT OF GOLD

Fossils of the vulturelike *Teratornis merriami* were found at the Rancho La Brea tar pits in California, along with those of 104 other species of ancient birds.

TELL-TAIL SIGNS

Confuciusornis was found in China. This bird is believed to be 65 million years old. The fossil shows the remains of two creatures—their skeletons and the blackish outlines of their feathered bodies. One of the birds has a long pair of quills projecting from its tail. Scientists think that the long-tailed fossil may have been a male, because in most modern birds, the male has the longer tail.

CLINGING ON

A Hoatzin nestling has three claws on the end of its wings. They drop off when the bird grows older. *Archaeopteryx* and *Confuciusornis* also had three separate claws on their wing fingers. Scientists often compare features they see in fossils with creatures that are alive today in the hope of discovering more about the history of life on Earth.

Inner Workings

BIRDS NEED WINGS to fly, but wings are only one reason for their skillful soaring ability. Every part of a flying bird's body—from its heart and lungs to its light bones—is well adapted to make flight possible. But flying requires an enormous amount of energy. To make that energy, birds need lots of food, lots of oxygen, and an efficient system to get these fuel-making materials to their muscles.

A bird's respiratory or breathing system is amazingly well organized. When a bird flies, it breathes in and out with each beat of its wings. From the lungs, oxygen gets into the bloodstream. The blood, rich in oxygen and in sugars from the bird's food, is pumped by a powerful heart to the bird's muscles. The muscles then burn the oxygen and the sugars to create the energy the bird needs for flight.

A bird's lungs are connected to many air sacs that extend into its abdomen and large bones. Air in these sacs helps keep the bird's busy engine cool. The sacs also help to keep the bird's body light and evenly balanced for flight.

A bird's skeleton and feathers also play an important part in flight. A bird's body is compact and made of light bones. And the feathers provide a smooth surface so that the bird can slice gracefully through the air with the least amount of wind resistance.

THE BARE BONES

Compared to a reptile or mammal, a bird has fewer bones. Parts of its backbone are fused together, helping to provide a sturdy, compact frame for flying. A bird's collarbone is also fused into a furculum, which most people call a wishbone. As the bird flies, this bone acts like a spring, bending together to store energy when the wings come down, then releasing energy on the upstroke.

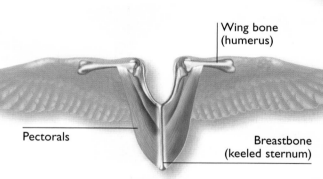

Wing bone (humerus)

Pectorals

Breastbone (keeled sternum)

POWER TO THE WINGS

Most of a bird's weight is in the center of its body, where the heavy flight muscles (pectorals) power its wings. The ends of these muscles are connected to the wing bone and to the sternum or breastbone. A bird's sternum is broad and curved like the keel of a ship, and it provides a secure anchor for the powerful muscles that give the bird strength enough to fly.

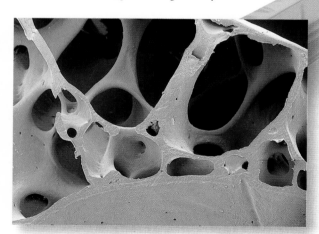

LIGHT AND STRONG

If a bird had solid bones like ours, it would be too heavy to fly. So most birds have bones that are hollow and light. You might think that hollow bones would bend or break easily, but in fact, they are amazingly strong. Inside, they have a honeycomb structure which adds lots of strength but only a little weight.

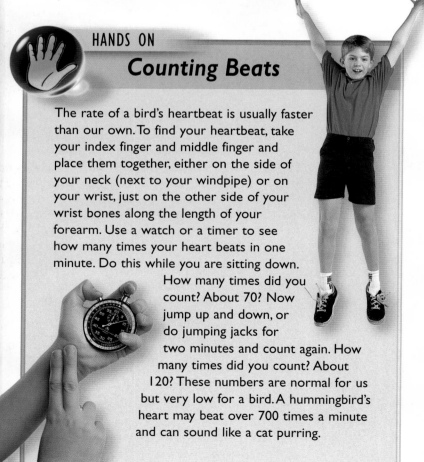

HANDS ON

Counting Beats

The rate of a bird's heartbeat is usually faster than our own. To find your heartbeat, take your index finger and middle finger and place them together, either on the side of your neck (next to your windpipe) or on your wrist, just on the other side of your wrist bones along the length of your forearm. Use a watch or a timer to see how many times your heart beats in one minute. Do this while you are sitting down. How many times did you count? About 70? Now jump up and down, or do jumping jacks for two minutes and count again. How many times did you count? About 120? These numbers are normal for us but very low for a bird. A hummingbird's heart may beat over 700 times a minute and can sound like a cat purring.

- Biologists study life and living things. The word **biology** comes from two Greek words. *Bios* means "life," and *logos* means "word" or "study."
- **Vertebrae** are the connected bones that make up the spine. The Latin word *vertebra* means "a joint." This word is related to *vertare*, which means "to turn." At a joint, bones are connected in a way that allows them to turn.

That's Amazing!

- In 1758, a famous English surgeon named John Hunter found that a bird with a blocked windpipe could still breathe if it had a hole in a wing bone or leg bone. This led to the discovery of birds' complex, connected system of lungs, bones, and air sacs.
- Some ancient birds had teeth, but none of today's birds do. Teeth would make the front of a bird heavier, and therefore less capable of flight.

- Everyone knows that birds have feathers, but what are feathers made of? Turn to pages 16–17.
- Birds' powerful muscles, light bones, keeled sternum, and efficient heart and lungs give them the power to fly. But how do they fly? See pages 20–21.
- To see how a bird develops from an egg into a fully grown bird, turn to pages 32–33 and 34–35.

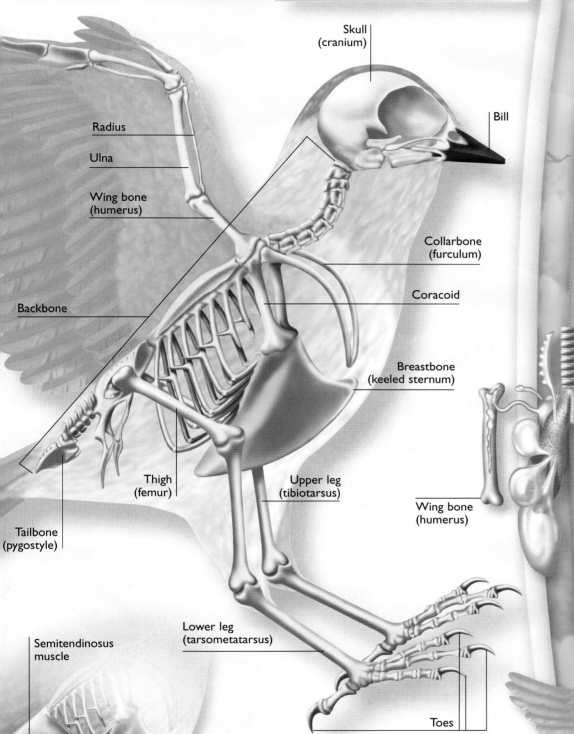

Skull (cranium)
Bill
Radius
Ulna
Wing bone (humerus)
Backbone
Collarbone (furculum)
Coracoid
Breastbone (keeled sternum)
Thigh (femur)
Upper leg (tibiotarsus)
Tailbone (pygostyle)
Lower leg (tarsometatarsus)
Toes
Semitendinosus muscle

LEG MUSCLES

All birds, whether adapted for perching, running, or swimming, have two powerful muscles in the legs that control movement. These muscles are in the top part of the leg, near a bird's center of gravity. They connect to the toes by long tendons that stretch over the ankle.

Flexor muscles
Flexor tendon

INTERNAL ORGANS

THE PUMP OF LIFE

Birds' hearts are much like our own, with two pumps working to move blood through the body. On the left side, oxygen-rich blood (yellow) is pumped from the lungs into the body. On the right side, oxygen-poor blood (blue) is pumped from the body to the lungs to receive more oxygen.

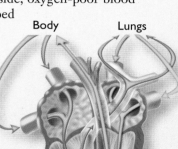

Body
Lungs
Right side
Left side

Trachea
Air sac
Wing bone (humerus)
Lung
Air sac

BREATHING DEEP

Birds have small, rigid lungs compared with humans. But the air sacs connected to the lungs help them work more efficiently. The sacs extend into birds' bones.

FUELING THE SYSTEM

Food travels down the esophagus to the crop, where it may be stored, or directly to the gizzard, which grinds food to a pulp. In the intestines, the bloodstream picks up fuel and carries it to the muscles. Wastes pass out through the cloaca.

Esophagus
Crop
Liver
Gizzard
Intestines
Cloaca

Cockatiel's wing feather   *Pheasant's tail feather*   *Macaw's body feather*   *Eagle's down feather*

Scapulars

Crest

Crown

Alula

Fascinating Feathers

BIRDS ARE THE only animals that have feathers. Feathers cover most of a bird's body, and they perform many important tasks. They can protect a bird from the heat and cold, and from water. They give a bird color and shape so that it can attract a mate, or hide from an enemy. And feathers are also a bird's main tool for flight.

There are three main kinds of feathers. Closest to the body are the down feathers. These light, fluffy feathers protect a bird from the cold. Over the down are the contour feathers. These are short and round. They are tougher than down, and they help give a bird its sleek, streamlined shape when flying.

The flight feathers on a bird's wings and tail are the most important for flying. The vanes of these feathers are locked together by tiny hooklets, so they are smooth and airtight when a bird is flying. When a bird wants to slow down or land, it spreads these feathers to create a drag. Swimming birds, such as penguins, use these same feathers to help them travel under the water.

INSIDE STORY
Feather Sleuth

Birds sometimes collide with aircraft. This can cause damage to jet engines, and may even cause a crash. So it is important for an airline to know which species of bird was involved so that any future accidents can be avoided. Who do the airlines call to investigate? Roxie Laybourne, a researcher at the Smithsonian Institution in Washington, D.C. in the United States of America.

Laybourne has been studying the structure of feathers for 40 years, and she has collected thousands of feather samples. As each kind of bird has a distinctive feather composition, she can usually uncover the identity of the culprit from just a few plumes. Laybourne has even helped solve crimes by humans where feathers have been presented as evidence.

THE ONLY WAY TO FLY
The body feathers of this Blue Jay, like those of all flying birds, point backward and neatly overlap each other. This creates a streamlined effect, allowing air to flow smoothly over the feathers when the bird is flying. If the feathers faced forward, they would catch the wind, create a drag, and make flying impossible. On the wings and tail, the bases of these important flight feathers are protected by covert feathers. The feathers that form a bridge between the back of the bird and the wing feathers are called scapulars.

BATH TIME
Feathers are important to a bird's survival, so they have to be kept in peak condition. Birds groom themselves every day, and they have developed a range of preening methods to clean and repair their feathers.

A GOOD SOAK
Bathing in water is a common preening method. This Mute Swan is cleaning its plumage by shaking itself around in the water. A good bath can also help cool a bird that is overheated.

- The word **molt** comes from the Latin word *mutare*, which means "to change."
- Scapular feathers cover the upper back area of a bird. The word **scapular** comes from the Latin word *scapulae*, which means "shoulders."
- A shaft is also known as a rachis. The word **rachis** comes from the German word *rhachis*, meaning "spine."

- Grebes sometimes eat their feathers. Scientists believe this protects their stomachs from being damaged by the bones of any fish that they eat.
- Some songbirds preen their feathers by a process called anting. They pick up ants or other insects and rub them onto their feathers. Some birds have even been observed sitting right on top of anthills. It is thought that the insects may secrete chemicals that kill harmful bacteria, mites, or fungi.

- How are feathers used by birds during courtship rituals? Check out the answers on pages 28–29.
- Some birds are born covered with a layer of feathers, but others are born naked. To find out more about this, go to pages 34–35.
- Which bird has a special type of feather that makes its flight almost impossible to hear? See pages 40–41 for the answer.

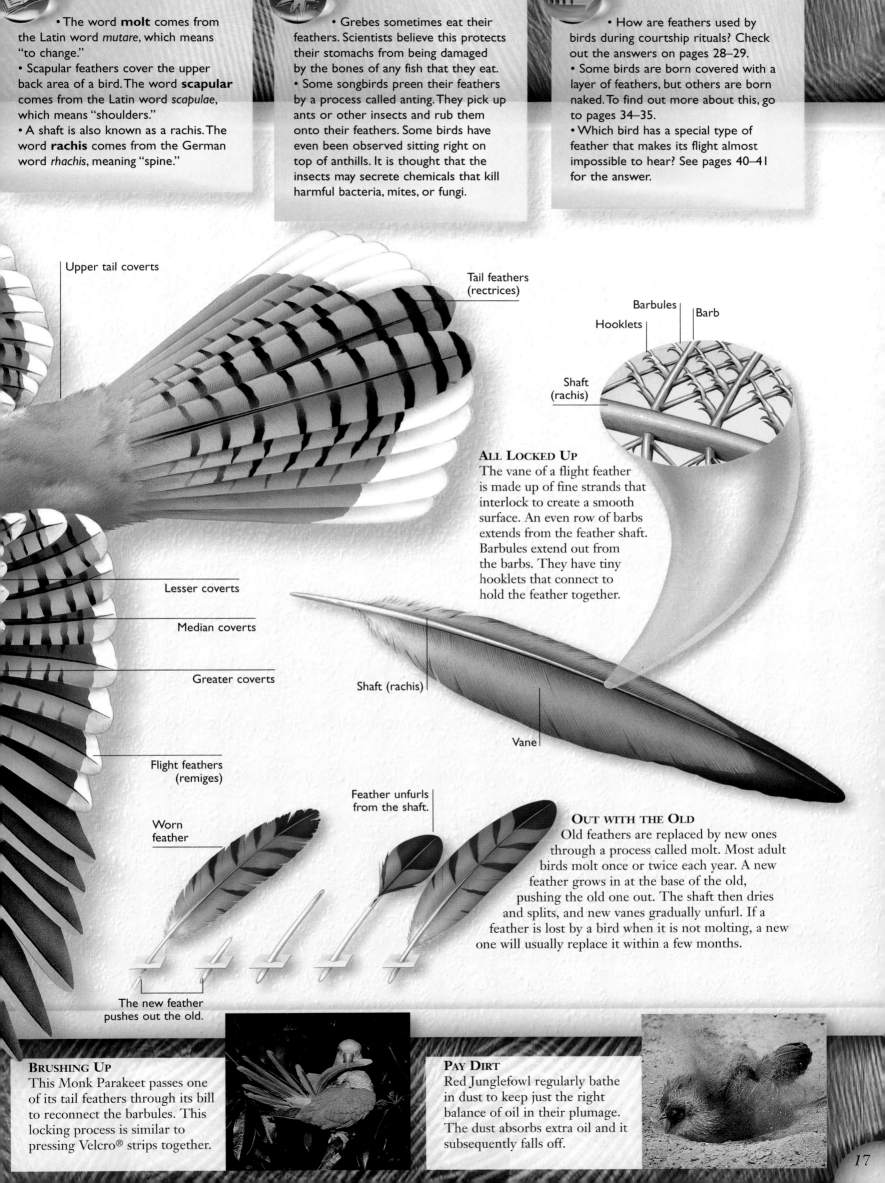

Upper tail coverts

Tail feathers (rectrices)

Barbules

Barb

Hooklets

Shaft (rachis)

Lesser coverts

Median coverts

Greater coverts

Shaft (rachis)

Vane

Flight feathers (remiges)

ALL LOCKED UP

The vane of a flight feather is made up of fine strands that interlock to create a smooth surface. An even row of barbs extends from the feather shaft. Barbules extend out from the barbs. They have tiny hooklets that connect to hold the feather together.

Feather unfurls from the shaft.

Worn feather

The new feather pushes out the old.

OUT WITH THE OLD

Old feathers are replaced by new ones through a process called molt. Most adult birds molt once or twice each year. A new feather grows in at the base of the old, pushing the old one out. The shaft then dries and splits, and new vanes gradually unfurl. If a feather is lost by a bird when it is not molting, a new one will usually replace it within a few months.

BRUSHING UP

This Monk Parakeet passes one of its tail feathers through its bill to reconnect the barbules. This locking process is similar to pressing Velcro® strips together.

PAY DIRT

Red Junglefowl regularly bathe in dust to keep just the right balance of oil in their plumage. The dust absorbs extra oil and it subsequently falls off.

17

Brilliant Plumage

A BEAUTIFUL BIRD flashes by and captures your attention. But how can you identify that bird? The entire feathery covering of a bird is called plumage. The plumage of each bird species is a distinctive color and shape, and provides valuable clues to help you find out the name of the bird you've just glimpsed.

The color of plumage is produced by two kinds of pigments—carotenoids and melanins—and by the structure of the feathers themselves. Carotenoids make the colors red, orange, and yellow. Melanins make black to pale brown. A combination of these two pigment types creates even more colors—except for blues and purples. These colors only occur if the feathers are structured so that they can scatter and reflect light in a special way.

Plumage comes in all shapes and colors for many reasons. It allows birds to identify other birds from their own species, and to communicate with them. It also serves as camouflage, helping birds to hide within their habitat. Male birds usually have brighter colors and use their plumage to attract a female. Some birds puff up their plumage to ward off other birds that may be encroaching on their territory.

The male Indian Peafowl, widely known as the peacock, has extraordinary plumage. He spreads more than 200 train feathers to form a 6-foot (1.8-m) fan adorned with patterns that look like eyes.

TECHNICOLOR DREAM COATS

There are 43 bird of paradise species. Each is spectacularly colored and shaped. The male Raggiana Bird of Paradise lives in Papua New Guinea. His body feathers are an orange-red color, and his head feathers are yellow, green, and black. The long feathers on his flanks, the lower part of a bird's sides, shimmer in the sunlight. When the male is not displaying his feathers, he keeps them sleek against his body.

INSIDE STORY

A Feather in the Cap

Many peoples throughout history have used birds' feathers for decoration. Today some tribes in Papua New Guinea still wear the plumes of birds of paradise during their dances and ceremonies. The tribes' hunters select and kill only a few adult male birds, leaving many younger birds to reproduce. But elsewhere in the world, other cultures have not behaved so responsibly. In the 1800s, the fashion for using feathers to

decorate ladies' hats resulted in millions of birds being shot. Some species died out altogether—they became extinct. The first Audubon Societies in America were formed in the early 1900s in protest against the killing of egrets for their fancy plumes. The work of these societies led to the formation of hundreds of groups devoted to the important job of protecting birds—especially those in danger of extinction.

PAINT A PICTURE

The black feathers on the male Wilson's Bird of Paradise make his bright colors look even more vivid. His blue cap, yellow nape, and scarlet back look as though they have been painted on him.

Word Builders

- The word **plumage** is from the Latin word *pluma*, meaning "soft feather." **Plume** means "pen" as well as "feather," because the shafts, or quills, of some bird feathers used to be dipped in ink and used for writing.
- **Iridescent** comes from the Greek word *iris*, meaning "rainbow." Iris is also the colored portion of a human eye, and it is the name of a flower.

That's Amazing!

- The color of a bird's plumage is sometimes the result of the food it eats. The Greater Flamingo and the Roseate Spoonbill must eat the right kinds of crustaceans and microscopic food from the seabed or they will lose their bright pink coloration.
- Birds see the same range of colors that we do, but they also see ultraviolet light. Colors may appear more intense to them than they do to us.

Pathfinder

- Plumage color and pattern give some birds extraordinary camouflage abilities. Which night bird can disguise itself as a stump of wood during the day? Go to page 40.
- Which species of bird turns white during winter to blend in with the snow? Turn to page 63 to find out.

COLORFUL ILLUSIONS

Female birds are usually less colorful than males, mainly so that they can remain hidden from predators when they are incubating eggs or rearing young. Both the colors and patterns of their plumage help birds blend in with their habitat.

SECRET TREASURES

The faces and body feathers of male and female Resplendent Quetzals look similar, but the male is more iridescent and he has long tail streamers. Like many rain forest birds, these quetzals are often hard to spot among the lush, sun-dappled foliage.

MIRROR MAGIC

The female Harlequin Duck is plain, but the male has white markings. This is called ruptive coloration and is a subtle form of camouflage. The male can be difficult to see against surfaces that are not a solid color, such as rippling water.

TURNING BLUE

Most of the year, the male Indigo Bunting is brown, like the female, and is difficult to see in his scrub habitat. But during the mating season, he sheds his drab plumage and turns a glorious blue.

HIDE IN PLAIN SIGHT

The fine patterns on the plumage of the male and female Pin-tailed Sandgrouse help conceal them among the sand, pebbles, and sparse vegetation of their dry habitat.

DANCING IN THE TREES

In a dance designed to attract a female, the male Blue Bird of Paradise makes himself look larger by raising his azure wings and long, black tail feathers. All birds of paradise have special dances that display their plumage to the best advantage.

Indian flying fox (bat)

Blue morpho butterfly (insect)

Flying dragon (lizard)

Flying gurnard (fish)

Rulers of the Sky

BIRDS ARE THE most amazing flying creatures on Earth. Insects and bats can fly, too, and some lizards, frogs, and squirrels can glide. But few can fly as high or as far or as fast as a bird. Birds may use flight to find food, to get away from enemies, or to migrate thousands of miles.

Most birds flap their wings to stay airborne, using their tail to help them change direction. But some birds are better at hovering, swooping, or gliding than others. The shape and size of a bird's wings determine the kind of flight to which it is best suited.

Birds with small, short, rounded wings are best suited for short flights, although they sometimes migrate hundreds of miles. Birds with longer wings can take advantage of air currents to travel far. Albatrosses have very long, narrow wings. They can use the wild energy generated by the interaction between wind and waves to stay airborne. They rise on powerful updrafts, and when they can go no higher, they glide down. To get lift again, they simply dip one wing and bank sharply into another updraft. This kind of flying is called dynamic soaring. The great arcs of this flight pattern look like a series of rainbows laid end to end.

GOING UP

Bird wings are nearly flat underneath and curved across the top. This means that air must travel more quickly across the top than across the bottom as the bird flies forward. This creates a lower pressure above the wing, providing the lift that keeps the bird in the air.

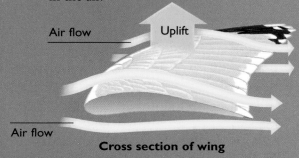

Air flow — Uplift

Air flow

Cross section of wing

HIGHER AND HIGHER

The Wandering Albatross has the largest wingspan of any bird—up to 11 feet (3.3 m) wide. This seabird can fly effortlessly over the southern oceans, where strong winds and gales are common. While traveling for hundreds of miles in search of food, it can glide for hours without beating its wings.

INSIDE STORY
Dreaming of Flight

Since ancient times, humans have wanted to fly. They admired birds and sometimes worshipped them. The brilliant Italian inventor and artist named Leonardo da Vinci (1452–1519) was ahead of his time in thinking about how humans could fly. He closely observed birds in flight, and studied how their bodies were constructed. Then he sketched designs for wings that look surprisingly similar to today's aircraft. But in Leonardo's time there were no engines that could power flight. It took another 400 years before two brothers, Orville and Wilbur Wright, successfully flew the world's first airplane, the *Flyer*, in 1903.

TO FLAP OR NOT TO FLAP?

Wings folded

American Crow

Scarlet Minivet

BEST WINGS FORWARD
Birds flap their wings to stay in the air and move forward. Huge muscles power the stroke, pulling the wings forward and down and upward and back. The downstroke takes more energy and gives lift. The upstroke isn't such hard work. Feathers streamline the body, making flight easier.

A TUCK IN TIME
A small bird can fold its wings in short bursts to save energy. When flapping, the bird rises. When its wings are tucked close to its body, the bird falls. These rests are brief and hard to spot, but the bird's flight pattern is easy to see. It is up and down rather than straight forward.

Word Builders

• The word **aviation** comes from the Greek word *avis*, meaning "bird." Other words use *avi-* as their stem word: **aviator**, a pilot; **aviary**, a large bird cage; and **aviculture**, the rearing or keeping of birds.
• The name **albatross** is a variation of the Portuguese word *alcatraz*, meaning "seafowl." The *c* may have been changed to a *b* because of the bird's coloring— the Latin word for white is *alba*.

That's Amazing!

It is difficult to measure how fast a bird can fly because it depends upon the circumstances under which the bird is traveling. Some birds can fly as fast as small airplanes when they are being chased, or are chasing. In 1961, a pilot clocked a male Red-breasted Merganser, startled by his plane, flying up to 80 miles per hour (129 km/h). Peregrine Falcons can reach speeds above 110 miles per hour (180 km/h) when diving for prey.

Pathfinder

• To learn more about the muscles that allow birds to take off, fly, and land, turn to pages 14–15.
• Which bird has a special wing design that makes it hard for its prey to hear its approaching flight? See pages 40–41.
• How far do birds fly when migrating? The answers are on pages 42–43.

WE HAVE LIFTOFF
Most birds seem to take off effortlessly. They simply leap into the air. But the pelican spends a lot of time in water, and that makes it more difficult for this large bird to get airborne. Using its feet to help lift its body above the water's surface, the pelican has to flap its massive wings fast to get liftoff. Once in the air, it is a strong flier and glider.

HITTING THE BRAKES
Birds need to fly fast in order to stay in the air. To land, they usually drop their tails and open out their wings. The air strikes the underside of their wings, slowing them down so they can alight safely. Airplanes open flaps on their wings during landing to accomplish the same thing.

Hot air rising

Golden Eagle

HITCHING A RIDE
The most energy-efficient method of flying is to glide on rising hot air currents known as thermals. Birds with long, wide wings, such as eagles, can fly in a circular pattern to stay inside the column of rising air as they are lifted higher and higher. From a great height, they can then glide slowly downward for long distances before hitching a ride on another thermal.

HOVERING STATIONS
Some birds can hover like insects. To do this, the bird must beat its wings rapidly, then rotate them in a number of different ways at the shoulder joint. Hovering requires lots of energy. Hummingbirds such as the Purple-backed Thornbill are able to hover. They can also fly forward, backward, and straight up or down.

Purple-backed Thornbill

Grounded

IT SEEMS ONLY natural for birds to fly. But quite a few birds never take to the air. No one is sure why they developed this way. The most likely theory, though, is that they lost the ability to fly simply because they stopped needing it.

Many flightless birds evolved on remote islands, such as the Galápagos Islands or New Zealand. Island birds were safe on the ground as there were no humans or other predators such as cats, rats, or foxes. And they didn't need to fly to gather food as supplies were always close by. So they gradually quit flying because it takes so much energy. When humans and other predators arrived, flightless birds couldn't escape them. Some, like New Zealand's Moa, became extinct as the newcomers took their places in their old habitats.

Some birds lost the ability to fly and then grew huge. This happened to the Ostriches, which can grow to be about 9 feet (2.75 m) tall. They survived because they developed long, powerful legs on which they could run faster than a racehorse to escape predators. When cornered, they could also defend themselves by kicking. They still have small wings, though, which they use mainly for balance.

INSIDE STORY

Seeding the Fruit

Cassowaries are large, flightless birds that move quickly along rain forest floors. They eat large amounts of fruit, and can, after digesting, disperse seeds a long way from the parent tree. Dr. David Westcott, who works for the Tropical Forest Research Center in north Queensland, Australia, studies these birds to measure the effect they have on rain forest tree populations. To monitor a bird, Dr. Westcott catches it. He feeds it and notes how long it takes food to travel through its digestive system. Then he attaches a radio transmitter and releases the bird into the wild. Dr. Westcott tracks the birds and notes where they drop seeds in their waste. He learns more about how cassowaries live, and can measure the way they affect the rain forest's ecology.

FLYING UNDERWATER

There are 18 species of penguins, and none of them can fly. The largest is the Emperor Penguin, which lives in Antarctica. It endures temperatures as low as -80°F (-62°C) during the bleakest winter months. All penguins have small, stiff, flipperlike wings. These wings enable them to be superb swimmers. Penguins dive into the water to catch their food, surfacing often to breathe. They can travel underwater at speeds of up to 20 miles per hour (32 km/h).

FLIGHTLESS IN NEW ZEALAND

There are five flightless birds living in New Zealand's Fiordland National Park—the Little Penguin, Kakapo, Takahe, Weka, and Brown Kiwi. The Kiwi is the country's national bird. It is nocturnal, and is one of only a few bird species to have a good sense of smell.

The Kakapo is the largest parrot in the world, and the only one that cannot fly. It can, however, climb trees and glide to the ground. Because it lives on the ground and nests in holes, it is vulnerable to predators—there are fewer than 50 still alive.

Word Builders

Kakapo, **Weka**, and **Kiwi** are names taken from the Maori language. The Maoris were the first humans to live on the islands of New Zealand. *Kakapo* is a combination of two Maori words, *kaka*, meaning "parrot," and *po*, meaning "night." *Weka* means "hen." *Kiwi* was originally the name the Maoris gave the country. The name was then given to the bird that became New Zealand's national mascot. *Kiwi* is also a nickname given to all New Zealanders.

That's Amazing!

• The Emperor Penguin can dive to a depth of up to 1,750 feet (530 m), and can stay underwater for nearly 20 minutes.
• The female Brown Kiwi lays enormous eggs, which are almost one-sixth of her own body weight. These eggs take 11 weeks to incubate, the longest time for any bird. In comparison, Yellow-breasted Chats' eggs take just 11 days, and chickens' eggs take 21 days.

Pathfinder

• The Ostrich lays the largest egg. Which bird lays the smallest? See page 32.
• The Brown Kiwi is a nocturnal bird. What does this mean? Are there other nocturnal birds? See page 40–41.
• Many birds, not just flightless ones, are in danger of extinction. To find out more about birds in danger, turn to pages 46–47.
• Which bird is known as the "penguin of the north?" Turn to page 51.

Emu

Ostrich

Rhea

INTERNATIONAL RELATIONS
Rheas, the Emu, and the Ostrich are very large flightless birds. They live on the continents of South America, Australia, and Africa, respectively. Because they look alike, it's possible they came from a common ancestor when the continents were joined. Or they may have evolved to be so similar to one another because they all live in open grassland, and feed on grass and insects.

The Takahe is a large, flightless rail. It was thought to have been extinct for 50 years, but in 1948, a small number were found. Today, there are about 180 Takahes living in a grassy hillside reserve near Te Anau. These solitary birds nest between tufts of grass, but live in the forests during winter.

The Weka is a flightless rail that has well-developed wings, but only uses them for balance when running. It survives because it is a strong fighter. Wekas are known to kill rats as well as other birds that live on the ground.

Bills and Feet

TRY TO PICK up an apple without using your hands. It's not easy. Birds don't have hands. They use their bills and feet to hold what they eat, to move things around, to scratch for food, and to defend themselves. The size and shape of a bird's bill and feet can tell you a lot about the bird's lifestyle.

The upper half of a bird's bill is called the maxilla, and the lower half is called the mandible—although the term mandible is often used for both. The bill is made of keratin, the same substance of which feathers are made. The Pileated Woodpecker's strong, straight bill is ideal for hammering into tree bark to dislodge insects. The Palm Cockatoo uses its stout bill to crush fruit, seeds, and berries, and the Far Eastern Curlew finds food by probing deep into the mud flats of waterways with its long, curved bill. The African Spoonbill has a flat, round bulge on the end of its long bill. It sweeps the floor of a lake with its lower mandible, and then traps food between the two spoonlike tips. The Bald Eagle has a hook-shaped bill, well designed to tear apart prey.

The upper part of a bird's leg is covered by body feathers. The lower part is covered by small scales. The joint that seems to be halfway up its leg is its ankle. Extending from the ankle is a long foot, then two, three or four toes. Birds use these toes in many different ways.

HOLDING ON
Birds do not have real teeth. The Common Merganser, however, has a row of spikes on both mandibles that point backward. The bird uses these serrated edges and the hooked tip of its bill to hold on to slippery fishes.

SPEAR FISHING
The bill, head, and neck are all that can be seen of the Anhinga when it swims with its body submerged. This is why it is sometimes known as the "snakebird." It dives underwater to spear fishes on its sharp bill before resurfacing to feed.

HANDS ON
Collecting Footprints

When birds walk on wet ground, they leave behind telltale tracks. To make a cast of a bird's footprints, mix about 1 1/2 cups of plaster of paris with 1 cup of water in a bucket. When the mixture is smooth, pour it over the footprints. When the cast has hardened sufficiently, lift it up and leave it in a safe place to dry completely. Then brush off any sand or dirt. Now try to identify the species of bird that left the prints.

Word Builders

• More than half the world's birds are classified as passerines. They are able to perch. The word **passerine** comes from the Latin *passerinus*, meaning "sparrowlike."
• The word **mandible** comes from the Latin *mandere*, meaning "to chew." The word **maxilla** comes from a Latin word meaning "jaw."

That's Amazing!

• The Eurasian Wallcreeper is as agile as Spiderman and can climb vertically up a rock face. It has three toes pointing forward and one pointing backward, each with sharp claws that enable the bird to keep its grip.
• Egyptian Vultures use their bills to pick up stones weighing up to 2 pounds (1 kg). They drop them onto Ostrich eggs, cracking open the thick shells so they can eat the contents.

Pathfinder

• Which bird turns its head upside down to strain its food from water in its specially adapted bill? Turn to pages 10–11 to find out more.
• Birds do not have teeth, so how do they grind their food? See page 15.
• One bird is so skilled in using its bill that it can weave leaves together to make its nest. Go to pages 30–31.

BEST FOOT FORWARD

The reptilian ancestors of birds had five toes, and their feet were well adapted to walking on the ground. Today, birds' feet have evolved into a variety of shapes for different tasks such as swimming, climbing, perching, and running, as well as landing and taking off.

PADDLE PERFECT

The Mallard has webbed feet, like all other ducks. The skin between their toes lets them use their feet like paddles when they are in water.

PADDED FOR COMFORT

Rheas are very large, heavy birds with powerful legs. Because they do not fly, their feet do a lot of hard work. Extra flesh on the feet helps absorb the impact of the bird's weight when it is running.

GETTING A GRIP

The Black-capped Lorikeet has two toes pointing forward and two turned backward. This allows the bird to grasp a branch firmly, and to hold food securely when it is feeding.

WALKING ON WATER

Northern Jacanas are wading birds. They have long toes and claws, so they can walk on lily leaves and other floating plants without sinking.

EXACT CONTROL

The Toco Toucan's large bill has made this bird famous worldwide. Despite its size, the hollow bill is remarkably light. It is strengthened internally by a honeycomblike support similar to that found in the bones of flying birds. The toucan picks up food in the tip of its bill. It moves the food into position with its tongue, which is about 6 inches (15 cm) long with brushlike bristles on the end. Once the food is in the right position, the toucan throws its head back and tosses the food down its throat. Toucans have two toes pointing forward and two pointing backward, giving the bird a good grip on branches while it feeds.

TWIST AND TURN

The African Gymnogene is a bird of prey with unique legs. It can bend its legs at extraordinary angles. Because it can twist 70 degrees behind and 30 degrees from side to side, it can forage in enclosed places such as tree hollows, which its prey might mistakenly think are safe havens.

The Way Birds Act

A BIRD SWOOPS past you, heading off to perform some important task. Is it trying to find material for building a nest? Does it have young to feed? Is it about to migrate to a warmer climate? Every action a bird makes tells us something fascinating about the way it lives its life. Look more closely and you'll see that behavior that seems strange to us makes perfect sense to a bird.

27

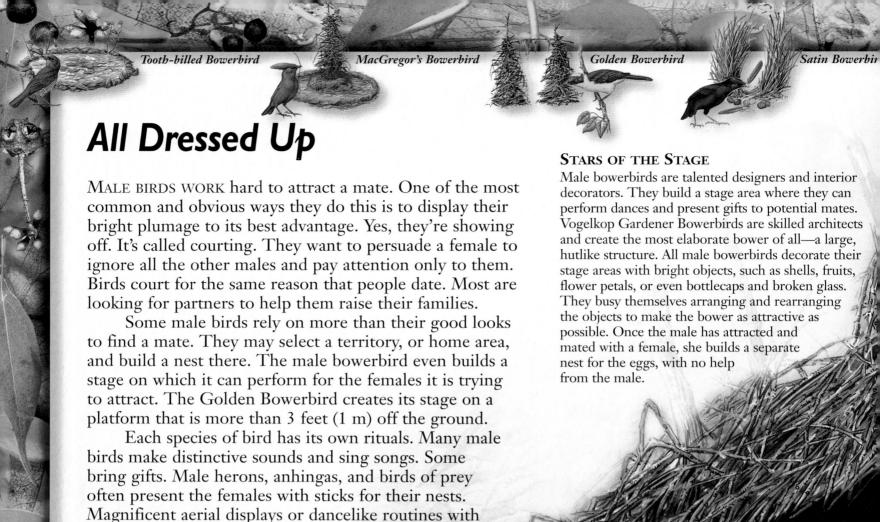

All Dressed Up

MALE BIRDS WORK hard to attract a mate. One of the most common and obvious ways they do this is to display their bright plumage to its best advantage. Yes, they're showing off. It's called courting. They want to persuade a female to ignore all the other males and pay attention only to them. Birds court for the same reason that people date. Most are looking for partners to help them raise their families.

Some male birds rely on more than their good looks to find a mate. They may select a territory, or home area, and build a nest there. The male bowerbird even builds a stage on which it can perform for the females it is trying to attract. The Golden Bowerbird creates its stage on a platform that is more than 3 feet (1 m) off the ground.

Each species of bird has its own rituals. Many male birds make distinctive sounds and sing songs. Some bring gifts. Male herons, anhingas, and birds of prey often present the females with sticks for their nests. Magnificent aerial displays or dancelike routines with their intended partner are also part of some birds' display strategy. Albatrosses nibble on each others' necks, a practice known as allopreening.

After mating, many birds stay together to incubate the eggs and raise their young. But in some species, the females raise their young by themselves.

STARS OF THE STAGE

Male bowerbirds are talented designers and interior decorators. They build a stage area where they can perform dances and present gifts to potential mates. Vogelkop Gardener Bowerbirds are skilled architects and create the most elaborate bower of all—a large, hutlike structure. All male bowerbirds decorate their stage areas with bright objects, such as shells, fruits, flower petals, or even bottlecaps and broken glass. They busy themselves arranging and rearranging the objects to make the bower as attractive as possible. Once the male has attracted and mated with a female, she builds a separate nest for the eggs, with no help from the male.

RED ALERT
After a male Great Frigatebird has constructed a nest, he inflates his red throat pouch, shakes his wings, and calls to circling females by making loud, gobbling noises.

DANCING DAYS

THE LONGEST WALTZ
Each year albatrosses renew their bonds with the partner they have chosen for life by performing complex mating rituals. These can last for days and usually involve both birds. The male Royal Albatross has a special, elaborate display. He begins by stretching out his massive wings and throwing his head and bill up toward the sky. Next, he lowers his head and marches around the nest like a toy soldier. Then he cocks his tail and shivers like a dog shaking off water.

Word Builders

• When birds **preen**, they clean and oil their feathers. The word is related to *prune*, "to trim away." In the word **allopreening**, *allo-* is a prefix from the Greek word "other." When birds allopreen, they clean each other's feathers.
• **Territory** comes from the Latin word *territorium*, which means "the land around a town." *Territorium*, in turn, comes from the Latin word *terra*, meaning "land."

That's Amazing!

• In a few bird species, the female has plumage more colorful than the male's. Among phalaropes, the females are the more brightly colored and use their plumage to attract a mate. The males care for the young, and their dull colors help hide them from predators.
• Albatrosses take one partner for life. But after most hummingbirds mate, they may not see their partners again.

Pathfinder

• The male bird that displays the finest feathers usually gets a mate. But how do birds keep their feathers in peak condition? See pages 16–17.
• Which male bird has feathers that shimmer in the sunlight when he is displaying? Turn to pages 18–19.
• Some male birds sing during courtship. To learn more about songbirds, turn to page 55.

INSIDE STORY
Shooting Stars

Film allows bird watchers to study and understand birds in distant parts of the world. But a lot of patience is required when trying to capture birds in their natural surroundings. For instance, during courtship, several male manakins gather in a lek—a place where they display for females. If you manage to find a lek to film, you also have to be there at the right time to see the males displaying. When photographer Marie Read set out to record Long-tail Manakins in their leks, she visited the dense forests of Costa Rica several times before she was successful. Read then shot a series of beautiful and informative photographs of the manakins' elaborate leapfrogging dance. Since then, she has also documented the Red-capped and Golden-collared Manakins in their leks.

FAN MALE
In the breeding season, male Great Egrets grow long, white feathers, called aigrettes, on their backs. The birds spread them like a fan to entice the female.

SYNCHRONIZED BALLET
Western Grebes perform a beautiful series of dances together on top of the water. Early in the nesting season, the two birds stage a little ballet, holding long strands of vegetation in their bills. This is called weed dancing. At the height of courtship, they rise in a graceful pose, called rushing, and run across the water's surface for some distance before diving below. Rival males also use this dance to defend their territories.

IN A WHIRL
Many raptors, such as these African Fish-Eagles, perform incredible aerial feats during courtship. The bonding pair may fly together in circles, or in tandem, one above the other. They may even hook talons and do cartwheels in midair like circus acrobats. Two rival males may also lock talons when they are battling over the right to a territory.

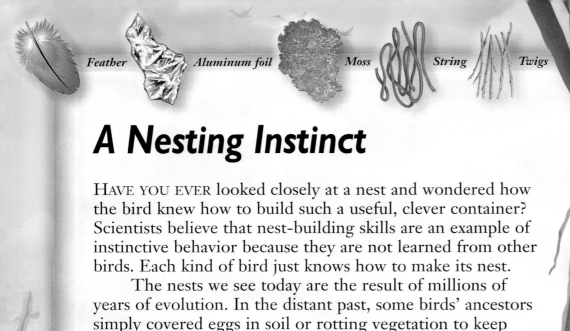

Feather   *Aluminum foil*   *Moss*   *String*   *Twigs*

A Nesting Instinct

HAVE YOU EVER looked closely at a nest and wondered how the bird knew how to build such a useful, clever container? Scientists believe that nest-building skills are an example of instinctive behavior because they are not learned from other birds. Each kind of bird just knows how to make its nest.

The nests we see today are the result of millions of years of evolution. In the distant past, some birds' ancestors simply covered eggs in soil or rotting vegetation to keep them warm, while others used natural cavities in trees as a place to lay their eggs. As birds began to use their body heat to incubate their eggs, they gradually developed the skills needed for more sophisticated nest building.

Most birds construct a nest of some sort. If you have seen one, it was probably cup-shaped and made of twigs or grass. But there are hundreds of kinds of nests, all with different designs and built with a variety of materials. Some are just scrapes in the sand or big piles of sticks. Some are tiny, weighing not much more than a paper cup. Others are enormous and can be the weight of a horse. Many contain found objects, such as hair, paper, foil, string, or feathers.

Cliff Swallows make jugs out of mud, attaching them to bridges. Puffins and kingfishers dig tunnels and place their nests inside. Orioles build deep baskets that hang from tree forks. Bushtits create long sacks from twigs, roots, and moss that they paste together with spiderwebs. No matter what their shape, nests help the adult birds keep their eggs warm, and most protect the eggs and chicks from predators.

HANDS ON
Making a Nest

Birds are master weavers. To appreciate their amazing skills, try building your own nest.

1. You will need a stick that has a fork of two or three strong branches; lots of tiny flexible twigs; and some grass, leaves, reeds, and whatever else birds may use—mud, string, dry moss, or even some of your own hair (if you have just had it cut).

2. Arrange the twigs, using the forked branches of your stick as a foundation. You could start with a flat platform, as some birds do, or try to bend the twigs around the branches to form a cup. The idea is to make a little basket.

3. Keep weaving material into the nest to make the sides strong. Line the nest with moss or grass.

You may make lots of nests that fall apart before you manage to come up with a good, strong design.

MASTER WEAVER
The male Black-headed Weaver, or Village Weaver, stitches strips of vegetation together to make a roofed basket. He ties knots, using grasses, to make the nest secure. Then he displays in front of the nest to attract a mate. The males usually pair with many females during the mating season. This system is called polygyny. These weavers nest in colonies. The females raise their young alone and work with other females in the colony to look out for predators. The seeds that the Black-headed Weaver eats are in very rich supply, so the males have no need to defend a territory and food source.

Word Builders

• Cavity nesters are birds that nest in holes in trees or cliffs, or in bird boxes. These holes are called cavities. **Cavity** comes from the Latin word *cavus*, meaning "a hollow place."
• Some birds practice polygyny, in which one male mates with many females. The word **polygyny** comes from the Greek words *poly*, meaning "many," and *gyne*, meaning "female."

That's Amazing!

• Some tropical birds, such as flycatchers and wrens, nest near bees' and wasps' nests. These insects probably keep away flies and predators.
• Some birds of prey allow other birds, such as sparrows, to place nests inside their own nests, which are much larger than those of their guests. The little birds may warn the larger birds by chirping loudly when danger is near.

Pathfinder

• Which bird builds a nestlike structure that never houses eggs or young birds? Go to pages 28–29.
• How do cliff-nesting birds that don't build nests keep their eggs from rolling off into the ocean? Go to page 32.
• Which bird nests on the ledges of some of the tallest buildings in the world? See pages 48–49.

HOME SWEET HOME

PRIME REAL ESTATE
Some raptors, such as the Verreaux's Eagle of southern Africa, build large nests on cliff edges. These sites, called eyries, are sometimes used for centuries. Each year, the eagles add more twigs and other building material.

SAFE AND SOUND
The Scarlet Tanager of North America likes to build its nests in oak trees, anywhere from 8 to 75 feet (2.6 to 22.5 m) above the ground. The nests are cup-shaped, like those of most tree-nesting birds. This shape is perfect for preventing the eggs from rolling out.

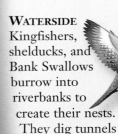

WATERSIDE
Kingfishers, shelducks, and Bank Swallows burrow into riverbanks to create their nests. They dig tunnels above the waterline to avoid the risk of flooding. Other birds, such as Manx Shearwaters, use old rabbit burrows.

AIMING HIGH
The Black-winged Stilt scrapes a hollow on an open, dry site or in low vegetation. Sometimes it makes a cup nest on a mud bank or mound. This nest can be built up higher if the water level rises.

IN THE OVEN
The Rufous Hornero, an ovenbird, lives in South America. It builds its nest in a tree or on top of a telephone pole. The nest resembles an old-fashioned baker's oven. It is made of mud mixed with grass and animal hairs. Inside the entrance is a grass-lined chamber where the eggs are laid.

SECURE HOLDINGS
The Reed Warbler's nest is built in tall reeds, right over water, so that the young birds are safe from predators. The Reed Warbler is an excellent weaver and can make its nest incredibly secure so the young don't fall into the water on windy days.

Before They Hatch

THE EGGS THAT a female bird lays may seem like lifeless things. But their smooth exterior hides something wonderful. A tiny embryo is alive inside each egg and is growing into a bird. The embryo has everything it needs to grow until it fills the egg completely and is ready to hatch. Well, almost everything. An egg will grow into a live chick only if it is incubated, which means it must be kept warm.

The female usually lays her fertilized eggs in a nest. Then, either the male or the female parent bird can keep the eggs warm, or they may share the task. Before a bird begins incubating, it may lose feathers on its belly. This area is called a brood patch. When the bird presses its brood patch against the eggs, the warmth from its body helps to keep the eggs at just the right temperature. The bird simply turns the eggs to warm them all over. A few bird species cover eggs under mounds of leaf litter and leave them to incubate.

Incubation can take just over a week for the egg of a small bird and 12 weeks for that of a large one. A chick may start to make noises several days before it hatches. To hatch, it has to peck at the shell and make a crack around the larger end. Some parent birds may hear the chick's cheeps and help to remove parts of the shell.

HANDS ON

Egg Hideout

Children in some countries paint eggs with bright colors to use for Easter egg hunts. In the wild, most eggs are not bright at all. They need to fade into the background so they cannot be seen easily by predators.

See if you can paint eggs a color that will make them blend in with a natural environment. You will need eggs from a supermarket, a paintbrush, and watercolor paints. Look for a good nest site, perhaps some dried leaves at the base of a tree. Study the colors and patterns of the site. Then paint your eggs to match. Start with a neutral base color, such as brown or gray, then dot, streak, and blotch with greens, darker browns, or black. Now place your eggs at the site and see if a friend can find them.

A PEEK INSIDE

1 An egg contains the growing bird (embryo), a yellow yolk, and albumen (egg white). The chick uses the yolk and albumen as food before it hatches.
2 As the chick uses the yolk and albumen, it produces wastes, which are stored in a special sac.
3 When the chick is close to hatching, it almost fills the entire shell.
4 Unhatched chicks have a special egg tooth that helps them break free. After they hatch, the tooth falls off.

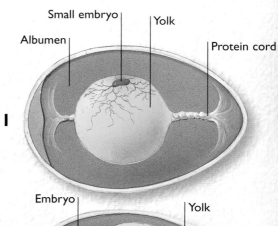

Small embryo   Yolk
Albumen   Protein cord

1

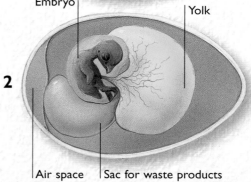

Embryo   Yolk

2

Air space   Sac for waste products

3

Developing chick

Egg tooth

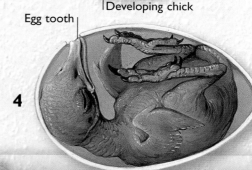

4

DIVERSITY RULES

Birds' eggs come in many different shapes, colors, and sizes. These variations are important to the survival of each species. The variations help keep eggs safe from predators and protect them in specific environments.

GOING NOWHERE

One end of the egg of the Common Murre is narrow and pointed. This shape stops it from being accidentally knocked off the cliff edge on which it is laid. If the egg should start to roll, it will move in a circle, rather than a straight line.

Word Builders

• **Incubate** comes from the Latin word *cubare*, meaning "to lie" or "recline." *In-* is a prefix meaning "on."
• **Brood** comes from the German word *Brut*, which means "breed." A brood is a group of birds that hatch together. The verb "to brood" means to keep young birds warm by covering them up after they have hatched.

That's Amazing!

• The largest bird eggs ever found belonged to the extinct elephant birds. Their eggs could hold over two gallons (8 l) of fluid. That's the contents of two of the biggest cartons of milk you can buy from a grocery store.
• The Ostrich lays the largest egg of any living bird. Just how big is it? Try to imagine an egg that can hold the contents of 12–18 chicken eggs.

Pathfinder

• Some birds build elaborate nests to protect their unhatched eggs. Find out more on pages 30–31.
• Which bird builds mounds of leaves in which to bury its eggs to keep them warm? The answer is on page 47.
• Which male bird incubates its single egg on its feet? See page 62.

BRAVING THE NEW WORLD

It can take several days for a young chick, such as this Downy Woodpecker, to break through the tough shell of an egg. First, the chick must turn to face the blunter end of the egg. It then pierces the air space in which it lies, enabling it to breathe for the first time. Next, the chick pecks at the shell, using its egg tooth and powerful neck muscles to help it break through. The chick turns in a circle by pushing itself with its feet so that the crack it is making will run right around the shell. Once the circle is complete, the chick pushes its way out of the egg. It usually emerges headfirst.

FOSTER CARE
Some cuckoos are nest parasites, laying their eggs in other birds' nests. The nest owners may not notice, even when the cuckoo eggs are larger than their own. They will usually raise the young cuckoo.

LOOK-ALIKES
Common Terns lay their eggs right on the ground. The eggs are often hard to see among pebbles, because the spotting on the eggs blends in with the patterns on the pebbles. This is perfect camouflage.

Growing Up

THE HATCHING OF a young bird is a remarkable event. Some birds, such as ducks, are born with their eyes open. These young birds run and swim as soon as they are born. They are described as precocial. Precocial birds are already covered with downy feathers when they hatch. These are eventually replaced by their adult feathers.

Other birds, like the songbirds, are born with their eyes closed. These newborn birds are too weak to move around after they hatch. They are known as altricial birds. Most altricial birds, including the Eurasian Bullfinch, hatch naked or have a very sparse down cover. The feathers of altricial birds grow out of tracts along the bird's wings and body.

Chicks depend on older birds for food and safety until they can fend for themselves. In most species, both parents tend and feed their young. Among ducks and some other species, only the females raise the chicks. Among phalaropes, only males raise the chicks. Among Florida Scrub-Jays, the parents get help from the chicks' older brothers and sisters. Pelicans nest in large colonies. When chicks have left the nest, parents gather them in a group called a crèche. Then all the adult birds can be on the lookout for predators that might harm the young. However, pelican parents still bring food to their own chicks.

Day by day, young birds grow bigger and stronger and learn the many skills they will need to survive.

A COOL SHOWER

Although the Shoebill looks clumsy, it is surprisingly skilled and delicate in its movements. Young Shoebills are often exposed to the fierce African heat. The parent bird fetches cool, refreshing water in its enormous, hook-tipped bill and showers it over its young. At other times, it shades the young with its huge body and large, broad wings.

BACKING THE FUTURE

The parent bird has to work hard to keep its chicks from harm. Although the young Common Loon can swim almost from the moment it is born, it cannot fend for itself. When the parent senses danger, it carries the young bird to safety on its back.

FOOD DELIVERY SERVICE

Some young birds cannot digest solid food. Adult pelicans change food into a liquid. They let the liquid food trickle down their large bills for the young to eat. As the young grow, they begin to eat solid food from a parent's pouch.

ACTING ON CUE

The Killdeer has developed a way to trick creatures that prey on its young. It diverts the predator's attention by pretending to have a broken wing, which would make it easier to catch. Once the predator has been lured away from the nest, the Killdeer stops its pretense and flies off.

Word Builders

• **Altricial** comes from the Latin word *altricies*, which means "feeders" or "nurses." A chick that is altricial is helpless and needs a parent to care for its every need.
• **Precocial** comes from the Latin word *praecoci*, which means "ripened early." A chick that is precocial can move around and leave the nest soon after it hatches.

That's Amazing!

• In Greenland, Barnacle Geese lay their eggs on cliffs to protect them from foxes. When goslings first leave the nest, they half jump and half fly hundreds of feet to the sea below. They often hit rocks on the way down, but their body fat and soft plumage cushion the blows.
• Young male songbirds in the wild copy the male adults' songs. Caged birds seldom have the same calls as their own kind in the wild because they have not heard them sing.

Pathfinder

• A young South American rain forest nestling provides a clue about the evolution of birds. See page 13.
• The instinct to fly is strong, but how do birds manage to do what so few other vertebrates can? Find out more on pages 20–21.
• When winter approaches, many birds migrate. How do young birds learn the migration routes? Turn to pages 42–43.

SCHOOL IN SESSION

Young birds need many skills to survive. Some skills are instinctive, some are learned, and some require both instinct and learning.

DUCKS TO WATER

Water birds take to the water soon after they hatch because there are often predators waiting to catch them. Swimming is an instinctual behavior, like nest building. But a duckling needs to learn from its parent where to go to find food and shelter, and how to stay safe from predators.

COME FLY WITH ME

When fledgling Banded Honeyeaters leave the nest, they do not return. Their ability to fly is inherited, but mastering the skill takes practice. These nomadic birds need to fly well—they cover vast distances to find the flowers and blossoms on which they feed.

LET ME SHOW YOU

Young birds often pick up skills by watching and copying their parents.
Green Herons in Florida, for example, learned by accident that dropping bread into a pond attracted fish. Their young copied this skill so they could catch fish.

INSIDE STORY

Are You My Mother?

When a chick hatches, does it know what species of bird it is? Does a gosling know that it's a goose? Konrad Lorenz (1903–1989), an Austrian zoologist, explored this kind of question in his work. He set up an experiment in which he incubated some goose eggs in a laboratory incubator. When the chicks hatched, he was there to feed them, keep them warm and protect them. He even made sounds and movements like an adult goose. The goslings soon accepted him as their parent and followed him everywhere. By fooling the goslings, Lorenz showed that young birds learn who they are by a process called imprinting. That is, they attach themselves to a figure who cares for them—usually their parent—and think that they are the same kind of creature. For this ingenious experiment and many others in animal behavior, Lorenz won a Nobel Prize in 1973.

Eating Like a Bird

IF SOMEONE SAYS, "you eat like a bird," they mean you pick at your food and eat very little. But in fact, birds eat a lot more food than humans do when you compare their body size with the amount of food they consume. Birds have to eat lots to supply the energy they need for flying, building nests, and keeping warm in winter.

Birds eat all kinds of things—seeds, fruits, and plants, as well as animals called invertebrates. These include worms, clams, shrimps, and insects. The size and shape of birds' bills and feet vary according to what they usually eat. The Tufted Titmouse has strong feet for gripping thin twigs while hanging at difficult angles to reach insects on leaves. Warblers have slender bills for delving among leafy branches to find juicy caterpillars. Birds such as flycatchers, swifts, swallows, and nightjars, which eat mostly insects, have a wide, rather gaping bill. When flying, these birds open their bills and use them to catch the insects.

For some birds, it can be a challenge to find the food they eat. Limpkins and Snail Kites are particular about their diet, living mainly on snails. For the seed and fruit eaters, it can be difficult to find enough food in winter or when plants fail to bear fruit. Waxwings and crossbills are nomadic in their hunt for food. They travel beyond their nesting areas after they have finished all the pine cones or berries there.

HANDS ON
Feed the Birds

To make a simple bird feeder, you will need a clean, dry plastic milk carton, one straight stick or dowel, scissors, and some string.

❶ On one side of the carton, about 1 inch (2.5 cm) from the bottom, cut out a 3-inch (7.5-cm) square opening. Make a second square on the opposite side of the carton.

❷ Just below each opening, punch a hole into which your stick or dowel will fit. Push the stick or dowel through the holes to make a perch for the birds.

❸ Fill the bottom of the feeder, up to the level of the openings, with seed, fresh fruit, or meal worms. Tie one end of the string onto the handle of the carton, and hang the feeder from a tree or post.

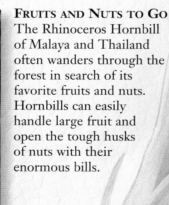

FRUITS AND NUTS TO GO
The Rhinoceros Hornbill of Malaya and Thailand often wanders through the forest in search of its favorite fruits and nuts. Hornbills can easily handle large fruit and open the tough husks of nuts with their enormous bills.

IT'S ALL IN THE METHOD

CATCH OF THE DAY
Sometimes the tastiest tidbits require a little extra effort. Oystercatchers feed mostly on the shellfishes that they find on mud flats and beaches. The Eurasian Oystercatcher opens the shells of mussels and oysters with its stout, chisel-like bill. It either stabs and cuts the muscle that holds the two halves of the shell together, or it shatters the shell against a rock.

HITTING THE MARK
The Red-breasted Sapsucker drills row upon row of small holes into trees that produce sap. Each hole is drilled at an incline so that the sap can drip out. The bird eats the sap, along with any insects that are attracted to it, mopping them up with its bristle-covered tongue.

Word Builders

• The Latin suffix -*vore* means "eating." Birds that eat insects are known as **insectivores**, while birds that eat fruit, which is *frux* in Latin, are called **frugivores**.

• **Invertebrates** are animals that do not have backbones. The word is derived from the Latin prefix *in-*, which means "without," and the Latin word *vertebratus*, meaning "jointed."

That's Amazing!

Some birds and plants have evolved so closely that their habits help each other to survive. For example, Clark's Nutcrackers rely on the fruit of the whitebark pine as a winter food. They bury the fruit by the thousands in late summer, then dig it up to eat in the winter. Buried fruit that is not eaten in the winter may sprout in the spring, helping the pine to reproduce. These new trees will provide food for future generations of Clark's Nutcrackers.

Pathfinder

• Birds do not have teeth to grind food, so how is food processed by their bodies? Turn to page 15.

• Bird bills have adapted so that birds can eat particular types of food. To learn more go to pages 24–25.

• Some birds are carnivores, which means they eat meat. How do they catch their supper? See pages 38–41.

CRACKERS
Seeds can provide the main diet of birds. The strong, cone-shaped beak of the Purple Grenadier is perfect for cracking open seeds. This secretive bird searches for its food close to the ground, in the undergrowth and thickets.

STING OR BE STUNG
Many birds eat insects, but eating a bee could invite a painful sting. The European Bee-eater has learned a way to solve this problem. It holds the bee at the tip of its long beak and removes the stinger by rubbing it against a branch. It then squeezes the body of the bee to get rid of any poison before eating.

THE NECTAR OF LIFE
Hummingbirds, such as the Broad-billed Hummingbird, are very active. Each day they need to eat almost as much as their body weight in nectar—a sugary fuel—to keep up their strength. Hummingbirds can hover, which allows them to remain in one place while they insert their long bills into the trumpet-shaped flowers they visit. They can also fly backward, enabling them to back out of the flowers.

TOOL BIRD
The Woodpecker Finch of the Galápagos Islands is named for its habit of eating grubs that live in wood. But the finch, unlike woodpeckers, does not have a long tongue or a bill that is suitable for getting hold of the grubs. Instead, it uses a cactus spine or twig that is just the right shape to dig the grubs out.

HELPING HAND
The Yellow-billed Oxpecker, a relative of the starling, collects its food and helps other animals at the same time. The oxpecker feeds on the irritating ticks and lice that live in the skin and hair of giraffe, buffalo, antelope, and rhinoceros.

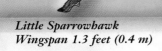

Little Sparrowhawk
Wingspan 1.3 feet (0.4 m)

Secretary Bird
6.6 feet (2 m)

Andean Condor
10 feet (3 m)

Mighty Hunters

THE HUNTING BIRDS are flying warriors. They are strong, fearless, and perfectly adapted to kill live creatures. The best hunters are the raptors, which include eagles, hawks, falcons, and owls. Their vision is up to three times better than that of humans. They can spot prey from a great distance. There is nothing pretty about what the raptors do. They grab and kill their victims with their needle-sharp claws called talons. They can also kill instantly with their strong, hooked bills, severing the neck with a single, mighty crunch. With their bills, they tear their kill into bite-size portions.

Kingfishers, herons, and storks are less dramatic, but they are equally skilled hunters. They hunt fishes, frogs, and other aquatic creatures. Sharp eyesight and lightning reflexes help them capture their slippery, fast-moving target. Storks are unusually quick. They can feel their prey in muddy waters and react with speeds that have been measured in thousandths of a second.

Some seabirds, such as the Great Skua, hunt other seabirds, along with the eggs and young of other birds. Skuas, giant-petrels, and albatrosses, like the land-based vultures, are often scavengers. In addition to hunting live prey, they eat carrion, the remains of dead animals.

GOTCHA!
The Azure Kingfisher is a clever hunter of fishes. It watches intently from a perch over water, then plunges bill-first to capture its prey.

INSIDE STORY

Game for a Sport

Falconry is an ancient sport that dates back many centuries. A falconer trains a falcon or hawk to capture prey, then fly back to its master with the kill. The master rewards the bird with food and keeps it in captivity until the next outing. Before the invention of accurate guns for hunting, falconry was popular for centuries. Falconers were among the first people to study birds seriously, learning their habits and skills. Today, only a small number of people continue the sport, and strict rules apply to protect the birds.

LETHAL WEAPONS
Many raptors hunt by day. They eat live prey that they catch with their strong feet. They are skilled hunters.

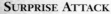

SURPRISE ATTACK
The African Pygmy Falcon uses its speed to surprise prey. It perches out in the open on dead trees, then suddenly pounces on its victim. This tiny falcon is about 8 inches (19 cm) long. It lives throughout the plains of eastern Africa, wherever the White-headed Buffalo-Weavers or Sociable Weavers are found. It uses these species' old nests for breeding.

HOOKED ON YOU
The beautiful Osprey hunts only fishes. The bird drops, feet first, into the water to grip a wriggling fish and carries it off for eating. The talons of the Osprey have special thorny growths called "spicules."

Word Builders

• The word **raptor** comes from the Latin word *raptare*, meaning "to seize and carry away."
• **Prey** is an animal killed for food by another animal. The word comes from the Latin *praeda*, meaning "booty," the food and valuables soldiers carry off when they conquer a territory.
• The name **Hamerkop** is an Afrikaans word meaning "hammerhead." This name refers to the shape of the bird's head when seen in profile.

That's Amazing!

• The two vulture species of North America hunt in different ways. The Turkey Vulture sniffs the air for the scent of carrion. The Black Vulture uses its keen eyesight. Sometimes Black Vultures wait for Turkey Vultures to pick up a scent and then follow them to the carcass.
• The Common Buzzard's territory extends 785 feet (240 m) above the ground. It will chase away any intruder that flies within this zone.

Pathfinder

• How do large raptors living in mountainous regions manage to fly so high and stay airborne for so long? The remarkable answer is on page 21.
• Birds that hunt during the night have developed special techniques for locating their prey. How do they do it? Fast-forward to pages 40–41.
• Some birds of prey, such as the Peregrine Falcon, have adapted well to life in the inner cities. Turn to pages 48–49 to find out more.

BORN TO RULE

In 1782, the Bald Eagle won the contest to become the national bird of the United States of America. Its fierce expression helped it triumph over the Wild Turkey, its rival for the honor. The Bald Eagle hunts mainly fishes and will sometimes take ducks or carrion. It will also steal food from other birds if it gets the chance.

STOP, THIEF!

The Antarctic Skua, like all skuas, has many ways of getting food. It often raids penguin colonies for both chicks and eggs, and also eats whatever carrion it can find. Most skuas will attack birds that have food to try to steal it from them.

FROGS' LEGS, ANYONE?

Hamerkops are small, storklike birds that live on the savannas of Africa, where they feed mainly on frogs. They also hunt fishes, shellfishes, and large insects. They build enormous stick-and-mud nests with small entrances in the forks of trees near their feeding grounds.

STOMPING GROUNDS

The Secretary Bird of the African savannas hunts snakes—even the venomous cobra—and other reptiles. Standing nearly 4.5 feet (1.3 m) tall, it stalks the grasslands, watching for signs of movement. The Secretary Bird's claws are weak and blunt. To make a kill, it stomps on its victim, breaking its neck.

CRUISE MISSILES

The Andean Condor travels great distances over the peaks of the Andes in South America looking for dead animals such as sheep and llamas. The Condor drops as soon as it spots a carcass. Unlike many other species, condors are prepared to share and rarely squabble with each other while feeding.

Oilbird   *Feline Owlet-Nightjar*   *Kagu*   *Night Parrot*

Night Raiders

IF YOU STEP outside on a moonless night, you have trouble seeing more than a few feet in front of you. But an owl's powerful night vision helps it detect a mouse moving far below on the forest floor. If the mouse makes the slightest rustle in the leaves, the owl can hear it, too. Some night birds, such as a cave-dwelling Oilbird, use echolocation—a way of using sound bouncing off objects—to find their way around in total darkness.

Birds that become active as darkness falls are called crepuscular (twilight active) or nocturnal (night active) birds. To protect them as they sleep during the day, owls, nightjars, and frogmouths have dull colored plumage that helps them fade into their surroundings. The green Night Parrot of Australia hides in the dense foliage of the saltbush. Most night birds, like the Kagu of New Caledonia, make spooky calls that can be heard over great distances.

There are advantages to birds hunting at night. The animals they prey on are more active in the dark. Most other birds are asleep, so they aren't competing with the night birds for food. Most bird predators are asleep as well.

NOW YOU SEE ME...
Like many night birds, the Tawny Frogmouth is very difficult to spot during the day. It is easily mistaken for a branch of the tree it perches on—unless it opens its large mouth.

...NOW YOU DON'T
The Common Potoo also adopts a pose like a stump of wood to make it hard to see during the day. It has a broad, flattened bill which is surrounded by a few bristles. These are used to funnel food into its mouth. Common Potoos use a swooping flight pattern to catch insects.

INSIDE STORY
Seeing in the Dark

Rose Ann Rowlett of the United States of America has been organizing birding expeditions worldwide for more than 20 years. She is skilled in locating birds that are seldom seen. Some live hidden in heavily forested regions, while others are shy and secretive or only come out at night.

To find night birds such as the Nocturnal Curassow in South America, or the Feline Owlet-Nightjar in New Guinea, Rowlett uses her knowledge of their habits, habitats, and sounds. She has a tape recorder with a sensitive microphone for recording sounds and a strong flashlight for illuminating the birds. Her work has led to exciting discoveries. In Panama, she and her colleagues made the first sound recording of the Crested Owl.

higher and larger ear opening

nostrils

eye socket

lower ear opening

70° binocular vision range

110° field of vision range

HUNTERS OF THE NIGHT
Many species of owls have ears that are asymmetrical. One is higher and larger than the other. This results in a slight difference in time between sound reaching each ear and helps owls judge the location of their prey with amazing accuracy.

Most birds' eyes are on the sides of their heads, but owls' eyes face forward. Their binocular vision—seeing an object with both eyes at the same time—helps them judge distance.

Word Builders

• Binocular vision is vision that uses both eyes at the same time. The word **binocular** comes from the Latin prefix *bi-*, meaning "two," and the Latin word *oculi*, meaning "eyes."
• **Crepuscular** birds come out during times of low light, such as dusk and dawn, or even when the sun is eclipsed. The word comes from the Latin root word *crepus*, meaning "dark," and the suffix *-culus*, which means "small."

That's Amazing!

• Barn Owls swallow their prey whole. After digesting the edible parts, they cough up a large pellet containing the fur, skull, and bigger bones. By dissecting these pellets, you can work out what an owl had for dinner.
• In one of its courtship rituals, the Common Nighthawk dives out of the sky and turns upward just before it hits the ground. At the bottom of the dive, wind rushing through its feathers makes a booming sound.

Pathfinder

• Cryptic coloration helps night birds hide during the day when they are resting. Do birds active during the day use plumage camouflage as well? The answer is on pages 18–19.
• The national bird of New Zealand is a nocturnal bird. Do you know its name? Go to page 22.
• Which nocturnal bird has mastered the art of hibernation? See page 63.

BURNING THE MIDNIGHT OIL

Is that a ghost in the night sky? No, it's just a Barn Owl out hunting. Hovering overhead, white underparts standing out against the darkness, Barn Owls are an eerie sight. And just as you recover from the shock of seeing one, chances are it will let out a shriek that makes your hair stand on end. Barn Owls are widespread throughout the world, living in open areas.

SUNSET WANDERINGS

Although the Black-crowned Night Heron is active during daylight hours, it usually waits until dusk to leave its roost and hunt for food. At this hour there is less competition from other heron species.

Owls swoop silently on their prey because their outer flight feathers have a serrated, or jagged, edge. This slows the flow of air over their wings, minimizing the noise they make as they flap. Most flying birds have smooth edges to their flight feathers.

Owls mostly hunt rodents. Once they have located their prey, they glide silently in for the kill. Raising their wings, they extend their sharp, curved talons to spike their target. A bite to the neck with their hooked bill finishes the job.

Bobolink

Arctic Tern

Rufous Hummingbird

Barn Swallow

Globetrotters

LIKE SOME PEOPLE, many birds have two homes—one for the summer and another for the winter. Flying makes it easy for them to travel from place to place. In the autumn they leave their summer nesting grounds and migrate to warmer places where they'll find more food. When the weather changes there, they migrate back again. Most birds migrate at precisely the same times every year. When the hours of sunlight get shorter in their nesting grounds, they know it's time to fly to warmer territory.

Some birds migrate in large flocks of one or more species, with first-time travelers and experienced birds flying together. Others, such as the Common Cuckoo, fly alone. When they meet other solitary travelers, they call back and forth. Small birds usually migrate at night because most of their predators are asleep and it is cooler, so flying is less tiring.

Birds are remarkable navigators. Some species orient their flight paths with the Sun, Moon, and stars. Others watch for large landmarks, such as mountain ranges or coastlines. Homing pigeons and a few other species have a tiny magnetic crystal in their heads. This may point toward Earth's magnetic pole, like a compass, allowing the birds to sense directions.

Not all birds migrate. About half the birds in the world remain close to one home for their whole lives.

Word Builders

- The word **migrate** comes from the Latin word *migrare*, which means "to change where one lives."
- The word **navigate** is from the Latin verb *navigare*, meaning "to sail."
- **Radar** tracks an object by measuring the time it takes for the echo of a radio wave to return from it. The word is the shortened form of the phrase *ra(dio) d(etecting) a(nd) r(anging)*.

That's Amazing!

- Dunlins, knots, and other small migrating birds have been seen at heights of over 21,000 feet (6,400 m). One pilot who was flying over the Outer Hebrides at 24,000 feet (7,300 m) saw a flock of migrating Whooper Swans sharing his air space.
- When a Manx Shearwater was taken from Britain to the United States and released, it found its way home—a trip of 3,200 miles (5,150 km) across the Atlantic Ocean—in only 12 days.

Pathfinder

- The words "lift," "vortex," and "updraft" are all connected with flight. To find out what they mean, turn to pages 20–21.
- Does flying come naturally to young birds? The answer is on pages 34–35.
- Some birds travel long distances on a daily basis, particularly seabirds when searching for food. How do they live over the oceans? See pages 50–51.

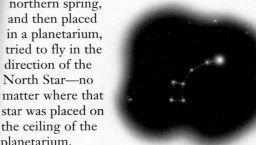

Rufous Hummingbird

Bobolink

Barn Swallow

Common Cuckoo

Latham's Snipe

Far Eastern Curlew

SUPER SKYWAYS

Huge numbers of migrating birds use a few main routes. They run along coastal areas and follow landmasses, avoiding long flights over water and high mountain ranges. The largest migrations are between North and South America, Eurasia and Africa, and East Asia and Australia. A few birds take other more difficult routes.

READING THE SIGNS

CELESTIAL BEACON

Experiments with nocturnal migrants, such as sparrows and warblers, showed that birds captured while migrating in the northern spring, and then placed in a planetarium, tried to fly in the direction of the North Star—no matter where that star was placed on the ceiling of the planetarium.

POLES APART

To test the theory that some birds navigate by the Earth's magnetic field, researchers attached a small magnet to the head of a pigeon. They found that the magnet caused the bird to lose its way. A piece of brass, with no magnetic force, had no effect on the pigeon's sense of direction.

FOLLOW THE LEADER

Some young birds learn the migration routes from their parents or other adult members of their species. Sandhill Cranes and Caspian Terns follow their parents from Canada to the south of the United States, calling to each other during the day and night.

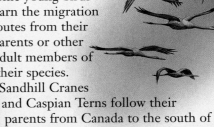

LINING UP

Some aspects of bird behavior are a mystery to us. Flocks of Barnacle Geese, for example, fly in a V formation when they migrate to and from Greenland and Europe. Scientists are not sure why they and other species do this. Some believe the wings of the lead bird create swirling wind currents called vortices. These can cause updrafts of air, making flying easier for the bird behind. Other scientists think that birds fly in a V formation to see more clearly what is in front of them, and to avoid colliding with the birds ahead of them.

CHARTING THE LAND

Rivers, mountains, and coastlines seem to help birds migrating during daylight. Many of these landmarks run in a north-south direction, like the migration routes.

43

Where Birds Live

WHAT DO FORESTS, deserts, oceans, and cities have in common? They are all places where you will find birds. These, and many other environments, are called habitats. Where birds live affects the way they look and behave. Birds adapt to their habitats. Desert birds, for example, have clever ways to find water. Some city birds even nest on window ledges instead of cliffs. Turn the page and begin to explore some of the places that birds call home.

Camera   Telephoto lens   Binoculars   Tape recorder   Notebook

Bird Watching

YOU BELONG TO one of the biggest clubs in the world—a club you joined the first time you watched a robin on the lawn. Those who watch birds often call it birding. Some serious birders are amateur scientists, who do invaluable work that helps identify and protect birds. Some musicians are also birders. They are inspired by birdsong and calls. Artists and photographers are attracted to birds, too, because of the beautiful colors of their plumage. For all of us, birding can be a fascinating hobby, as simple or complex as we want it to be.

Dedicated birders often spend their weekends at wildlife refuges. They don't just watch birds. They record their sounds and try to identify different species. It takes practice to tell birds apart. Birders like to share their observations with others. Their findings can be useful to ornithologists in understanding birds and to conservationists who work to ensure that birds and their habitats are protected.

But remember, birds are shy around people. You'll have to stay still and quiet when you watch them.

The Rules of the Game

Going birding is fun and exciting, but there are a few rules that all birders should follow.

❶ Always use your common sense and behave in ways that do not endanger any birds, other wildlife, or people.

❷ Don't chase or flush birds. Stay away from nests and nesting colonies. You can watch and photograph birds without disturbing them.

❸ If you use tape recordings to attract birds, do not play them too often.

❹ Never handle birds or their eggs unless you are involved in recognized research work with qualified experts.

❺ Be sure to dress warmly because the best time to watch birds is in the cool morning or evening when birds are active.

INSIDE STORY

A World Without Song

In 1962, American biologist Rachel Carson published a book called *Silent Spring*. In it, she drew attention to the disappearance of many kinds of birds that were being poisoned by insecticides—chemicals used to kill insect pests. Describing the result, she wrote, "On the mornings that had once throbbed with the dawn chorus of robins, catbirds, doves, jays, wrens, and scores of other voices, there was now no sound; only silence lay over the fields and woods and marsh." When birds ate insects killed by the chemicals, the birds got sick or could not reproduce. Carson warned that such poisons can travel up the food chain and endanger many living things. Her book led to many international laws against the use of some insecticides and encouraged people to help protect the environment.

GOING, GOING …
Many birds are under the threat of extinction. Some species have survived because scientists and birders kept a careful watch on their numbers and habitats.

WORKING TOGETHER
In 1986, a pair of Gurney's Pittas was found in Thailand. This species had not been seen since 1952. Then 30 more pairs were found. Today, farmers work with conservationists to protect the birds' forest habitat.

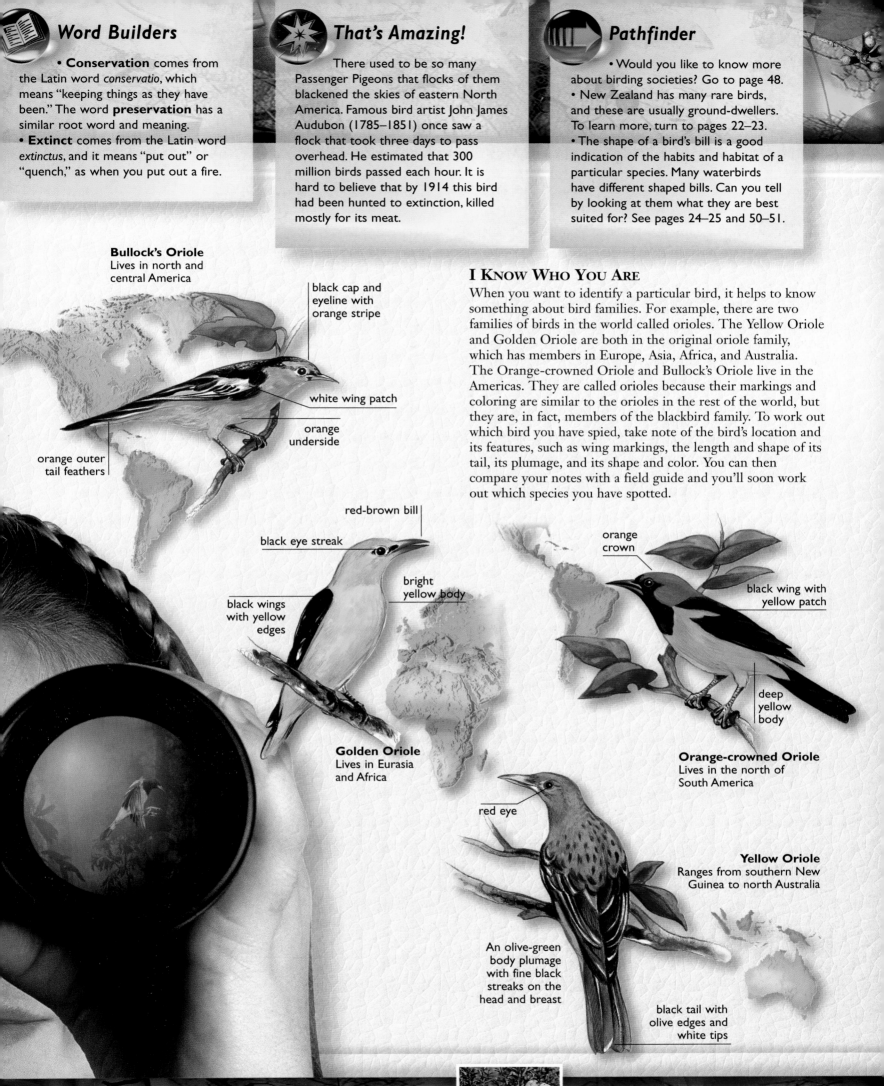

Word Builders

- **Conservation** comes from the Latin word *conservatio*, which means "keeping things as they have been." The word **preservation** has a similar root word and meaning.
- **Extinct** comes from the Latin word *extinctus*, and it means "put out" or "quench," as when you put out a fire.

That's Amazing!

There used to be so many Passenger Pigeons that flocks of them blackened the skies of eastern North America. Famous bird artist John James Audubon (1785–1851) once saw a flock that took three days to pass overhead. He estimated that 300 million birds passed each hour. It is hard to believe that by 1914 this bird had been hunted to extinction, killed mostly for its meat.

Pathfinder

- Would you like to know more about birding societies? Go to page 48.
- New Zealand has many rare birds, and these are usually ground-dwellers. To learn more, turn to pages 22–23.
- The shape of a bird's bill is a good indication of the habits and habitat of a particular species. Many waterbirds have different shaped bills. Can you tell by looking at them what they are best suited for? See pages 24–25 and 50–51.

Bullock's Oriole
Lives in north and central America

black cap and eyeline with orange stripe

white wing patch

orange underside

orange outer tail feathers

I KNOW WHO YOU ARE

When you want to identify a particular bird, it helps to know something about bird families. For example, there are two families of birds in the world called orioles. The Yellow Oriole and Golden Oriole are both in the original oriole family, which has members in Europe, Asia, Africa, and Australia. The Orange-crowned Oriole and Bullock's Oriole live in the Americas. They are called orioles because their markings and coloring are similar to the orioles in the rest of the world, but they are, in fact, members of the blackbird family. To work out which bird you have spied, take note of the bird's location and its features, such as wing markings, the length and shape of its tail, its plumage, and its shape and color. You can then compare your notes with a field guide and you'll soon work out which species you have spotted.

red-brown bill

black eye streak

bright yellow body

black wings with yellow edges

Golden Oriole
Lives in Eurasia and Africa

orange crown

black wing with yellow patch

deep yellow body

Orange-crowned Oriole
Lives in the north of South America

red eye

Yellow Oriole
Ranges from southern New Guinea to north Australia

An olive-green body plumage with fine black streaks on the head and breast

black tail with olive edges and white tips

LEARNING FROM PAST MISTAKES
The Malleefowl buries its eggs under mounds of leaves to incubate them. Species numbers fell when farmers burned the leaves to clear land. Areas are now left untouched for nesting.

FOR THE NEXT GENERATION
In the 1970s the California Condor was near extinction. To prevent this, scientists captured pairs and protected them while they raised their young. Then the healthy young birds were set free.

Barn Swallow *Black Kite* *Black-billed Magpie* *House Sparrow*

City Slickers

IT TOOK BIRDS millions of years to adapt to their natural environments. So what happens when their natural world suddenly changes? Urban areas—cities and suburbs that are crammed with people, traffic, and buildings—have existed for only about 150 years. Birds haven't had much time to become accustomed to them.

Some birds couldn't adjust to city life, so they moved to other regions or died out. But many other birds are now at home in busy cities. You can find House Sparrows in cities in many parts of the world. The appearance of Barn Swallows, coming to make their nests in buildings, is a sign to some city dwellers that spring has arrived.

City birds have learned to take advantage of human behavior to make their lives easier. For example, sparrows and magpies congregate in parks and gardens because the soft soil makes it easy to catch worms. Others peck up crumbs spilled from office workers' lunches or are bold enough to eat straight out of people's hands. Black Kites scavenge scraps from garbage.

People who live in cities often try to make them as bird-friendly as possible. They put out birdbaths, bird feeders, and nesting boxes. In many places, areas of natural habitat have been saved from development so that birds can live and raise their young without harm. These areas, called bird refuges, are the homes of the greatest variety of birds.

CITY BOUND

New York City is the most heavily populated area in North America. But people are not the only ones attracted to the city. Central Park is in the center of New York. Almost 300 bird species have been spotted there. Some species live in the park all year, but most are migrating visitors. Birds seen there include Rock Doves, American Robins, Northern Mockingbirds, and Great Horned Owls. Peregrine Falcons can even be seen nesting on the ledges of the city's skyscrapers. These birds were introduced into the city in the 1960s. They were taught to use ledges because they were on the brink of extinction in their natural habitats, due to the use of pesticides.

Northern Mockingbird

Peregrine Falcon

Mallards

HANDS ON
Tracking Trends

In cities around the world, various programs keep track of where birds live. With your parents' help, you can find a program in your area. In North America there is a program called Project Feeder Watch. Thousands of people participate in this program by sending in reports about birds that visit bird feeders in their yards and gardens. Through efforts like these, scientists can monitor the health of different bird groups and can follow the northward expansion of species such as the Carolina Wren, Northern Mockingbird, Northern Cardinal, Tufted Titmouse, and Red-bellied Woodpecker. Counting birds is not as easy as you might think. If you see 15 chickadees in one hour, it doesn't automatically mean that 15 individuals have paid you a visit. Some of the 15 you counted may be birds that have stopped by twice or more in the hour.

Word Builders

• The Peregrine Falcon migrates from the Arctic to southern Europe, North America, and Asia. **Peregrine** comes from the Latin word *peregrinor,* meaning "to wander or travel."
• The word **urban** comes from the Latin word *urbs,* meaning "city" or "town." The Latin prefix *sub* means "beneath" or "below." The word **suburbs** means the outlying areas of a city.

That's Amazing!

• Legend has it that the city of Rome was saved in the early part of the first millennium by a flock of geese. The Goths of northern Europe were about to attack. The geese heard them coming, and honked so loudly that they woke the Roman soldiers.
• The Northern Mockingbird is a superb mimic. If it copies another bird's song, it can be impossible to tell which bird is doing the singing.

Pathfinder

• Do you know how to make a simple bird feeder? See page 36.
• What tools do birdwatchers need when they are in the field? Look at pages 46–47 to find out more.
• Gulls are seabirds that have adapted well to city life. If you would like to know more about seabirds, turn to pages 50–51.

Rock Doves

American Robin

Great Horned Owl

House Finches

The Human Touch

Cities are difficult places for birds to live, but people often help to make things easier for them.

Turning Over a New Leaf

Many woodland birds that have come to live in cities take advantage of the hard work of suburban gardeners. This European Robin is carefully inspecting freshly turned garden soil in search of worms.

Operation Bird Rescue

Birds face many dangers in cities, including collisions with cars and power lines and attacks from cats. Every day, wildlife services around the world come to the aid of many injured birds. This eagle is being prepared for an operation.

Just Give a Little Whistle

The White-faced Whistling-Duck is a naturally timid bird. In parks in Durban, South Africa, it has gradually gotten used to people and is happy to be fed by hand.

49

By the Sea

PERHAPS WE SHOULDN'T call our planet Earth, because more than seven-tenths of its surface is covered by water. Oceans and seas surround the land, and wherever there is seawater, there are places that attract birds: steep cliffs, tropical reefs, oceanic islands, mangrove swamps, and salt marshes. Birds flock to these habitats, attracted by plenty of food and moderate weather.

These birds have learned to gather their food in different ways. Plovers and sandpipers run along the water's edge in search of insects and shellfish buried in the sand. Gulls swoop down to scoop food off the surface of the water, while terns make shallow dives to catch fishes in the shallows. Blue-footed Boobies and Northern Gannets are also divers. Gannets sometimes dive from more than 100 feet (30 m) in the air to claim a fish from the water. Cormorants swim along the surface, diving from water level to browse along the coastal seabeds.

Shorebirds and seabirds have adapted well to their watery environments. The Hudsonian Godwit has a long, upwardly curved bill, ideal for probing deep into mud for food. As its name suggests, the Ruddy Turnstone turns over stones with its bill to get at the food underneath. The Black-necked Stilt has extremely long legs. It can wade into deep, still water without getting its body wet.

BEACH HOUSES

The shores of the Mediterranean Sea, enclosed between the south of Europe and the north of Africa, are lined with small evergreen shrubs, heathers, and scented herbs. These plants provide well-hidden nesting sites for many birds. Little Terns lay their eggs on the pebbles of the shore, where they are well camouflaged. The cliffs provide excellent nesting sites. On some of the sea's islands, there are huge colonies of Cory's Shearwaters. These birds nest in holes and cracks in the rocks. Many shearwater species are active at night at their nesting sites, and are seldom seen there during the day.

Northern Gannets
Little Tern
Little Terns

INSIDE STORY
Return Visitors

Ilsa Craig is an island off the coast of Scotland. It is a nesting site for Northern Gannets, and is the oldest known gannetry in the world. Researchers, under the guidance of Dr. Bernard Zonfrillo from the University of Glasgow, have been putting bands on the legs of Ilsa Craig's gannets for many years. Some of these banded birds have been spotted as far away as the Mediterranean Sea, a distance of more than 500 miles (800 km). But Dr. Zonfrillo has found that his gannets return to the island every year, and often nest in the same spot as they did in earlier years.

THE CALL OF THE OCEAN

LONE WANDERERS

Some birds live most of their lives far out at sea. Red-billed Tropicbirds roam, either alone or in pairs, over the oceans near the equator. They have long, pointed wings that help them fly quickly. Though these tropicbirds are good fliers, their short legs are set far back, making them very clumsy on land.

OCEAN FISHERS

Atlantic Puffins live in large colonies near the North Atlantic coasts. They find food out at sea, collecting fishes near the surface. Then they return to their nests to feed their young. Puffins can hold lots of fishes in their bills. The bills have backward-facing serrations, a bit like a comb's teeth.

Word Builders

• The word **booby** comes from the Spanish word *bobo*, which means "clown" or "stupid fellow." The Blue-footed Booby got its name from sailors who were amused by its clownish antics. The birds seem to fence each other with their bills.

• If something is difficult to see because of its color, it is described as having **cryptic** coloration. The word comes from the Latin word *crypta* and the Greek word *kryptos*, meaning "hidden."

That's Amazing!

• Razorbills, seabirds of the North Atlantic, look like penguins, but they can fly—most of the time. When a Razorbill molts each year, it loses all its flight feathers at the same time. So for about 45 days, until its new feathers grow in, it is as flightless as a penguin.

• Pelicans and cormorants have air sacs under their skin that enable them to float.

Pathfinder

• Which bird lives out over the ocean for most of the year, and has the largest wingspan of all birds? The answer is on pages 20–21.

• Which seabird is the fastest swimmer, even though it cannot fly? Turn to pages 22–23.

Cory's Shearwater

Black-bellied Plovers

Pied Avocets

Eurasian Curlew

Common Ringed Plovers

Yellow-legged Gull

Great Cormorants

PENGUINS OF THE NORTH

There are no penguins in the Northern Hemisphere, but Dovekies, which live in the Arctic, resemble penguins. They are black and white, and stand upright. Unlike penguins, Dovekies can fly.

SEA PIRATES

The Giant Petrel is a large, powerful bird that lives in the southern oceans. It is a scavenger. Scavengers eat dead fishes and other animals. Scavenging seabirds often follow fishing trawlers, ready to eat fishes caught in the nets, or garbage the crew throws overboard.

Purple Heron   *Saddle-billed Stork*   *Roseate Spoonbill*   *Japanese Crane*

Freshwater Homes

SWAMPS AND MARSHES are among the world's many different types of freshwater habitats. Rivers, creeks, lakes, and ponds are other expanses of fresh water. All are home to a great variety of birds. In the shallower waters, especially along the water's edge, dabbling ducks, such as the Mallard and teal, feed on plants and small aquatic animals. Deeper water is the territory of diving ducks and swans. Mud flats on the edge of these waterways provide shorebirds, such as yellowlegs, with worms, insects, and other invertebrates.

In all of these habitats you can see herons, egrets, ibis, and storks. These are wading birds with long legs and long bills. They can high-step through the water without getting their plumage wet. Herons and egrets use their long bills to stab fishes. Curlews and ibis have long, curved bills which they can stick in the mud to find tiny crabs and worms.

If you wanted to hide in these habitats, reed beds would be a good place to choose. Bitterns and rails hide from predators among grasses and reeds in such beds. Other birds live in marshlands, too. Wrens, sparrows, and blackbirds can sometimes be spotted nesting in trees that grow on dry hummocks.

Black Kites

Little Egrets

Magpie Geese

INSIDE STORY

Saving the Everglades

In 1947, an American named Marjorie Stoneman Douglas wrote a book called *The Everglades: River of Grass*. She described the beauty of this area of wetlands in southern Florida and warned of the damage that was being done to the freshwater environment as a result of real-estate developments and agricultural pollution. Most people at that time saw the Everglades as an unpleasant place full of alligators. But President Harry S. Truman was so moved by Douglas's words that he acted to protect the Everglades as a national park. Douglas supported the conservation of the Everglades until her death in 1998 at the age of 108. The United States government continues to help fund work aimed at reversing decades of damage to birds and other wildlife and their habitats. The Everglades is improving, but there is still much to do.

GONE FISHING
UNDER MY WING
When they fish, Black Herons spread their wings to reduce water reflections. This helps them to see fishes and may even attract smaller fishes into the shade.

WHAT'S UP?
The Cinnamon Teal is like all dabbling ducks. It almost never dives underwater for food. It feeds near the surface and reaches plants farther down by going tail up.

Word Builders

• The Black-necked Stork is Australia's only stork. It is known in that country as the **Jabiru**. This second name comes from the name Amazonian Indians gave to a South American stork.
• A **hummock** is a raised area, like a small hill. The word may come from an Old English word *humm*, which is related to the word "hump."

That's Amazing!

Anhingas are cormorant-like birds that live in freshwater wetlands in the Americas. They need to dive underwater to catch fishes. To help them do this, their feathers have tiny gaps that open to let the water in so they can sink, or close so they can float. When they want to fly, Anhingas must come out of the water and spread their wings to dry.

Pathfinder

• Which bird seems to run across water during courtship? Go to page 29.
• There are many ways for birds to catch slippery fishes. See pages 38–39 and 50–51 to find out more.
• A drink is always available to birds that live near fresh water. But where do ocean and desert birds find the moisture they need? For answers, turn to pages 50–51 and 62–63.

Black-necked Stork

Brolga

Comb-crested Jacana

Radjah Shelducks

PLAIN SAILING

Wetlands are rare in Australia. But the East and South Alligator rivers in the far north create vast lagoons at Kakadu, a national park covering nearly 1.6 million acres (645,000 ha). Kakadu is a birder's paradise. Its many types of habitats, such as mangrove forests, grass flood plains, and swamps, teem with more than a million water birds. You will often see great flocks flying overhead. The dry season runs from May to September. The floodwaters recede at this time, leaving only billabongs, or small ponds.

SCOOPING THE POOL

The lower part of the Black Skimmer's bill is longer than the upper part. The bird is able to fly with the lower part in the water, and when it feels a fish, it snaps its bill shut like a pair of scissors.

MUDDY WATERS

The Limpkin probes the water's edge with its long bill in search of food. It is fond of large snails, called apple snails, and other aquatic animals, such as crustaceans, frogs, freshwater clams, and insects.

Into the Woods

WOODLANDS ARE AS varied and as busy as the streets of a city. They seem peaceful enough, and you may think they all look much like one another. But look more closely and you'll find that each wooded area is a world of its own. Even within a single acre, there are many different trees and habitats supporting many different birds. Some species live on the lower levels of the forest and on the forest floor, while others dwell in the upper branches of the trees, finding many different sources of food.

In Europe and large parts of North America, the most common forest trees are maple, beech, and oak. These trees are all deciduous, which means they lose their leaves in the autumn. When new shoots sprout from their branches in spring, migrating birds start to return. They come for the rich supply of food, especially the insects. Woodland birds of prey also return. They know there will be many other birds on which they can prey. In the spring and summer, birds nest and rear their young in these woodlands.

In the autumn, before the trees shed their leaves, birds eat as much as they can to build up their stores of body fat. This fat becomes the fuel they will use as they make the long journey to warmer regions. Not all woodland birds migrate. For those that stay, food is scarce during winter, and they must search constantly for it. Sometimes, small groups of birds of different species roam together, each group looking in a different part of a tree for food.

European Robin

Eurasian Woodcock

HANDS ON

A Stroll in the Forest

Birds love trees. They are wonderful places in which they can hide, hunt for food, and nest. Because they are colored to blend into the woodland background, the birds can be difficult to see. This camouflage protects them from predators. The first sign of the bird may be its call. But if you know something about its shape, color, and habits, you are more likely to spot it.

Many birding clubs organize bird walks for beginners. You can learn a lot about identifying birds from the experts there and from other birders. You could also plan your own bird-finding mission. You'll need a field guide, binoculars, a journal, and a pen.

Field guides are books that have details of birds' appearances, habits, and habitats. Your local library or bookshop should stock them. Before you set out, make a list of the birds in the area you are planning to investigate. Keep this list handy when you go for your stroll. When you spot a bird, quickly draw it or write down its features in your journal for later reference. You never know—this first sighting may inspire a career in bird studies.

Word Builders

• The word **prothonotary** comes from the name of an important official in the Roman Catholic Church. The Prothonotary Warbler male's deep yellow color resembles the robes worn by the official on special days.
• The word **deciduous** comes from the Latin *decidere*, meaning "to fall from." The leaves of a deciduous tree fall off in the autumn.

That's Amazing!

The Ruffed Grouse performs a unique territorial display. This woodland bird perches on a hollow log and thumps its wings on its breast like Tarzan. The resulting sound is like a low-pitched drum beating faster and faster. The hollow log works to amplify the drumbeats. As this eerie sound reverberates through the forest, it tells other Ruffed Grouse males that this territory belongs to the thumper.

Pathfinder

• The Eurasian Sparrowhawk is a raptor, or bird of prey. To learn more about raptors, turn to pages 38–39.
• The Northern Mockingbird and the American Robin are woodland birds that can live in the city of New York. How have they and other birds adapted to city life? See pages 48–49.

SINGING FOR A LIVING

The bird calls and songs you can hear in the forest convey messages, just as human sounds and words do. Birds vocalize to signal danger, to identify other birds within their group, to defend their territories, or to court a mate.

WATER MUSIC

In the southern river woodlands of North America, the rich "sweet-sweet-sweet-sweet" song of the Prothonotary Warbler resounds throughout the swampy area.

FLUTE ORCHESTRA

The male Hermit Thrush begins its song with a crisp, clean note. It then sings in ascending and descending tones that sound like flutes playing in the distance. When migrating, these birds use their call to make sure they stay together.

LOVE SERENADES

As night falls, the male Nightingale sings to mark its territory and to charm a partner. Its sweet calls have inspired many love poems.

WARNING CHIMES

If you hear a chorus of "twit-twit-twit" echoing through a woodland area, it may well belong to a group of Eurasian Nuthatches. These agile birds flit up and down tree trunks, warning one another of approaching danger.

Winter Wren

Mistle Thrush

Eurasian Sparrowhawk

Blue Tit

HUNTING GROUNDS

An English forest is a deceptively tranquil place. One resident, the Eurasian Sparrowhawk, attacks small birds without warning. This sparrowhawk has short, rounded wings that allow it to twist and turn around the trees with great ease. The forest is a bit like an apartment block. Birds live on all levels. You might spy thrushes or woodcocks foraging for food on the ground, or wrens looking for insects in the understory, slightly above ground level. Blue Tits live in the upper levels, and robins in the mid-levels.

Great Tinamou   Sunbittern   Hoatzin   Guianan Cock-of-the-Rock

Deep in the Jungles

THERE ARE PLACES on Earth that may be home to species of birds that no one has ever seen. These remote places are the dense, tropical rain forests in Central and South America, southern Asia, northern Australia, and central and western Africa. They provide homes for almost half the life-forms on Earth. But they are rapidly disappearing because land is being cleared by timber companies and farmers.

Tropical rain forests have no spring, summer, autumn, or winter—it is either the wet or dry season. Because of this, rain forests are filled with lush, green trees that can grow as tall as 200 feet (60 m). The trees are often covered in brilliant swags of flowers. Birds, such as hawk-eagles, soar above their branches, and thick vines wind up their trunks. The top layer of the forest is called the canopy.

The closer you get to the ground, though, the darker it becomes. Shade-loving trees thrive in a level called the understory. In the dappled light and dense foliage, brightly colored birds, such as the trogons of South America, search for fruit and insects. But the sunlight can barely reach the small shrubs and leaf litter that carpet the forest floor. Here, thousands of insects scurry and flit about. They are easy pickings for birds, such as the Great Tinamou. Where there are creeks or rivers, Sunbitterns search for fishes.

TREE HOUSES

A vast array of tropical birds, such as the Harpy Eagle, lives high in the canopy of the Central and South American rain forests. This is an area of abundant light, warmth, and food. Birds, such as the Chestnut-eared Araçari, Chestnut-capped Puffbird, White-tipped Sicklebill, and Blue-crowned Trogon, also live among the trees. Some of these birds are brightly colored, but they can be difficult to spot among the green leaves and bright streaks of sunlight. Parrots, such as the Hyacinth Macaw, are perhaps the best known of rain forest birds.

Hyacinth Macaw

INSIDE STORY

Surrounded by Sound

Ted Parker (1953–93) worked for Conservation International. He recorded birds around the world, and gradually learned the songs and calls of over 4,000 species—more than any other person in history. But he is most noted for his work in the rain forest and mountain habitats of South America. Here, more than one-third of all bird species live in a region that is only one-sixth of the Earth's landmass. Parker discovered many species in these dense, remote locations that no one knew existed. By the 1980s, he became concerned about the effect that the loss of habitats was having on wildlife. His studies into this area enabled scientists and governments to determine which habitats and bird species needed urgent protection.

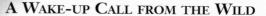

A WAKE-UP CALL FROM THE WILD

Every day, around the world, 214,000 acres (87,000 ha) of rain forest are destroyed. This is almost the same size as New York City in the U.S.A. Once a forest is cleared, the birds and other wildlife lose their habitats and may even become extinct. Because most of these rain forests are so dense, it is likely that some animals will die out before scientists have had a chance to discover them. To help prevent this situation from getting worse, some countries have set aside pockets of rain forest as reserves. This may help save some tropical birds and wildlife from extinction.

PLOWING AFRICA

The largest of the turaco species, the shy Great Blue Turaco, lives in western and central Africa. The rain forests in these regions have been cut down in order to create farmlands to feed the almost one billion people who live in Africa.

Word Builders

• The word **jungle** makes you think of a dense, lush, tropical forest. But it comes from the Sanskrit word *jangala*, which means desert.
• **Hoatzin** is a Nahuatl word. Nahuatl was spoken by the Aztecs of Mexico and Central America. This language has given us words such as coyote and chocolate.
• A **canopy** is a rooflike covering. The word comes from the Greek *konopeion*, meaning "mosquito net."

That's Amazing!

• When displaying, a Guianan Cock-of-the-Rock is quite a sight. It extends its crest forward so that it completely covers its bill, and narrows its round eyes to become slits.
• Because of the downward curve of its bill, the White-tipped Sicklebill is a hummingbird that has trouble hovering. To feed from tubular flowers, it has to use its strong feet to clamber over the flowerheads.

Pathfinder

• Do you know what a young Hoatzin looks like? Go to page 13.
• Birds of Paradise are among the most colorful and fascinating birds on Earth. They live in the rain forests of New Guinea and northern Australia. To learn more, see pages 18–19.
• Which South American rain forest bird has a very large bill that has made it famous worldwide? Turn to pages 24–25 to find out.

Chestnut-eared Araçari

Chestnut-capped Puffbird

Harpy Eagle

White-tipped Sicklebill

Blue-crowned Trogon

MADAGASCAR MARVEL
Almost half of Africa's Madagascar Island birds are threatened with habitat loss. The Sunbird Asity is only one of a few birds that can adapt to life after logging. It can live in new growth forests.

HANGING ON
The Blue-crowned Hanging-Parrot lives in Malaya, Sumatra, and Borneo. Forests there have existed in their present form for 70–100 million years. If these ecosystems are destroyed, they can never be recreated.

FIGHTING CHANCE
The Double-wattled Cassowary is a flightless bird that lives in New Guinea and northern Australia. Its habitat in Australia is a World Heritage site, which helps protect the birds.

Wide Open Spaces

GRASSLANDS HAVE DIFFERENT names in different parts of the world. They are known as savannas, prairies, pampas, and steppes. They can be harsh habitats, occurring where climates are too dry and soils too poor for trees to grow.

On the enormous African savannas, Ostriches and White-quilled Bustards feed on plants and insects. Hungry vultures circle in the sky, waiting for lions to leave their kill. And many other birds, including sandgrouse and a variety of brilliantly colored finches, feast on the largest food supply of this region—grass seeds.

In South America there are the vast, rolling pampas, where the Rufous Hornero builds its strange mud nests. But in North America and Europe there are few unspoiled grasslands. Much of the land has been taken over for farming. These large farms and other human developments have taken away the nesting areas and natural food sources of many birds, causing some to be in danger of extinction. The Greater Prairie-Chickens that still survive have learned to eat the grain in farm fields, especially after heavy snowfall, and some farmers consider them a pest.

The Russian steppes, which stretch into northern Asia, are cooler in temperature than most grasslands because they lie farther from the equator. The nights here can be freezing cold. The Rosy Starling eats almost anything it can find. It has adapted to the treeless habitat by wedging its nests in cracks in rocky outcrops.

MAKING A BEELINE

All animals must be resourceful in order to survive the harsh conditions of the African savannas. The Greater Honeyguide eats insects like many other birds but is unique in its ability to digest beeswax. To get the wax, the honeyguide leads a honeybadger, mongoose, or even a person to a beehive, catching their attention with its chattering calls and repeated spurts of flight. The honeyguide waits for the nest to be opened by the honey seeker, and then seizes its chance to feed on the beeswax.

Superb Starling

Gray Crowned-Cranes

HANDS ON

A Place to Hide

Birds will come near you only if they think you're not there. You need to sit still and quiet, and out of sight, perhaps behind some bushes or a fence. In open spaces like grasslands, a blind can provide an ideal place from which to secretly observe birds.

❶ You'll need four sturdy poles, about 6 feet (1.8 m) long, string, one or two pieces of dark cloth, about the size of a double-bed sheet or larger, and some clothespins.

❷ Arrange your poles. Some people shape them like a tepee, tying the poles together at the top with string. Others prefer a box-shape, with the poles pushed firmly into the ground to keep them upright.

❸ Wrap your cloth around the poles, and secure with clothespins.

❹ Fold the cloth so that you create an entrance to your blind. On the opposite side, make a small observation window at eye level. Then wait patiently for the birds.

Word Builders

- The word **savanna** comes from the extinct Taino language. It was spoken by the Arawaks, people who lived on the islands of the Caribbean. Their word for grassland was *zabana*.
- The **Rufous Hornero** builds a nest that resembles a bread oven, hence the bird's name. The Spanish word for baker is *hornero*. Rufous comes from the Latin word *rufus*, meaning "red."

That's Amazing!

- The Red-billed Quelea lives on the plains of Africa. It gathers in roosts that number tens of millions of birds. These birds feed on grain and can strip a farmer's large crop in one day.
- The Burrowing Owls of North and South America have gone underground to nest and keep safe from predators. They live in the old burrows of prairie dogs or other mammals, emerging at night to feed.

Pathfinder

- If you want to know more about flightless grassland birds, such as rheas, check out pages 22–23.
- To see the strange mud nest that the Rufous Hornero builds, and many other nests, turn to pages 30–31.
- Which grassland bird hops on the back of antelope, giraffe, buffalo, and rhino when it is looking for something tasty to eat? See page 37.

Paradise Whydah

Greater Honeyguide

Ostriches

Helmeted Guinea-Fowl

IF THE BILL FITS

The bills of most seed-eating birds are shaped like a cone, and are usually short and stout. This shape enables the birds to exert pressure and crack the outer layer of the seeds to get at the nutritious contents. The grasslands of South America are home to a large number of seed-eating birds.

The Double-collared Seedeater's bill has a curved culmen, or upper ridge. This bill adaptation is perfectly suited for opening the seeds of a great variety of grasses and small plants.

The Great Pampa-Finch has a heavy, curved bill that copes well with the large seeds of the huge grasses that grow on many parts of the Pampas of Argentina.

The striking Red-crested Cardinal has a bill that is capable of husking a large variety of seeds. This bird can usually be seen feeding in pairs or small groups.

Rufous Rockjumper

Mountain Chickadee

Snow Finch

Alpine Accentor

On Higher Ground

MOST OF THE WORLD'S continents have their own great mountain range—the Rockies, Appalachians, and Andes in America, the Alps, Pyrenees, and Urals in Europe, and the mighty Himalayas in Asia. As you travel up a mountain, the temperature falls. This creates a vast range of habitats, allowing many bird species to find food and nesting sites.

At the base, forests tend to grow thickly. Many birds in North America and Europe feed on seeds from cold-forest trees known as conifers—pines, spruces, cedars, and firs. Depending on the season, some birds migrate between these forests and the meadows higher up. Mountain Chickadees and Alpine Accentors forage in the forests during the cooler months but travel above the tree-line in search of insects when it is warmer. The occasional bush and conifer on the meadows provide year-round shelter for birds such as the Snow Finch.

The meadows give way to rocky outcrops and steep cliffs. Rufous Rockjumpers build nests in the crevices lower down, but few birds live in the windswept heights. If they do, they need to defend large territories because food is scarce. Andean Condors search for many hours over vast areas before they find carrion on which to feed.

Spotted Forktail

INSIDE STORY
A Journey of Discovery

In 1803, United States president Thomas Jefferson planned a trip of exploration to find an overland route from the Mississippi River to the Pacific Ocean. Meriwether Lewis and William Clark were the leaders of the expedition, which set out in the spring of 1804. Along the way, they were helped by a young Shoshoni guide named Sacagawea.

Two years later, the expedition returned to the Mississippi with tales of amazing adventures and descriptions of mountain birds and wildlife that Easterners had never seen. Lewis was a keen observer of the newly found birds and brought back many sketches he had made of them. Two of the bird species were eventually named for the explorers—Clark's Nutcracker and Lewis's Woodpecker.

SUMMER RETREATS
Coniferous forests surround the base of mountains in temperate zones. The Japanese Waxwing of north Asia comes to these forests for fruit. These birds have waxlike droplets on the tip of some of their wing feathers, which explains their name.

The Steller's Jay lives in the Rocky Mountains. It is a very noisy bird. Sometimes it sounds like a hawk screeching while at other times it sings sweetly. The Steller's Jay likes stealing food from picnics.

Word Builders

- The word **condor** comes from the Quechua word *kuntur*. Quechua is a language of Indians who live in the South American Andes.
- The Indian Hill Myna has a syrinx, a specialized organ at the base of the windpipe, that allows it to mimic human speech so well that it's hard to tell the bird from the person. **Myna** comes from the Hindi word *maina*, which is the ancient name for this bird.

That's Amazing!

Some birds, such as the small Mountain Chickadees, survive dramatic drops in high-altitude temperatures by decreasing their body temperature by as much as 50 degrees Fahrenheit (10 degrees C). They do this by lowering their metabolism, breathing rate, and heart rate. This puts them into a state of inactivity that is known as torpor.

Pathfinder

- Which bird of prey can be found gliding high over the Himalayas? Turn to page 11 to find out.
- What sort of nests do birds build on mountain cliffs? See page 31.
- Coniferous forests stretch across the top of the Northern Hemisphere. Which type of forest lies near the equator, and how do birds live in that habitat? Pages 56–57 will reveal all.

Red-billed Magpie

Indian Hill Myna

Blue Whistling Thrushes

Wallcreeper

Himalayan Monals

PHEASANT LIFE

The Himalayas are the world's highest mountains. Many birds live on the slopes, including the Blue Whistling Thrush, Wallcreeper, Red-billed Magpie, Indian Hill Myna, and Spotted Forktail. Himalayan Monals live in the forests and meadows about halfway up. These ground-dwellers use their curved bills to dig up roots, bulbs, and insect grubs, often from snow-covered soil. When in danger, they run down the slopes, flapping their wings for speed. Then, when the scare is over, they waddle slowly back up to their feeding grounds.

Treecreepers do as their name suggests—they creep up the tree trunks. They climb in a spiral motion, probing the bark with their curved bills for insects and larvae. When they reach the top, they fly to the base of the next tree and start again.

The Red Crossbill has a bill that crosses at the tip. This shape, along with the birds' strong muscles, helps the crossbill to pry open fresh pine cones and get at the seeds inside. Other birds have to wait for the cones to open naturally.

 *Lichtenstein's Sandgrouse*

 *Houbara Bustard*

 *Harris's Hawk*

Gibber Chat

Fire and Ice

THE HARSHEST ENVIRONMENTS on Earth are the superhot deserts and the ice-capped Arctic and Antarctic regions—the North and South poles. The ground is either baked hard or frozen solid. Few plants or animals can live in these bleak habitats, so birds (and other creatures) must find clever ways to survive.

In the African deserts, the male Lichtenstein's Sandgrouse uses its belly feathers like a sponge. It lies in whatever water it can find and soaks its feathers. Then it carries the liquid back to its young. The Houbara Bustard lives in the wide arid belt between Algeria and central Asia, and gets the water it needs from water-filled insects and plants. Harris's Hawks nest among the spikes of cacti. They help each other to survive by hunting for prey in groups. The Gibber Chat, in the stony deserts of Australia, raises no young when conditions are too harsh.

Desert birds conserve energy by staying quiet during the heat of the day. The best time to see them is at sunrise or sunset, when the temperatures are cooler.

The polar regions are the coldest places on Earth. Huge ice sheets grow larger in winter, and shrink in summer. Most birds visit these regions in summer only, when the weather is milder and there is more food to eat. But the Adélie Penguin and the Emperor Penguin are hardy enough to live in Antarctica all year.

PRICKLY SITUATIONS

Cacti are plants with scales or spikes that people avoid touching. But in North America's western deserts, birds use these plants to help them survive. The Verdin hangs upside down from cactus branches while it looks for insects. The Gila Woodpecker makes two kinds of holes in the saguaro cactus. One is for hunting for insects; the other is a nest hole, in which it lays its eggs. Elf Owls use abandoned Gila Woodpecker holes for shelter and nesting. The Gambel's Quail lives among the cacti, feeding mostly on seeds and the occasional insect.

Cactus Wren

INSIDE STORY
Doing It the Hard Way

Because Emperor Penguins live in Antarctica, little was known about their nesting habits until the early 1900s. Three explorers—Edward Wilson, Apsley Cherry-Garrard, and Henry Bowers—made a harrowing climb around the edge of the Ross Ice Shelf in the winter of 1911. They climbed down a steep, icy ridge, and were amazed to discover a rookery—the place where penguins incubate their eggs and care for the hatchlings.

Hundreds of male Emperor Penguins were gathered in the cold, bleak weather. Each penguin had a single large egg resting on its feet. The egg was covered by a special flap of skin that kept it warm even when the temperature fell as low as -80 degrees Fahrenheit (-60 degrees C). Later, it was discovered that female Emperor Penguins, after having laid their eggs, spend the winter in the sea, leaving the males to hatch the eggs. They return later to help rear the young.

Word Builders

• The arid gibber plains of Australia are covered in weather-worn rocks and boulders. **Gibber** comes from the Australian Aboriginal Dharug word *giba*, meaning "stone."
• **Tundra** comes from a Russian word that means "marshy plain."
• **Arctic** is from the Greek word *arktikos*, meaning "bear." The northern constellation called the Great Bear can be seen above the Arctic.

That's Amazing!

• The Poorwill lives in the western deserts of North America. It is the Sleeping Beauty of the bird world. The only bird known to hibernate for long periods in winter, it sleeps so deeply that it doesn't wake even when someone picks it up and holds it.
• The Rock Ptarmigan flies into soft snowbanks to sleep. It can sleep safely, insulated by the snow, because it has left no tracks for predators to see.

Pathfinder

• The Persian Gulf in the Middle East is surrounded by hot, burning sands. One bird has found a clever way to keep its eggs cool there. See page 11.
• Which seabird steals into penguin colonies to take their eggs for supper? The answer is on page 39.

Elf Owl

Verdin

Roadrunner

Gila Woodpecker

Gambel's Quail

SUMMER HOMES
Vast treeless plains around the Arctic are called tundra. Some birds live there all year, but most come only during the summer.

CHANGING COLORS
The Rock Ptarmigan lives all year on the tundra. During summer, the brownish color of its plumage blends in with the rocks and lichens of its habitat. The ptarmigan molts during fall, turning white to match the winter snow.

NURTURING MALE
The Red-necked Phalarope lives in the Arctic during the warmer summer months. The female is more brightly colored than the male. She takes the lead in courtship rituals. The male incubates the eggs and takes care of the chicks.

SKILLFUL HUNTER
The Snowy Owl may kill up to 10 lemmings a day. When plenty of food is available, the females raise many chicks. When food is scarce, they hatch no young.

SUMMER MIGRANT
Lapland Longspurs migrate to the tundra to nest in summer. Because there are no trees, the male must hop up onto rocks when displaying or defending his territory.

bill   *clutch*   *crest*   *display*   *egg tooth*

Glossary

adaptation A change in a bird's or other animal's body that allows it to function and reproduce more successfully in a particular environment.

altricial Helpless at birth or hatching, and dependent on care from adults. Many bird hatchlings are altricial.

bill The horny covering of the jaws of a bird, comprising two halves—the maxilla and the mandible. Sometimes called a beak.

brood A number of young birds hatched in one clutch or group. As a verb, "to brood" means to shelter young birds from the sun, heat, or cold.

call A sound, other than a song, used by birds for communicating messages.

carrion The flesh of dead animals that is eaten by birds or other animals. Creatures that eat carrion are called scavengers.

class One of several divisions into which scientists divide animals. Birds are in a class of their own, which is called Aves.

clutch All the eggs laid by a bird in one breeding cycle.

conifer A tree or shrub, such as a pine, fir, or spruce, that produces cones.

conservation An effort by people to protect a natural area so that plants and animals can live there undisturbed by human development.

courtship The behavior patterns that male and female birds and other animals display when they are trying to attract a mate.

crepuscular Active at dusk or dawn, when the light level is low.

crest The elongated or erect feathers of a bird's crown.

cryptic The kind of marking or coloring that makes a bird difficult for a predator to see against the bird's natural surroundings.

deciduous A description of a tree that loses all its leaves at once, usually in the autumn. Maples, oaks, and birches are deciduous.

display A behavior or set of behaviors that aims to attract the attention of another bird. Also, it may threaten or distract another bird or animal.

distribution Where a species is found, including its habitat, range, and location at different seasons.

diurnal Active during the daytime.

ecosystem The carefully balanced interaction of plants, animals, and their environment, usually in a particular habitat.

egg The large, rounded shell that contains a yolk and a white, laid by a female bird. If it has been fertilized, the egg contains a tiny embryo that will grow into a baby bird, using the yolk and white as food. When mature, the baby will break out of the eggshell.

egg tooth A sharp, tooth-shaped calcium deposit that grows on the tip of the bill of an embryonic bird. The bird uses the tooth to help it break through the shell when it is hatching.

endemic Found only in one habitat or region. Most penguins are endemic to the cold waters of the Southern Hemisphere.

environment The whole of an animal's surroundings, which influences the animal's development and behavior.

evolution The constant genetic adaptation of species to their environments.

extinct No longer existing alive anywhere in the world. Many bird species are extinct.

feather One of the objects that make up a bird's covering or plumage. A feather is made of a horny substance called keratin, and has a long shaft to which two vanes are attached. The vanes, made up of many closely spaced barbs, give the feather its shape and color. Feathers have many uses. They keep birds warm and dry, and help them to fly.

field mark A particular feature of a bird species that helps birdwatchers tell it apart from other species.

fledgling A very young bird that has left the nest in which it hatched. Prior to leaving the nest, it is known as a nestling.

habitat The native or natural environment of a bird, other animal, or plant.

hatch To break free from the eggshell.

imprinting A process in which hatchlings or other very young animals attach themselves to a parental figure.

incubation Keeping eggs warm so that the embryos inside will grow and hatch. The parent bird usually uses its body to warm the eggs, but some birds use sand or rotting leaves and plants.

instinct An inborn (or innate) behavior that develops in a bird or other animal without learning. Ducklings begin to swim by instinct.

invertebrate An animal that does not have a backbone, such as a worm, crab, or jellyfish.

iridescent Showing different colors as light strikes from different angles, like a soap bubble or oil on a pool of water. The plumage of some birds is iridescent.

juvenile A young bird or other animal. Some juveniles have markings that are very different from those of adults of the same species, so they may be difficult to identify.

feather   *fledgling*   *invertebrate*   *juvenile*

molting   *nest*   *predator*   *shaft*

mandible The lower part of a bird's bill, usually a bit smaller than the upper part.

mate A bird's partner during courtship and mating.

maxilla The top part of a bird's bill, usually a bit larger than the lower part.

migration The movement of birds from one place to another, which usually occurs in the spring and autumn.

mobbing An action used by a flock of small birds to drive away a predator. They follow, surround, and attack the larger bird, which often flies away. The flock may also use mobbing to teach young birds which predators to be wary of.

molting The process by which birds shed old, worn feathers and replace them with new ones.

nectar The sweet, sugary secretions of flowering plants that attract birds and insects.

nest A pocketlike structure that is often made of branches, twigs, and grass. Many birds build nests in which to lay and incubate their eggs, and to feed their young.

nestling A young bird that has not yet left its nest after hatching. It relies on its parents for food and protection.

nocturnal Active at night.

ornithologist A person who makes a scientific study of birds.

pellet A small, hard object that some birds regurgitate (spit up) containing parts of their food that they could not digest, such as bones, fur, or shell.

pigment Any substance that creates color in the skin, feathers, or tissues of a bird, other animal, or plant.

pouch A sac-like area of skin stretched between the two sides of the lower jaw of a bird, such as the one on a pelican.

predator A creature that hunts and eats other live creatures. Birds of prey are predators that hunt other birds or mammals.

preen For a bird, to clean and restore the structure of its feathers so that they remain in good condition.

prey An animal that is killed by another animal to be eaten. The killer animal is called a predator.

range The entire geographic area across which a species is regularly found.

rectrix A technical term used by scientists to describe a bird's tail feathers.

remige A technical term used by scientists to describe a bird's flight feathers.

roost An area where birds come to socialize, preen, or sleep.

scavenger A bird or other animal that feeds on dead animals. Many vultures and crows are scavengers.

scrape A depression in the ground made by some bird species in which to lay their eggs.

shaft The long, slender, central part of the feather that holds the vanes.

solitary A bird that stays by itself at least during some seasons of the year.

song A sound or series of sounds made by a bird to announce its territory or seek a mate. Bird songs can be simple or elaborate, and some are very musical.

species A group of birds, other animals, or plants with common features that distinguish them from any other group.

sternum The breastbone. Flying birds have a large, deeply keeled sternum to anchor their powerful flight muscles.

tapered Becoming smaller or thinner toward one end.

territory An area that is defended by a bird or other animal species against other creatures of the same species, especially during the mating season.

thermal A column of warm air that is rising. Some birds ride upward in thermals, to gain height, then glide slowly downward again.

theropods A group that includes all meat-eating dinosaurs.

torpor A state of dormancy—a kind of sleep—in which a bird or other animal can lower its heart rate and body temperature to save energy, especially during the night or periods of cold temperatures.

tundra The vast, treeless Arctic plains of northern Asia, Europe, and North America.

vane The part of the feather that grows from the central shaft.

vertebrates Animals with backbones, including birds, fishes, reptiles, amphibians, and mammals. The vertebrae are the bones that make up the spine.

vortex Circular air currents made by the movement of the wingtips of a bird.

yolk The yellow part of an egg. If the egg is fertilized, a tiny embryo grows inside the egg, using the yolk (and the white) as food.

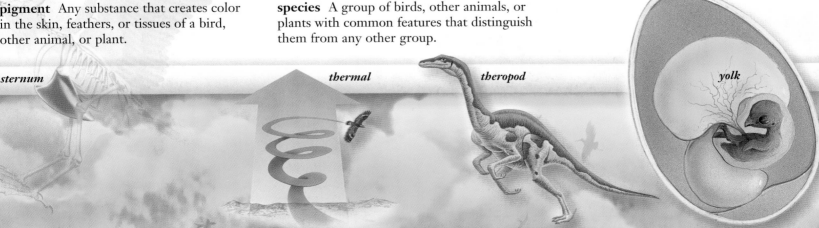

sternum   *thermal*   *theropod*   *yolk*

Index

Sharks
and Other Sea Creatures

Contents

Introducing...Sharks 70

Sharkworks 90

A Shark's World 110

Pick Your Path!

READY FOR A swim with *Sharks and Other Sea Creatures*? Plunge into the pages of this book for a look at some of nature's most efficient underwater predators. Cruise straight through with the gentle giants of the shark world, then come face to face with the scariest shark of them all—the great white. Or follow your interests. Have you always wondered how fishes breathe underwater? Dive right into "Deep Breathing" and read on from there.

You'll find plenty of other discovery paths to choose from in the special features sections. Read about real-life shark experts in "Inside Story," or get creative with "Hands On" activities. Delve into words with "Word Builders," or amaze your friends with fascinating facts from "That's Amazing!" You can choose a new path with every reading—READER'S DIGEST PATHFINDERS will take you wherever *you* want to go.

INSIDE STORY
Close Encounters

Find out what it takes to make an aquarium shark feel right at home. Picture yourself alongside scientists who spend 17 hours underwater in a small sub to learn about deep-sea creatures. Relive the excitement as one shark expert identifies a totally new species! INSIDE STORY introduces you to men and women who've devoted their lives to studying sharks. You'll also meet people who've come face to face with these incredible animals—and have lived to tell their tales.

HANDS ON
Things to Do

Create a vacuum with a rubber suction cup and discover first hand how a remora stays attached to a shark. Use makeup to help you fade into the background just like a carpet shark. Check out other underwater creatures for yourself—in person. The HANDS ON features offer experiments and projects—practical ways to help you appreciate the special requirements of a shark's underwater world.

Word Builders

What a strange word! What does it mean? Where did it come from? Find out by reading *Word Builders*.

That's Amazing!

Awesome facts, amazing records, fascinating figures—you'll find them all in *That's Amazing!*

Pathfinder

Use the *Pathfinder* section to find your way from one subject to another. It's all up to you.

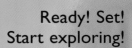

Ready! Set! Start exploring!

Introducing... Sharks

THERE'S MORE TO sharks than the toothy maw you've seen coming at you in the movies or on television. And now's your chance to get a glimpse of a few of them. First we'll meet sharks' ancestors, and then we'll cruise the deep alongside modern-day sharks. There are sharks with strangely shaped heads and others with tremendous tails. Some—the largest ones—have lost the need for teeth altogether. It's time to take the plunge...

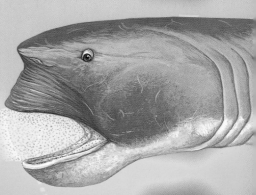

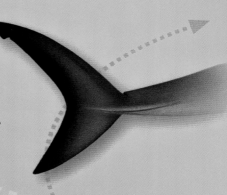

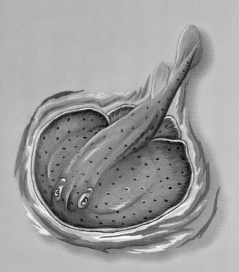

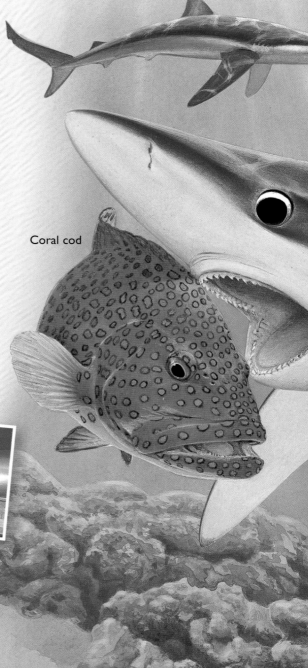
Coral cod

What Is a Shark?

WHAT IS IT about sharks that terrifies people? Is it the gaping maw, the jagged teeth, the cold eyes? Most people think of sharks as gigantic underwater man-eaters. But the truth is that only some sharks (but not all, or even most) are dangerous to humans.

Sharks are fishes, and like all fishes, they have a strong, sturdy skeleton. What sets sharks apart from other fishes is that their skeletons are made of a lighter and more flexible (yet durable) substance known as cartilage. Scientists call sharks cartilaginous fishes.

Scientists have identified about 340 species of sharks. All have a powerful tail, or caudal fin, and two sets of paired side fins. The pair toward the front of the body are called pectorals. The two toward the back are called pelvic fins. Most shark species also have two dorsal fins on their back and an anal fin on the underside near the tail. All sharks have at least five pairs of gills and gill openings so that they can breathe underwater.

All sharks are meat-eaters. Some eat prey as large as seals and dolphins. Others eat smaller sharks and fishes. A few—the biggest of them all—feed on tiny marine creatures, such as plankton, shrimps, and small fishes.

 INSIDE STORY
Seeing Sharks

Keeping sharks in aquariums is a tricky business. Many species don't even survive the trip to the aquarium because they simply can't get enough oxygen in a small tank. Those that do make it pose other challenges. They need an environment that mimics their native habitat, plus special shark-friendly tanks. Because sharks tend to rub against walls and bump into corners, aquarists try to build tanks that have smooth walls and no right angles. The walls of the tanks also need to be free of electric cables, because sharks are sensitive to electricity and will knock against the walls in search of the current. But aquarists and researchers are determined to overcome these problems. That way, we can observe, learn about, and protect all sharks—both in aquariums and in the wild.

SHOWCASE OF SHARKS

Not all sharks look alike. Some have flattened heads and wide, gaping mouths. Others have snouts like saw blades, or barbels on their chins. Sharks vary in size, too—some can fit into the palm of your hand, and others are bigger than a school bus!

Whale shark

FILTER FEEDERS
Some sharks don't need teeth to eat. Instead, they suck in huge mouthfuls of water filled with animals or small fishes. They use comblike sieves near their gills to strain the food from the water. A strong tongue flushes water through the gill slits.

Word Builders

- The Latin word for meat or flesh—*carn*—gives us **carnivorous,** meaning "meat-eating." All sharks are carnivorous animals. Their food ranges from tiny plankton to large dolphins.
- A **barbel** is a spine or bristle that hangs from a fish's jaw. The word comes from the Latin *barba*, meaning "beard."
- **Crustaceans** are animals, such as crabs and lobsters, that have hard external skeletons. The word comes from the Latin *crusta*, meaning "shell."

That's Amazing!

Scientists are still finding new species of sharks. The megamouth—a shark as big as a large car—was never seen until 1976, when one was caught accidentally in a fishing net in deep waters off Hawaii. A filter feeder that lives far away from the coast, the megamouth is still rarely sighted by divers. There is no telling how many unidentified sharks cruise the murky depths—yet to be discovered.

Pathfinder

- What were ancient sharks like, and how closely do they resemble the sharks of today? See pages 74–75.
- Rays and skates are related to sharks. Read about their similarities and differences on pages 88–89.
- Sharks have special adaptations that fit them for life underwater. Find out more on pages 92–93.

TAKING ITS TIME
The large Greenland shark is an example of how well sharks adapt to extremes in temperature. Seen here amid ice floes in the Atlantic, this shark moves slowly because of the cold, but it can catch fast prey such as seals. Scientists aren't sure how it does this. They think it might have to do with small crustaceans that live on the shark—they glow in the dark and might attract prey.

SILKY SKINNED
The streamlined silky shark fits everyone's notion of the perfect shark—smooth and graceful as it cruises through the sea. Silkies, so called for their smooth skins, live in warm waters all over the world, from 60 to 1,640 feet (18–500 m) deep. They grow to nearly 8 feet (2.4 m) long.

Blue shark

PREDATOR PREDICAMENT
To be successful hunters, or predators, sharks must find food, or prey, and then catch it. Smaller sharks also have to worry about becoming prey for larger sharks, dolphins, and killer whales. Sharks are extremely well equipped to meet these challenges. They have excellent sensory systems that zero in on prey, as well as powerful muscles and streamlined fins that help them to accelerate quickly.

FLAT SHARKS
Angel sharks are adapted for living, hiding, and feeding on the seafloor. Their speckled skin blends with their sandy home. They look like rays, but rays have gill slits on their undersides instead of on their sides. Aptly named for the shape of their pectoral fins, angel sharks are also known as monk sharks because the head looks like a monk's hood.

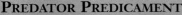

Angel shark

NOSING AROUND
Sawsharks drag their barbels—sensitive "whiskers" under their noses—through the sand to locate buried prey. Then they dig up the food with their long tooth-studded snouts.

Sawshark

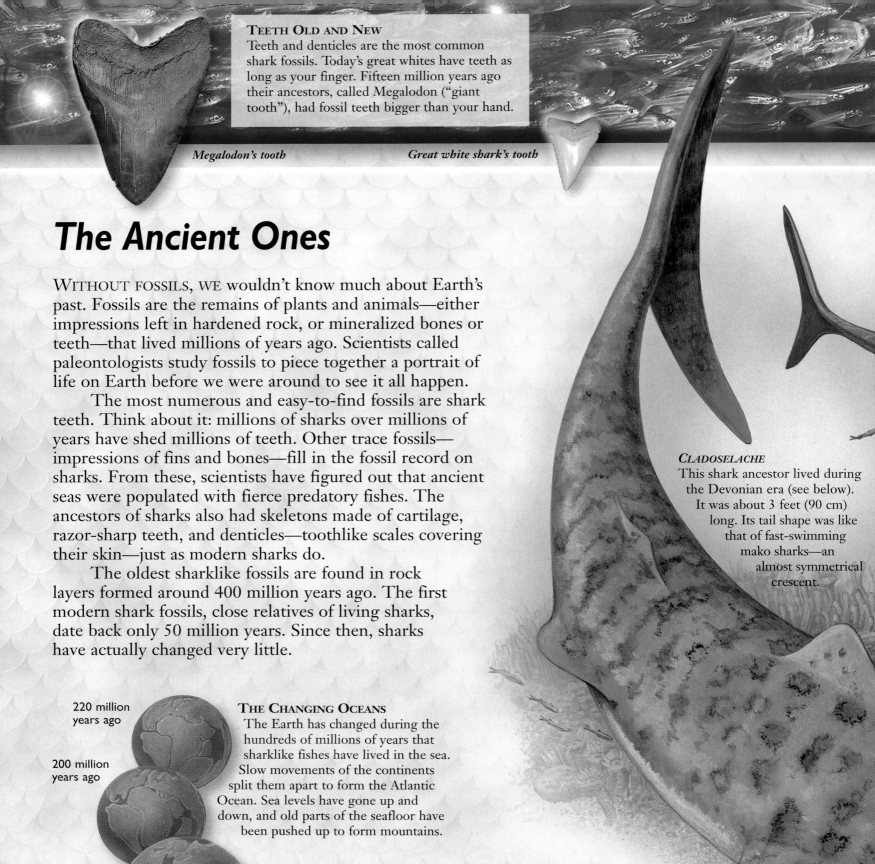

TEETH OLD AND NEW
Teeth and denticles are the most common shark fossils. Today's great whites have teeth as long as your finger. Fifteen million years ago their ancestors, called Megalodon ("giant tooth"), had fossil teeth bigger than your hand.

Megalodon's tooth   *Great white shark's tooth*

The Ancient Ones

WITHOUT FOSSILS, WE wouldn't know much about Earth's past. Fossils are the remains of plants and animals—either impressions left in hardened rock, or mineralized bones or teeth—that lived millions of years ago. Scientists called paleontologists study fossils to piece together a portrait of life on Earth before we were around to see it all happen.

The most numerous and easy-to-find fossils are shark teeth. Think about it: millions of sharks over millions of years have shed millions of teeth. Other trace fossils—impressions of fins and bones—fill in the fossil record on sharks. From these, scientists have figured out that ancient seas were populated with fierce predatory fishes. The ancestors of sharks also had skeletons made of cartilage, razor-sharp teeth, and denticles—toothlike scales covering their skin—just as modern sharks do.

The oldest sharklike fossils are found in rock layers formed around 400 million years ago. The first modern shark fossils, close relatives of living sharks, date back only 50 million years. Since then, sharks have actually changed very little.

CLADOSELACHE
This shark ancestor lived during the Devonian era (see below). It was about 3 feet (90 cm) long. Its tail shape was like that of fast-swimming mako sharks—an almost symmetrical crescent.

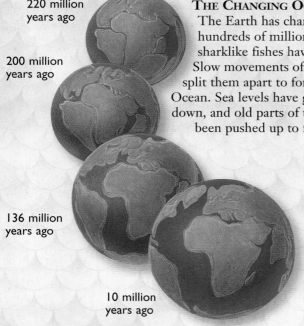

220 million years ago

200 million years ago

136 million years ago

10 million years ago

THE CHANGING OCEANS
The Earth has changed during the hundreds of millions of years that sharklike fishes have lived in the sea. Slow movements of the continents split them apart to form the Atlantic Ocean. Sea levels have gone up and down, and old parts of the seafloor have been pushed up to form mountains.

SHARK ANCESTORS
Judging from the fossil evidence, there were large fishes in ancient times that looked like modern sharks. Despite some physical differences, the size and shape of their teeth suggest that they—like today's sharks—were some of the sea's top predators. Modern sharks are thought to have descended from these ancient fishes.

SHARKS IN TIME
Each period of the Earth's history features fossils known from specially named layers of rock. The study of these layers is called stratigraphy. The earliest sharklike fossils are found in Devonian rocks. The species we see today arose eons later in the Cenozoic era.

Precambrian Time	Cambrian	Ordovician	Silurian	Devonia
				Paleozoic
4,600 million years ago 550 mya	505 mya	435 mya	408 mya	

Word Builders

- **Paleontology**, the word for the study of fossils and ancient life, is from the Greek words *paleo,* meaning "ancient," and *-logos,* meaning "word."
- **Devonian** fossils were first found in ancient rocks near Devon, England.
- **Stratigraphy** comes from the Latin *stratum,* meaning "layer," and the Greek *graphein,* meaning "to write."

That's Amazing!

The fossil record of sharks goes back almost 400 million years, making it three times as long as that of the dinosaurs and almost 100 times longer than that of humans. Horn sharks have the longest fossil record of any living shark. The skeleton and teeth of a 160-million-year-old fossil shark look almost exactly like those of a horn shark you could catch today.

Pathfinder

- Is the Megalodon's descendant, the great white shark, really as scary as people think? Turn to pages 78–79.
- Does the shape of a shark's tail affect how fast it swims? Find out on pages 84–85.
- Which modern shark resembles 200-million-year-old fossils? See page 118.

HYBODONTS

These shark forebears shared lakes, rivers, and the seas with dinosaurs and other creatures. They all died out at about the same time—65 million years ago. Hybodont remains have been found at dinosaur fossil sites in Wyoming. They grew up to 6¹/₂ feet (2 m) long.

XENACANTHIDS

Remains of this mostly freshwater fish have been found all over the world. Xenacanthids evolved from *Cladoselache* and lived from Devonian to Triassic times. They were about 10 feet (3 m) long.

QUITE A STRETCH

Megalodon was an ancestor of the great white shark. Only fossils of its teeth have been found. From these, people have been able to make models of its jaws. Some of these models are probably far too big, but they still give a good idea of just how huge this shark might have been.

INSIDE STORY

Detective Work

Shark ancestors swam in the sea for eons. Suddenly they were gone. What happened? Scientists think it went something like this: 65 million years ago a meteor slammed into Earth. Fires raged. The sky turned black. And creatures like the dinosaurs and shark ancestors may have died out as a result. We know something about the fishes that perished because they had body parts that fossilized. Hard parts of animals make the best fossils. Since sharks and their ancestors had few hard parts, complete fossilized skeletons are rare. The best fossils were formed when the fishes were buried in silt and calm water. Scientists can even tell what some fishes ate from their fossilized stomach contents.

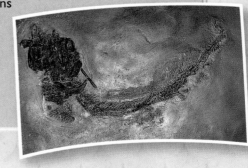

Carboniferous	Permian	Triassic	Jurassic	Cretaceous	Tertiary	Quaternary
		Mesozoic			Cenozoic	

| mya | 286 mya | 248 mya | 208 mya | 144 mya | 65 mya | 2 mya | 0 |

Putting Sharks in Order

EVERYONE HAS A family. Your immediate family includes your parents and siblings. Your other relatives—cousins, aunts, uncles, and grandparents—make up your extended family. Sharks are divided up into large, extended family groups, too. Scientists call these groups "orders." The sharks in each order share certain common features, and all have descended, long ago, from a single ancestor.

How do we tell the orders apart? Some sharks share certain features with other sharks, such as how many fins and gills they have, the location of their mouths, or the shape of their bodies, fins, and snouts. All these things help scientists decide to what order to assign each shark.

Scientists have grouped sharks into eight orders. Two of the orders—the Carcharhiniformes and the Lamniformes—have many features in common. They have an anal fin, five pairs of gill slits, two dorsal fins, no fin spines, and a mouth set behind their eyes. What sets them apart is eyelids! Lamniformes (including great whites and threshers) have none. Carcharhiniformes (including hammerheads and tiger sharks) have eyelids, so they can open and shut their eyes much as we do.

NICTITATING EYELID
All Carcharhiniformes, such as this oceanic whitetip, have a feature called a nictitating membrane—an eyelid that stretches, from bottom to top, over the eyeball and protects it. This is especially handy when the shark is eating a struggling fish that could poke and blind it.

Coastal sharks such as the lemon shark hunt for rays and bony fishes near the sunlit surface.

The oceanic whitetip hunts far from the coast, in open sea. It eats fishes, birds, and turtles.

INSIDE STORY
Adaptation Wins the Day

Many sharks eat fishes. To avoid competition, some sharks have changed to eating hard-shelled creatures. This nurse shark, for example, is munching on a lobster. Its change in diet and its teeth that are specially suited for crunching are examples of adaptation. When two kinds of sharks compete for the same food in the same place at the same time, one species will lose out. In order to survive, those sharks, their young, and future generations must change in some way.

Those that change their diet, or feed at a different time, avoid competition and improve their chances of survival.

FITTING IN
Over many generations a species changes for life in a special place. Great white sharks have adapted to live in cool waters, where seals and sea lions raise their young. Bramble sharks have adapted to become suction feeders of crabs and squids near the seafloor.

OUTWARD APPEARANCE

When trying to identify a shark, take a look at its physical features. Is the head conical, flattened, or blunt-nosed? Where is the mouth positioned? How many pairs of gill slits are there? How many dorsal fins are there? Are they the same size?

COUNT THOSE GILLS
All sharks have at least five pairs of gills. Some sharks have six, like this bluntnose sixgill shark, or even seven pairs. Bony fishes have several pairs of gills, too, but they are all protected by a bony cover with a single gill slit. Shark gill slits have no protection. Water comes out of the gill slits, taking with it dissolved waste products that the shark produces as it breathes and eats.

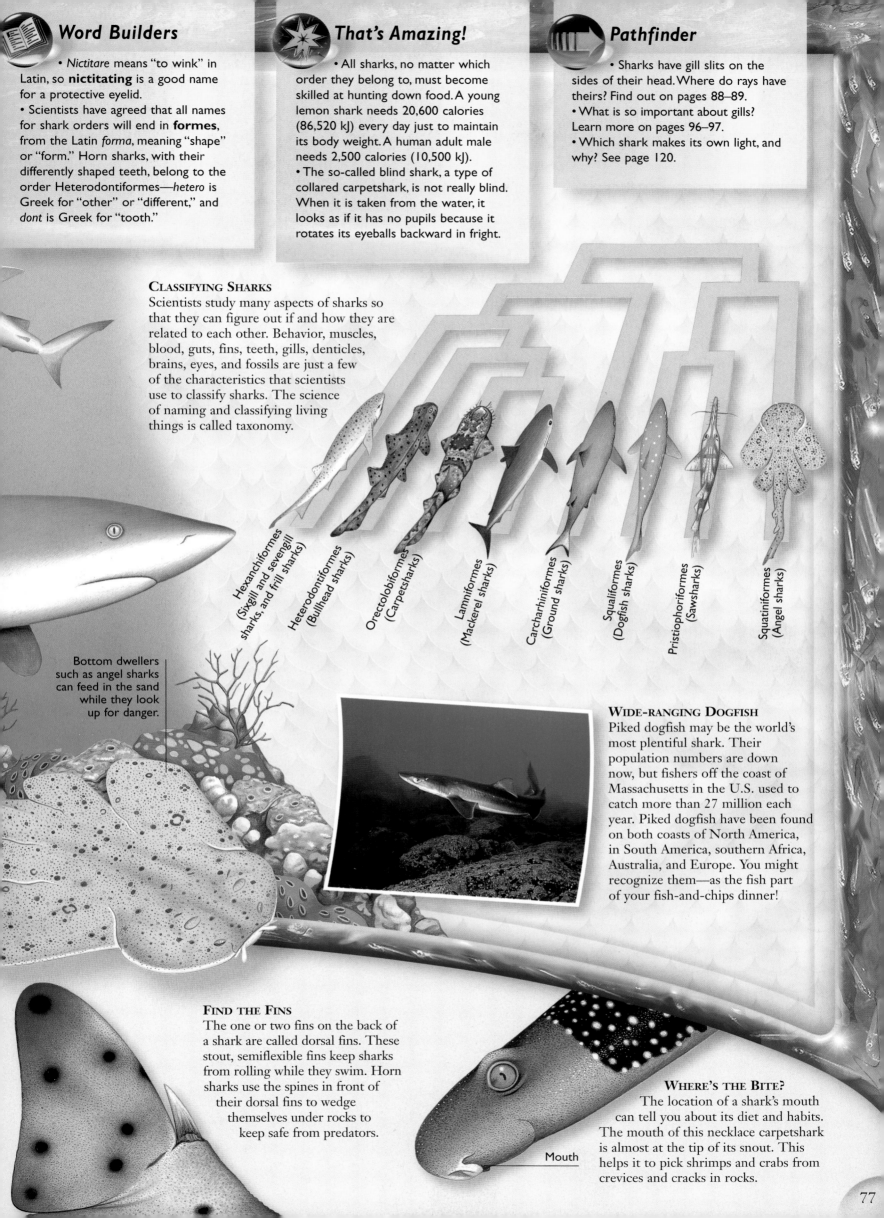

Word Builders

- *Nictitare* means "to wink" in Latin, so **nictitating** is a good name for a protective eyelid.
- Scientists have agreed that all names for shark orders will end in **formes**, from the Latin *forma*, meaning "shape" or "form." Horn sharks, with their differently shaped teeth, belong to the order Heterodontiformes—*hetero* is Greek for "other" or "different," and *dont* is Greek for "tooth."

That's Amazing!

- All sharks, no matter which order they belong to, must become skilled at hunting down food. A young lemon shark needs 20,600 calories (86,520 kJ) every day just to maintain its body weight. A human adult male needs 2,500 calories (10,500 kJ).
- The so-called blind shark, a type of collared carpetshark, is not really blind. When it is taken from the water, it looks as if it has no pupils because it rotates its eyeballs backward in fright.

Pathfinder

- Sharks have gill slits on the sides of their head. Where do rays have theirs? Find out on pages 88–89.
- What is so important about gills? Learn more on pages 96–97.
- Which shark makes its own light, and why? See page 120.

CLASSIFYING SHARKS

Scientists study many aspects of sharks so that they can figure out if and how they are related to each other. Behavior, muscles, blood, guts, fins, teeth, gills, denticles, brains, eyes, and fossils are just a few of the characteristics that scientists use to classify sharks. The science of naming and classifying living things is called taxonomy.

Hexanchiformes (Sixgill and sevengill sharks, and frill sharks)

Heterodontiformes (Bullhead sharks)

Orectolobiformes (Carpetsharks)

Lamniformes (Mackerel sharks)

Carcharhiniformes (Ground sharks)

Squaliformes (Dogfish sharks)

Pristiophoriformes (Sawsharks)

Squatiniformes (Angel sharks)

Bottom dwellers such as angel sharks can feed in the sand while they look up for danger.

WIDE-RANGING DOGFISH

Piked dogfish may be the world's most plentiful shark. Their population numbers are down now, but fishers off the coast of Massachusetts in the U.S. used to catch more than 27 million each year. Piked dogfish have been found on both coasts of North America, in South America, southern Africa, Australia, and Europe. You might recognize them—as the fish part of your fish-and-chips dinner!

FIND THE FINS

The one or two fins on the back of a shark are called dorsal fins. These stout, semiflexible fins keep sharks from rolling while they swim. Horn sharks use the spines in front of their dorsal fins to wedge themselves under rocks to keep safe from predators.

Mouth

WHERE'S THE BITE?

The location of a shark's mouth can tell you about its diet and habits. The mouth of this necklace carpetshark is almost at the tip of its snout. This helps it to pick shrimps and crabs from crevices and cracks in rocks.

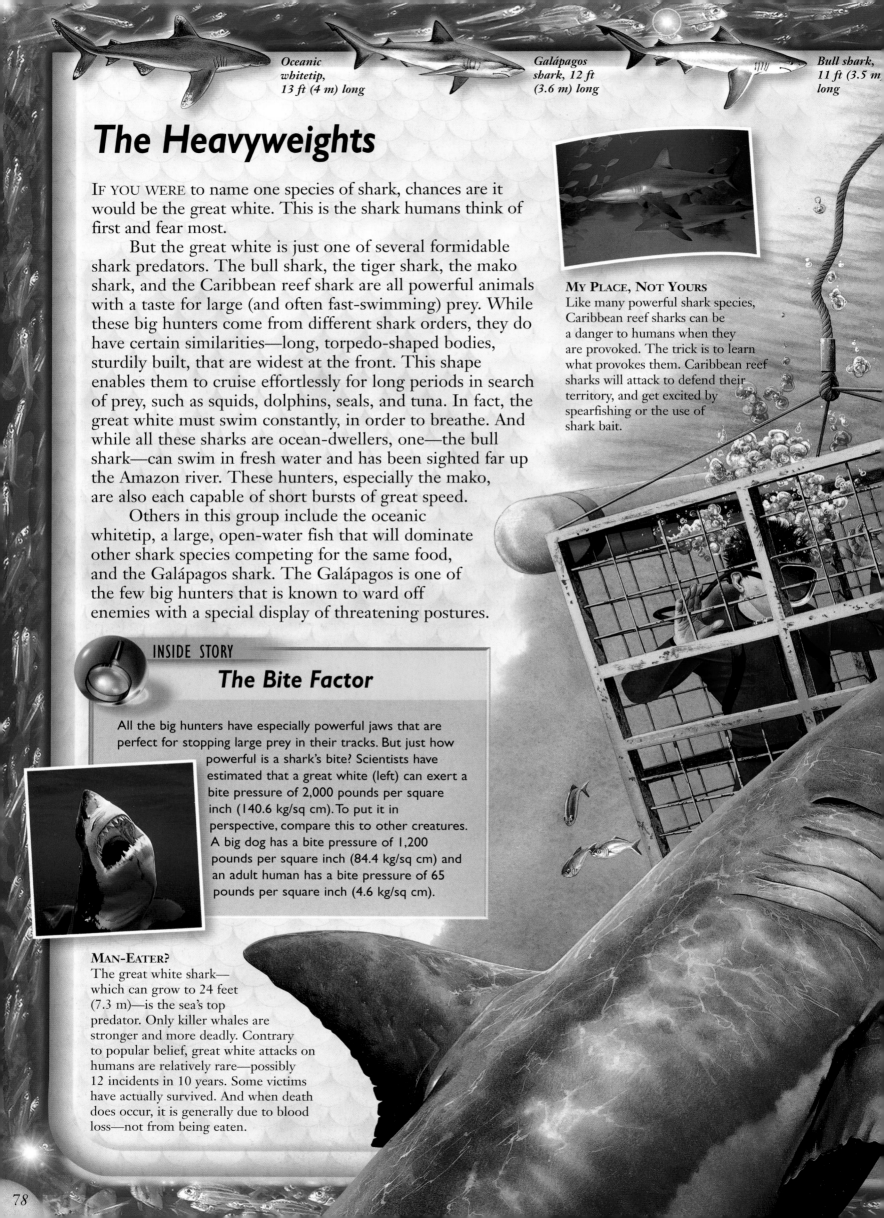

Oceanic whitetip, 13 ft (4 m) long

Galápagos shark, 12 ft (3.6 m) long

Bull shark, 11 ft (3.5 m) long

The Heavyweights

IF YOU WERE to name one species of shark, chances are it would be the great white. This is the shark humans think of first and fear most.

But the great white is just one of several formidable shark predators. The bull shark, the tiger shark, the mako shark, and the Caribbean reef shark are all powerful animals with a taste for large (and often fast-swimming) prey. While these big hunters come from different shark orders, they do have certain similarities—long, torpedo-shaped bodies, sturdily built, that are widest at the front. This shape enables them to cruise effortlessly for long periods in search of prey, such as squids, dolphins, seals, and tuna. In fact, the great white must swim constantly, in order to breathe. And while all these sharks are ocean-dwellers, one—the bull shark—can swim in fresh water and has been sighted far up the Amazon river. These hunters, especially the mako, are also each capable of short bursts of great speed.

Others in this group include the oceanic whitetip, a large, open-water fish that will dominate other shark species competing for the same food, and the Galápagos shark. The Galápagos is one of the few big hunters that is known to ward off enemies with a special display of threatening postures.

MY PLACE, NOT YOURS
Like many powerful shark species, Caribbean reef sharks can be a danger to humans when they are provoked. The trick is to learn what provokes them. Caribbean reef sharks will attack to defend their territory, and get excited by spearfishing or the use of shark bait.

INSIDE STORY

The Bite Factor

All the big hunters have especially powerful jaws that are perfect for stopping large prey in their tracks. But just how powerful is a shark's bite? Scientists have estimated that a great white (left) can exert a bite pressure of 2,000 pounds per square inch (140.6 kg/sq cm). To put it in perspective, compare this to other creatures. A big dog has a bite pressure of 1,200 pounds per square inch (84.4 kg/sq cm) and an adult human has a bite pressure of 65 pounds per square inch (4.6 kg/sq cm).

MAN-EATER?
The great white shark—which can grow to 24 feet (7.3 m)—is the sea's top predator. Only killer whales are stronger and more deadly. Contrary to popular belief, great white attacks on humans are relatively rare—possibly 12 incidents in 10 years. Some victims have actually survived. And when death does occur, it is generally due to blood loss—not from being eaten.

Word Builders

• A shark that defends the area around it is called **territorial**—from the Latin *terra,* for "land" or "property."
• Most great hunters have subtle skin patterns and coloration, but the mako is very distinctive, with a metallic blue top and a white underside. This shark is also known as the **bonito** shark. *Bonito* is Spanish for "pretty."

That's Amazing!

A gruesome murder was solved in Australia after scientists who worked at an aquarium caught a tiger shark in Sydney harbor. A week after the shark went on display, it vomited a man's tattooed arm. The bone had been cut through with a saw. A newspaper article about this event helped police catch the man's killer.

Pathfinder

• To catch fast prey, sharks need to be good swimmers. Find out how they swim on pages 98–99.
• Learn more about shark teeth on pages 100–01.
• Sharks are at more risk from us than we are from them. See pages 122–25.

ATTACKS ON PEOPLE

The International Shark Attack File has details of more than 3,100 attacks over the past 500 years—but how dangerous are sharks to humans? Numbers of shark attacks are on the rise because more people are using the sea than ever before. But the chances of being attacked by a shark are still extremely remote. Millions of people use the sea every day, but worldwide, only about six people per year are killed by sharks. Contrast that with 100 deaths from lightning each year in North America alone!

6 percent of attacks occur 500–1,000 feet (150–300 m) from the beach.

13 percent of attacks occur 200–500 feet (60–150 m) from the beach.

51 percent of attacks occur less than 200 feet (60 m) from the beach.

ATTACK STATISTICS

These statistical facts show that most people stay near the beach—not that it is safer to swim farther from the beach.

UNDER OBSERVATION

Great white sharks inhabit shallow, cool coastal waters, and are sometimes seen in warmer waters off Hawaii. Diving scientists and field biologists are learning more about their biology and behavior. One way to do this is to observe great whites closely from the safety of a steel cage. While this offers great photo opportunities, it's not always ideal for the scientist. The metal cage gives off electrical signals and the sharks, which are sensitive to electrical fields, will sometimes mistake the cage for lunch and attack.

THE TIGER OF THE SEAS

Tiger sharks are named for the black or dark gray vertical stripes seen on the bodies of juveniles. The stripes fade as the shark matures. Tiger sharks hunt at night and are the largest, most dangerous predators in tropical waters. They grow as large as the great white, and live up to 12 years.

SHARK'S EYE VIEW

Surfboarders are a relatively new sight for sharks—and an intriguing one at that. We can't blame them if they take a look and think what they see might make a good meal, like their usual diet of turtle or seal.

Huge but Harmless

YOU'RE SNORKELING IN warm, tropical waters when you see it. A giant shape looms before you, appearing suddenly out of the murk. It's a shark with a gaping mouth and a body the size of a school bus. You can actually see into its mouth and out through its gill slits. You and three friends could fit into the cavernous maw. Are you next on the menu?

No—this gentle giant is already getting its meal as it swims. The whale shark, which can grow to 40 feet (12 m), is one of three species of shark that filter their food from seawater. Swimming with its mouth open, the whale shark scoops and sucks up a living "soup" of water, tiny plant and animal plankton, fish eggs, and even small fishes. Then it flushes the water through its gill slits before swallowing the strained food.

Basking sharks are slightly smaller filter feeders that frequent cooler waters to feed on plankton and shrimps. Like the whale shark, they are surface feeders. Megamouths are the smallest of the three, averaging about 15 feet (4.5 m) in length. They feed on shrimps and small fishes in deeper waters.

Whale sharks are related to wobbegongs, but basking sharks and megamouths are Lamniformes, which means that they belong to the same order as some of the most dangerous sharks, such as great whites and makos. So why aren't they predators like those sharks? Some scientists think that filter feeding may be a primitive form of feeding that preceded the predatory ways of most modern sharks.

BIG MOUTHS, LITTLE FOOD

A 30-foot (9-m) fish needs a lot of food to survive, grow, and reproduce, but contrary to popular belief, the filter feeder does not feed continuously. On average, it feeds once or twice a week, but can go without food for weeks at a time if conditions demand it. To feed well, a filter-feeding shark needs to find a place where there is a high density of food. Plankton is not found everywhere—only in concentrated groups that scientists call patches.

Blue fish

MYSTERIOUS MEGAMOUTH

Since the first known specimen was discovered in 1976 in Hawaiian waters, just over a dozen megamouths have been caught in waters near California, Japan, Brazil, Africa, and Australia. Megamouths inhabit very deep waters, only coming to the surface at night. Perhaps that's why they are rarely seen.

Megamouth shark

INSIDE STORY

Secrets of the Deep

Does the sea still hold mysteries? Are there still unidentified creatures swimming in the depths? Marine biologist Leighton Taylor is convinced the answer is yes. And based on his own experience, he is probably right.

In 1976, Dr. Taylor was stunned to be the first person to recognize an entirely new kind of plankton-feeding shark, promptly nicknamed megamouth because of its large mouth. "Finding a new species of plant or animal is not that rare. But this shark represented not just a new species, but also a completely unknown family of sharks. Finding something that different was a tremendous surprise. After studying it carefully so that we could scientifically describe it, my colleagues and I decided it is related to the large group that includes makos, threshers, basking sharks, and great whites."

Word Builders

• *Densus* means "thick" in Latin. A small volume of the ocean with a large number of shrimps has a high **density** of the creatures.
• In Greek, *mega* is "very big." The **megamouth** shark's huge mouth gives it both its common name, megamouth, and its scientific name—*Megachasma pelagios*, from the Greek for "giant yawner of the open sea."

That's Amazing!

• Megamouth sharks have silver-colored reflective surfaces inside their mouths. Scientists think these may attract plankton and small fishes, which then become the shark's dinner.
• Basking sharks that have shed their gill rakers can't eat. Scientists think these huge sharks may lie dormant on the ocean floor, living off fat stored in their livers, until the rakers grow back.

Pathfinder

• Giant whale sharks have small relatives—wobbegongs. Read about them on page 87.
• Besides feeding, what else are gills used for? See pages 96–97.
• Whale sharks are as big as boats—and like boats, they carry passengers. Learn more on pages 112–13.

A VARIED DIET
Whale sharks mostly eat plankton and small fishes (such as anchovies and sardines). But they can also swallow larger fishes, such as mackerel and small tuna.

Whale shark

A WHALE OF A JOURNEY
No one knows how far a whale shark swims in search of food. Scientists think that the whale sharks of Ningaloo Bay, Australia, may travel as far as 9,000 miles (15,000 km) to waters off the coast of Indonesia.

Plankton

HEAD LIKE A SIEVE
Basking sharks have the longest snout and the biggest gill slits of the three filter-feeding sharks. Like all filter feeders, they travel over vast areas looking for dense patches of food. Basking sharks use their toothlike gill rakers to sieve food from seawater. They may grow a new set every year.

Filter feeders accidentally take in microscopic plants, or phytoplankton, along with zooplankton

MIGHTY MAWS
To get enough food, filter-feeding sharks must take in many gallons of seawater. Each of the three species of filter feeders does this in a different way. Even though they filter their food with gill rakers inside their mouths, these species still have teeth, just as other sharks do.

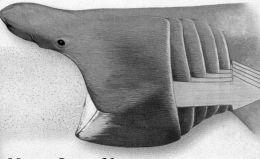

WIDE MOUTH
Whale sharks have been seen amid huge plankton patches, with their heads out of water. When they sink beneath the surface, the food falls into their mouths. Then they rise back up, letting the water strain out through their gills, and start all over again.

MOUTH LIKE A NET
The basking shark lifts its snout, lowers its chin, and widens its jaws to make a huge net for plankton.

SCOOP MOUTH
The megamouth sticks out its upper jaw and drops its lower jaw to scoop up midwater shrimps and plankton.

Head Hunters

YOU ARE SWIMMING through the water with a pair of hammer-shaped wings jutting from the sides of your face. Your eyes are set on the ends of these wings, so you have great side vision with which to track prey, but you can't see straight ahead because your eyes are too far apart. To compensate, you must swing your head back and forth to get a view of what's in front of you. The tiny sensory pores that every shark has are spread over the entire width of your broad head. That means you have a greater advantage in detecting the electricity emitted by creatures hidden in the sand or elsewhere in the dark waters. As you swim, propelled by sweeps of your tail, the wings on your face actually help give you extra lift, especially when you move fast. Welcome to the world of the hammerhead shark.

There are nine species of these unusual-looking sharks, and their names give clues to their different shapes—bonnethead, scalloped bonnethead, winghead, and scoophead sharks, and scalloped, whitefin, smooth, small-eye, and great hammerheads. Although many sharks are loners, hammerheads are not. In fact, scientists are just beginning to realize how complex hammerhead behavior and society really are.

IN THE SHALLOWS
The most widespread of the hammerheads, smooth hammerheads live in shallow, warm inshore waters around the world—in North and South America, Hawaii, Africa, Europe, Asia, Australia, and New Zealand. They hunt stingrays, skates, small sharks, sea bass, and small schooling fishes such as herring and menhaden.

PINNED!
Although great hammerhead sharks prey on other sharks, skates, and fishes, they are particularly fond of stingrays. Stingrays feed on the sea bottom, and although they have eyes on the top of their heads, they don't always see an approaching shark in time to make their getaway. A great hammerhead can pounce quickly and pin a fleeing ray to the sand with the side of its head. Then it will turn and bite a chunk from the ray's wing as if it were a large, fleshy cookie—one bite at a time until the ray is all gone. Divers must take care around great hammerheads—they are the only hammerhead known to attack people.

SEEING SIDEWAYS
Hammerheads have a broader sideways range of vision than most sharks, but they are unable to see straight ahead.

THAT'S USING YOUR HEAD!
Aside from improved side vision, the wing shape of a hammerhead's head, or cephalofoil, offers several advantages. It helps the shark to swim by lifting it through water, just as wings give an airplane lift. In fact, some experimental planes have an extra pair of wings set far forward like a hammerhead's. The shark also uses its head to change direction more easily—it tilts its head to one side much as an airplane banks when turning. Hammerheads even use their heads to find prey, dig it up, and hold it down.

Word Builders

• **Cephalofoil** is the name that scientists give to the head shape of the hammerhead. This comes from the Greek word *kephalos,* for "head," and the Latin word *foil,* for "leaf" or "thin sheet of metal," which refers to the flattened shape of the shark's head.
• **Hydrodynamics**—from the Greek word *hydor,* for "water," and *dunamis,* for "power"—is the study of the way things move through water.

That's Amazing!

• Even though the largest great hammerhead to be caught and measured was about 10 feet (3 m) in length, people have reported seeing much bigger ones—of up to 20 feet (6 m).
• Sometimes you really *are* what you eat. Take the small-eye hammerhead, also called the golden hammerhead. The small-eye gets its remarkable golden skin color from a substance found in its favorite food—shrimps!

Pathfinder

• How do sharks sense electrical currents in the water? Go to pages 94–95.
• Find out how other shark species and shark relatives are adapted for getting around on pages 98–99.
• Hammerheads often dig up buried food. What do other species do? Read more on pages 108–09.

KEEPING AN EYE OUT
Because the hammerhead's eyes grow on the two ends of a very wide head, this small-eye hammerhead would only have seen the photographer with its left eye. Its right eye saw something completely different.

LOOKING FOR LUNCH
Hammerheads like this bonnethead use their heads to find food much as a person uses a metal detector to find a watch buried in the sand. All creatures emit weak electrical currents, even when perfectly still. These faint currents are detected by the shark's electrosense system as it swims, moving its head back and forth over the sand. Bingo—lunchtime!

INSIDE STORY
Hammerhead Get-Together

Underwater photographer Bob Cranston and filmmaker Howard Hall have helped make famous the gatherings of scalloped hammerhead sharks in the Sea of Cortez. Most sharks are solitary, but scalloped hammerheads form true schools of up to 500 sharks, most of them female. Some scientists believe that the groups form to socialize and to avoid predators, but Cranston thinks the main reason is to mate. He has seen and filmed these sharks for himself: "Occasionally a male would bite a female on the pectoral fin, and then wrap its tail around her and begin to mate. Then the two sharks would sink to the bottom. One time, a pair actually crashed to the seafloor a short distance away from me."

Great hammerhead

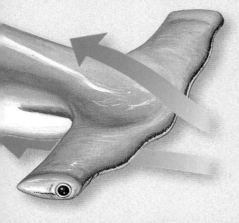
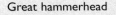

HYDRODYNAMICS
As the hammerhead's tail pushes it forward, water under the wing on its head rushes by at a slower rate than the water rushing over it. This lifts the shark's head and allows it to go faster with less effort.

DIGGING UP DINNER
When a bonnethead's electrical sense finds buried prey, the shark converts its head from an electrical detection device to a shovel with which to dig out the food.

Bonnethead

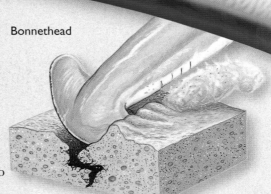

Tall Tails

IF YOU THINK the tail is the safe end of the shark, think again. In thresher sharks, the tail is a lethal weapon—and a small fish's worst nightmare.

All thresher sharks have extremely long tails that they use like whips to herd together the small schooling fishes—such as mackerel, herring, and tuna—they like to eat. Most threshers swim the open waters, and once they've herded together their prey near the surface, the sharks cut and slash at the fishes with their tails. This behavior is called "tail slapping," and the violent blows actually stun or even kill the prey. Threshers have even been seen using their tails to scoop food into their mouths.

Compared to bony fishes, sharks don't have much diversity in the tail department. Since they are at or near the top of the food chain, most species use their tail for one purpose: powering forward. The powerful swimmers have stiffened tails for maximum thrust through water. Ground dwellers such as nurse sharks and carpetsharks have narrower tails with small lower lobes. The more flexible nature of these tails allows bottom feeders to wriggle their way through cracks and over coral reefs as they hunt for food.

Yellowtail scad

TURNING TAIL
The thresher shark has by far the longest tail of any shark—its whiplike tail is as long as the rest of its body. Threshers can grow to a total length of up to 20 feet (6 m). Long-line fishers sometimes pull up thresher sharks that have been snagged by the tail after they have tail slapped the baited hook.

SPOTS AND STRIPES
Zebra sharks are named for the yellow-and-black stripes of the juveniles. As they mature, they develop a yellowish-brown color with dark brown spots. These tropical reef hunters have tails almost as long as the rest of their bodies. They are sometimes seen resting on the seafloor, propped up on their pectoral fins and facing into the current in order to get oxygen more easily from the water.

Upper lobe

INSIDE STORY

Surprise!

Skip Naftel, a fishing captain, helps biologists at the University of Hawaii by allowing them to study the sharks he catches. Grad students who regularly join Naftel's fishing trips are sometimes a source of entertainment for the captain and crew. Here, Naftel tells of a case of mistaken identity: "One time, off Waikiki Beach, we pulled the line and it was obvious to me that we'd hooked a thresher by the tail. One student looked over the rail and said 'Wow, this shark has a weird head!'—not realizing he was looking at the tail. All of a sudden, the shark arched around. When the student saw the teeth coming, he shrieked and jumped back!"

A shark's tail is divided into an upper lobe (usually larger) and a lower lobe. The spool-shaped bones in the tail are called vertebrae. They are a continuation of the backbone and extend to the tip of the tail's upper lobe.

Lower lobe

Word Builders

• To **thresh** means to cut down grains, such as wheat, oats, or barley, by slashing at them with a sharp blade. Thresher sharks strike at fishes with their long tails in a similar way, which is how they got their name.
• **Diversity** means difference or variety. It comes from *diversus*, the Latin for "turned in different directions."

That's Amazing!

Thresher sharks aren't the only sea creatures to use their tails for more than just swimming. Killer whales (orcas) hunt down fishes and kill them with powerful slaps of their tails. Great whites are also know to use tail slapping, though not to kill prey. Scientists think it may be one way that they communicate. Water is a good conductor of sound, so a loud tail slap might be heard miles away.

Pathfinder

• Do ancient and modern sharks have similar tails? Find out on page 74.
• Some shark relatives defend themselves with poisonous spines on their tails. See pages 88–89.
• Learn more about how a shark swims on pages 98–99.

TELLING TAILS

The shape of a shark's tail can give you clues about how active it is. Symmetrical, crescent-shaped tails usually belong to sharks such as makos and great whites, which need to swim fast because they hunt equally fast-moving prey. Long, low-set, thin tails generally belong to sluggish bottom dwellers that feed on shellfish, crustaceans, and other invertebrates.

There may not be safety in numbers for schooling fishes when a thresher shark is around.

WE HAVE LIFTOFF

Threshers gather so much momentum when they swim fast that they can jump right out of the water. They are prized by game fishers, who consider them a more exciting quarry than marlin or tuna because their strength and jumping ability mean that they put up a good fight.

Nurse shark
This shark swims with an eel-like motion, using its elongated tail to propel it slowly in search of food.

Tiger shark
The long upper lobe helps this shark to twist and turn rapidly in pursuit of fast and agile prey.

Paired pectoral fins help a shark steer by giving direction to the thrust of its tail. The "pecs" on a thresher are longer than on most species. This may compensate for the powerful thrust from the extra-long tail.

Mako shark
Makos have flattened ridges called caudal keels at the base of their tail. These may reduce drag and help them swim faster.

Common thresher shark

Caudal keel

Paired pelvic fins help stabilize a shark so that it doesn't roll from side to side.

*Graceful catshark,
2 feet (60 cm) long*

*Small spotted catshark, 3 feet
(90 cm) long*

*Coral catshark,
2 feet (60 cm) long*

Part of the Scenery

TO BE A successful predator, a shark must be fast enough to catch its lunch on a regular basis. But not all marine hunters are fast swimmers, so what's a slow-moving yet hungry shark to do? Blend in with the background—and then ambush lunch! Many sea creatures, including some sharks, have patterns on their skin that allow them to blend in with their environments. This is called camouflage.

Sometimes an ambusher will try to look like something that its prey finds attractive. For instance, nurse sharks are known to curl their pectoral fins under to form a dark area—the perfect hiding spot for small fishes. When a fish swims in—lunchtime!

Camouflage can also protect a shark from becoming another shark's dinner. Recently born zebra bullhead sharks and tiger sharks have distinctive color patterns that camouflage them from predators. As they get older, larger, and better equipped to defend themselves, the patterns often disappear or change.

ELEMENT OF SURPRISE
Even fast swimmers like this shortfin mako (above) make good use of camouflage. Many sharks are counter-shaded—they have dark backs and light undersides, which allows them to blend in with the water around them when seen from above or below. They seem to swim out of nowhere to surprise their prey.

Tasseled wobbegong

HANDS ON

Fading into the Background

Some sharks are born with natural camouflage, while other sea creatures can actually change their skin color to match the background. Humans can do this by wearing special clothing and makeup. You can try it, too. Here's how.

❶ Choose a background that you would like to match. You could try matching a wallpaper, foliage, or a checkerboard.

❷ Then use stage makeup to paint your skin the same color and pattern. Try to camouflage a small body part like a hand. Get a friend to take a photograph of you in your camouflage in front of your chosen background.

Stonefish

MASTERS OF DISGUISE

Camouflage is an adaptation, a combination of instinct and anatomy. Sharks are just one of many sea creatures that are able to camouflage themselves. Octopuses, for example, can change their color and pattern—even skin texture—faster than you can blink. Stonefishes can look just like rocks. This is a dangerous for waders in the tropics because stonefishes inject a deadly poison from their spines if stepped on. Flounders are able to create such a variety of colors that they can almost match a checkerboard.

Word Builders

- An **ambush** is an attack that surprises its victim because the attacker was hiding. It may come from the Latin word *imboscare*, meaning "to hide in the bushes."
- **Prey** is any animal that is hunted and eaten by another animal. It comes from the Latin word *prehendere*, which means "to grab hold of."

That's Amazing!

- According to Hawaiian myth, sharks can camouflage themselves as "shark men." They trick swimmers by asking where they are going so that later, in shark form, they can find and attack them.
- Some bony fishes have developed false eye spots on the tail or back of the fins, so that a predator is tricked into attacking a part of the fish's body that is less vulnerable than the head.

Pathfinder

- Wobbegongs are masters of ambush, but which sharks are speed kings? Find out on pages 78–79.
- What else besides camouflage protects young sharks from being eaten? Learn more on pages 106–07.
- Which shark uses its glowing belly to evade predators? See pages 120–21.

Black-backed butterflyfish

Oval spot butterflyfish

DEADLY DISGUISE

The tasseled wobbegong may be the best decorated of any shark. Its head and body have a fringe of fleshy lobes so that even when it is swimming it can look like a clump of marine plants or a floating rock. No wonder its prey can't see it coming! Tasseled wobbegongs live on the coral reefs of New Guinea, Australia, and Indonesia. They are aggressive feeders, with sharp, narrow teeth that help them snap up fishes, crabs, and shrimps. These wobbegongs rest during the day and swim out at night to catch prey.

SPOT THAT SHARK

To humans, leopard sharks may seem boldly patterned and easy to spot. They are often displayed in big aquariums where we can get a good, long look at them. But in the wild, where light dapples through floating kelp and shadows abound, a slow-moving leopard shark is very difficult to see.

Octopus

Flounder

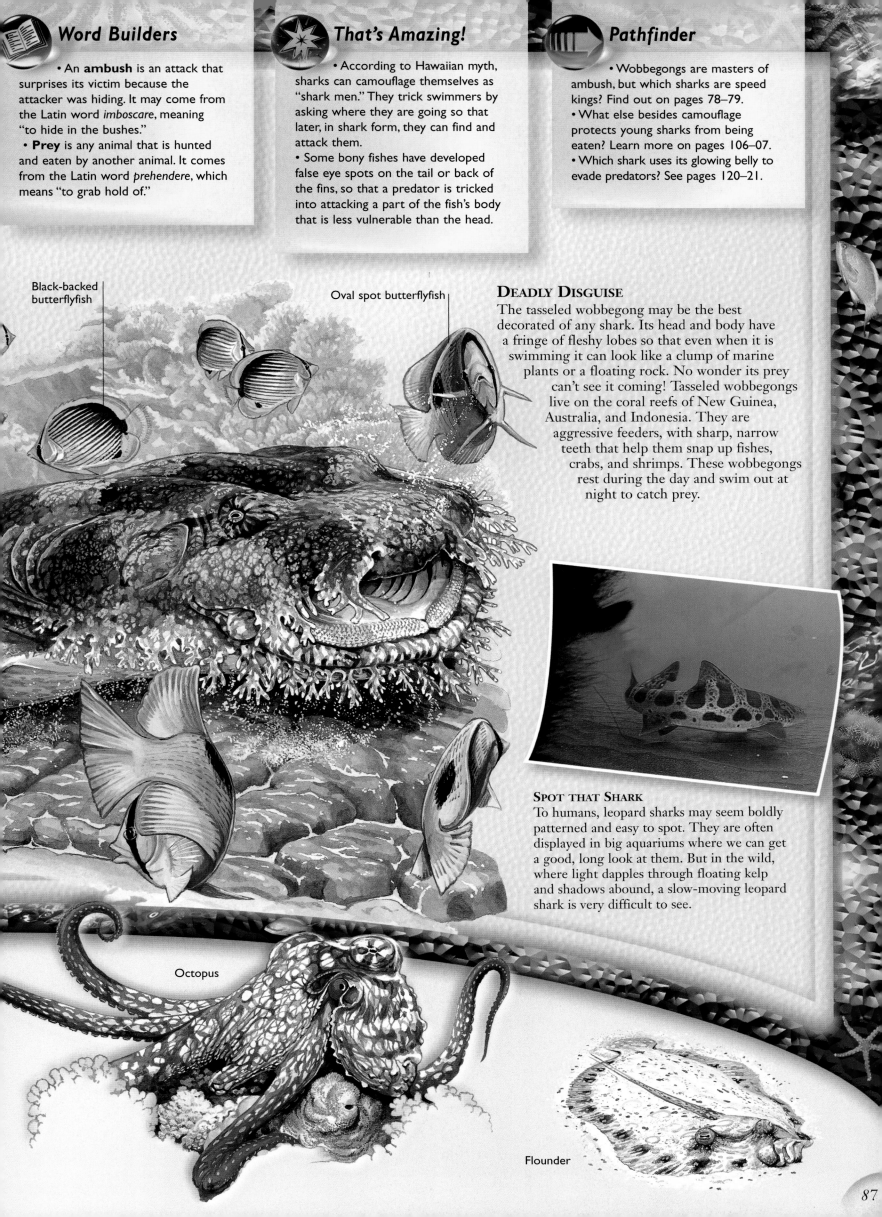

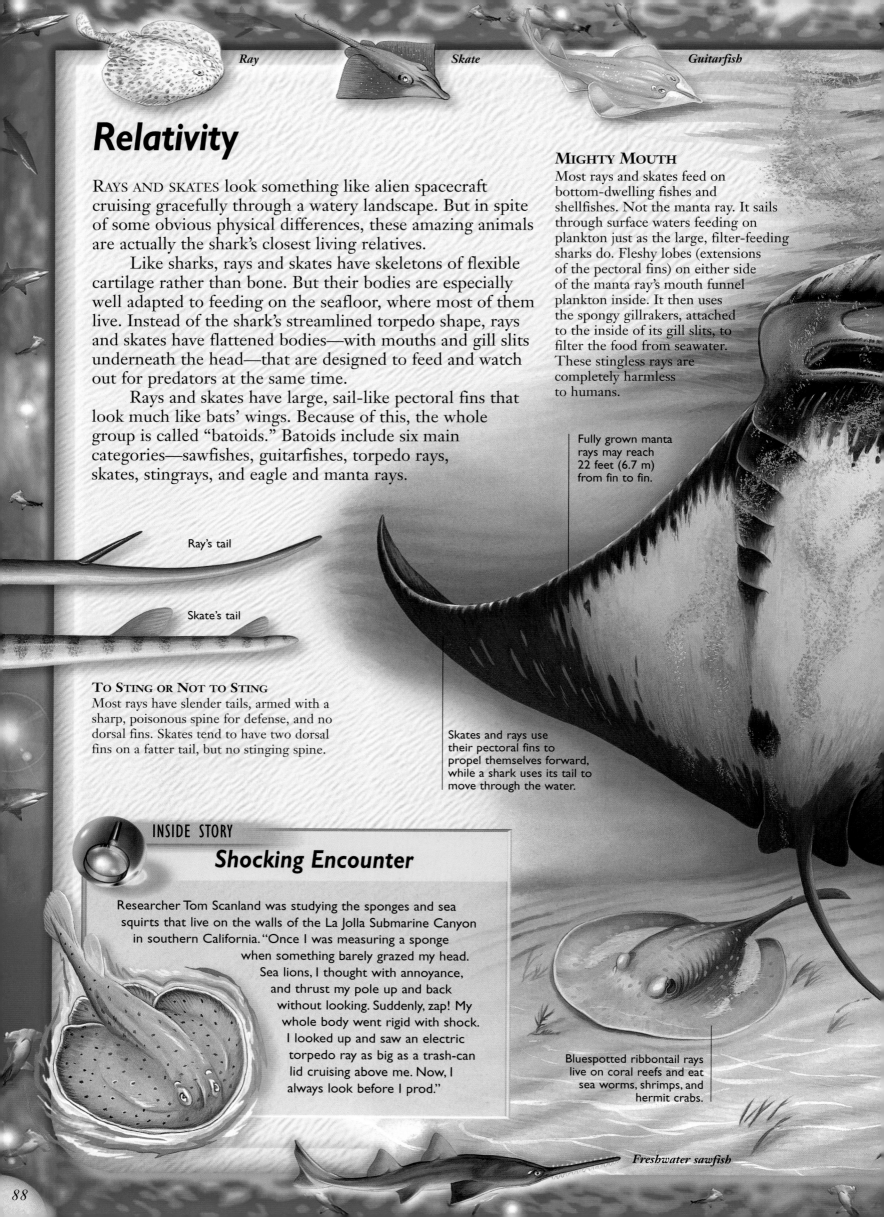

Ray *Skate* *Guitarfish*

Relativity

RAYS AND SKATES look something like alien spacecraft cruising gracefully through a watery landscape. But in spite of some obvious physical differences, these amazing animals are actually the shark's closest living relatives.

Like sharks, rays and skates have skeletons of flexible cartilage rather than bone. But their bodies are especially well adapted to feeding on the seafloor, where most of them live. Instead of the shark's streamlined torpedo shape, rays and skates have flattened bodies—with mouths and gill slits underneath the head—that are designed to feed and watch out for predators at the same time.

Rays and skates have large, sail-like pectoral fins that look much like bats' wings. Because of this, the whole group is called "batoids." Batoids include six main categories—sawfishes, guitarfishes, torpedo rays, skates, stingrays, and eagle and manta rays.

Ray's tail

Skate's tail

TO STING OR NOT TO STING
Most rays have slender tails, armed with a sharp, poisonous spine for defense, and no dorsal fins. Skates tend to have two dorsal fins on a fatter tail, but no stinging spine.

MIGHTY MOUTH
Most rays and skates feed on bottom-dwelling fishes and shellfishes. Not the manta ray. It sails through surface waters feeding on plankton just as the large, filter-feeding sharks do. Fleshy lobes (extensions of the pectoral fins) on either side of the manta ray's mouth funnel plankton inside. It then uses the spongy gillrakers, attached to the inside of its gill slits, to filter the food from seawater. These stingless rays are completely harmless to humans.

Fully grown manta rays may reach 22 feet (6.7 m) from fin to fin.

Skates and rays use their pectoral fins to propel themselves forward, while a shark uses its tail to move through the water.

INSIDE STORY
Shocking Encounter

Researcher Tom Scanland was studying the sponges and sea squirts that live on the walls of the La Jolla Submarine Canyon in southern California. "Once I was measuring a sponge when something barely grazed my head. Sea lions, I thought with annoyance, and thrust my pole up and back without looking. Suddenly, zap! My whole body went rigid with shock. I looked up and saw an electric torpedo ray as big as a trash-can lid cruising above me. Now, I always look before I prod."

Bluespotted ribbontail rays live on coral reefs and eat sea worms, shrimps, and hermit crabs.

Freshwater sawfish

Word Builders

Chimaeras get their name from their strange appearance. In Greek mythology, the Chimera was a fire-breathing monster with a lion's head, a goat's body, and a serpent's tail. These weird-looking shark relatives even have strange common names, including spookfish and ghostshark.

That's Amazing!

• Electric rays have special muscle cells in the center of both pectoral fins that form a batterylike electric organ. An Atlantic torpedo ray can discharge 220 volts of electricity. That's about twice the voltage used in the average household—and enough to knock out a diver.
• The whitespotted guitarfish is known for its curiosity. It will even prop itself up on the tips of its pectoral fins to get a better look at a diver on the seafloor.

Pathfinder

• How old are the most ancient ancestors of today's sharks and rays? Find out on pages 74–75.
• There are six main groups of batoids. But how many groups, or orders, are there of sharks? Turn to pages 76–77.
• Not all rays swim in exactly the same way. Check out the differences on pages 98–99.

Fleshy lobes called celaphalic fins guide plankton into the ray's mouth.

Plankton is the collective word for tiny plants, crabs, shrimps, eggs, baby fishes, and the young of many sea animals that drift in currents.

LOOPING THE LOOP
A manta ray can filter feed constantly by looping through a cloud of plankton. If the manta swam straight through, it would waste time turning around in water that contained no food.

A manta breathes in through its mouth, but breathes out through gill slits.

GHOSTS OF THE SEA

Sharks and rays have other, more distant relatives—the chimaeras. Although chimaeras share certain features with bony fishes—they have a single gill opening on each side and a movable dorsal fin— scientists place them in the same group as sharks and rays because they have a skeleton of cartilage, they lack a swim bladder, and their eggs have tough, flexible cases.

Family Ghost
The shortnose chimaera is also known as ghostshark or ratfish.

The height of a diver is just over one-fourth of the width of a very large manta.

Nosy Relation
The spookfish has a long nose—called a proboscis—with taste and touch sensors that help it find food.

Skates' fins are more pointed than those of rays.

MILES AWAY
Some ray species, such as the reticulated freshwater ray, live in the rivers and lakes of South America, more than 1,000 miles (1,610 km) from the sea. Rays like these stir the bottom with their pectoral fins to flush out the small creatures on which they feed.

Digging for Dinner
Also known as plownose, the elephantfish uses its nose to dig through the sand for food.

89

Sharkworks

SHARKS LIVE IN an environment that we can only visit—water. Not only can sharks breathe underwater, but they also can hear in it and see in it. They can even feel a possible dinner swimming through it. Some sharks species must swim constantly to survive, while others can lie still at rest. Still others have special coloration that helps them hide from larger, faster sharks. What makes it possible for sharks to do all these things and more? Read on and be amazed.

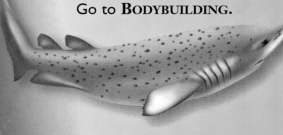

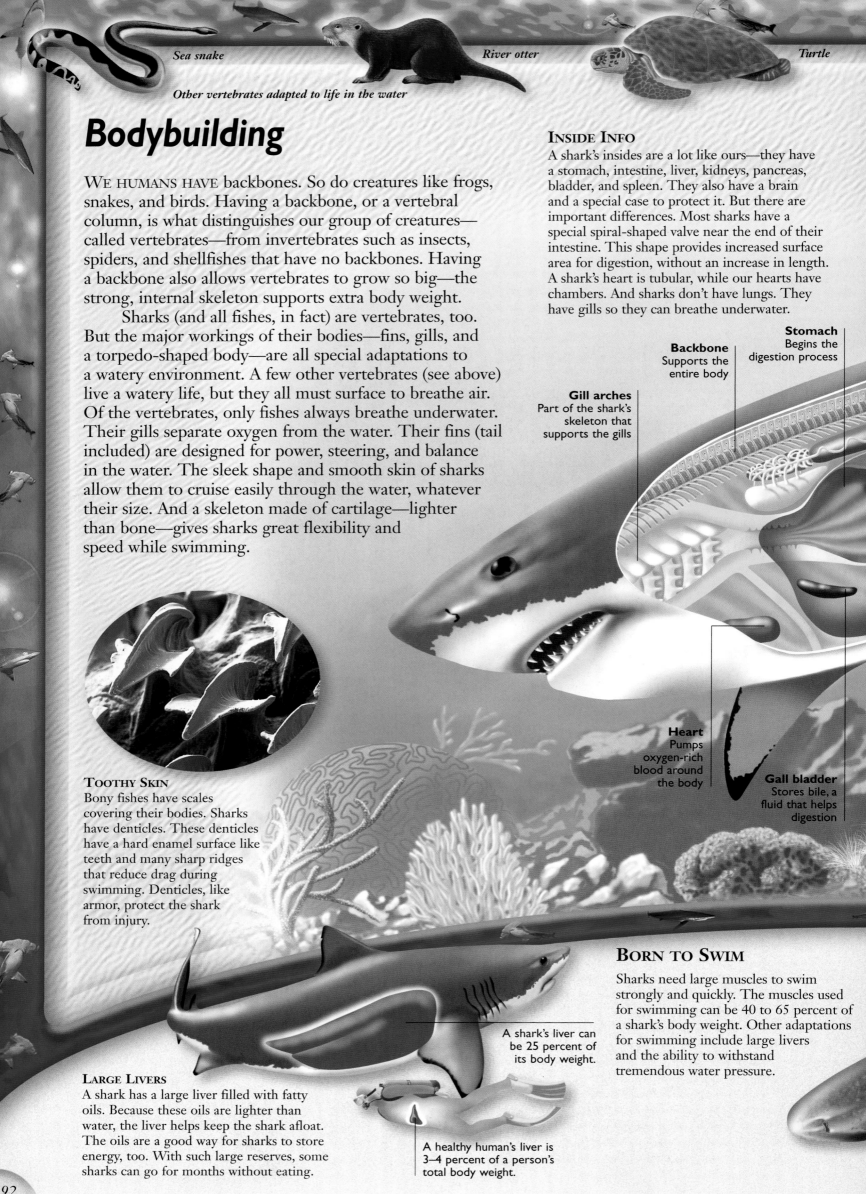

Sea snake

River otter

Turtle

Other vertebrates adapted to life in the water

Bodybuilding

WE HUMANS HAVE backbones. So do creatures like frogs, snakes, and birds. Having a backbone, or a vertebral column, is what distinguishes our group of creatures—called vertebrates—from invertebrates such as insects, spiders, and shellfishes that have no backbones. Having a backbone also allows vertebrates to grow so big—the strong, internal skeleton supports extra body weight.

Sharks (and all fishes, in fact) are vertebrates, too. But the major workings of their bodies—fins, gills, and a torpedo-shaped body—are all special adaptations to a watery environment. A few other vertebrates (see above) live a watery life, but they all must surface to breathe air. Of the vertebrates, only fishes always breathe underwater. Their gills separate oxygen from the water. Their fins (tail included) are designed for power, steering, and balance in the water. The sleek shape and smooth skin of sharks allow them to cruise easily through the water, whatever their size. And a skeleton made of cartilage—lighter than bone—gives sharks great flexibility and speed while swimming.

INSIDE INFO
A shark's insides are a lot like ours—they have a stomach, intestine, liver, kidneys, pancreas, bladder, and spleen. They also have a brain and a special case to protect it. But there are important differences. Most sharks have a special spiral-shaped valve near the end of their intestine. This shape provides increased surface area for digestion, without an increase in length. A shark's heart is tubular, while our hearts have chambers. And sharks don't have lungs. They have gills so they can breathe underwater.

Stomach
Begins the digestion process

Backbone
Supports the entire body

Gill arches
Part of the shark's skeleton that supports the gills

Heart
Pumps oxygen-rich blood around the body

Gall bladder
Stores bile, a fluid that helps digestion

TOOTHY SKIN
Bony fishes have scales covering their bodies. Sharks have denticles. These denticles have a hard enamel surface like teeth and many sharp ridges that reduce drag during swimming. Denticles, like armor, protect the shark from injury.

LARGE LIVERS
A shark has a large liver filled with fatty oils. Because these oils are lighter than water, the liver helps keep the shark afloat. The oils are a good way for sharks to store energy, too. With such large reserves, some sharks can go for months without eating.

A shark's liver can be 25 percent of its body weight.

A healthy human's liver is 3–4 percent of a person's total body weight.

BORN TO SWIM
Sharks need large muscles to swim strongly and quickly. The muscles used for swimming can be 40 to 65 percent of a shark's body weight. Other adaptations for swimming include large livers and the ability to withstand tremendous water pressure.

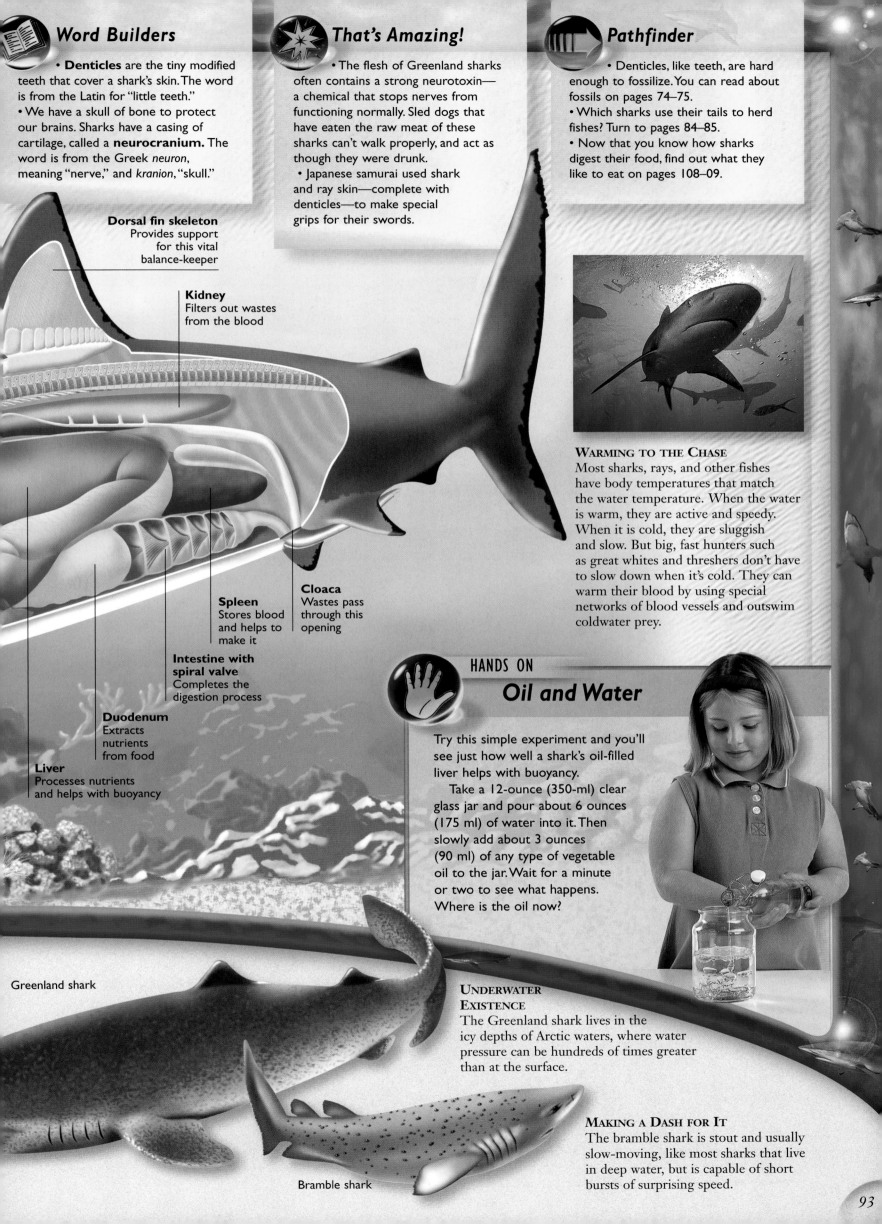

Word Builders

- **Denticles** are the tiny modified teeth that cover a shark's skin. The word is from the Latin for "little teeth."
- We have a skull of bone to protect our brains. Sharks have a casing of cartilage, called a **neurocranium.** The word is from the Greek *neuron*, meaning "nerve," and *kranion*, "skull."

That's Amazing!

- The flesh of Greenland sharks often contains a strong neurotoxin—a chemical that stops nerves from functioning normally. Sled dogs that have eaten the raw meat of these sharks can't walk properly, and act as though they were drunk.
- Japanese samurai used shark and ray skin—complete with denticles—to make special grips for their swords.

Pathfinder

- Denticles, like teeth, are hard enough to fossilize. You can read about fossils on pages 74–75.
- Which sharks use their tails to herd fishes? Turn to pages 84–85.
- Now that you know how sharks digest their food, find out what they like to eat on pages 108–09.

Dorsal fin skeleton
Provides support for this vital balance-keeper

Kidney
Filters out wastes from the blood

Spleen
Stores blood and helps to make it

Cloaca
Wastes pass through this opening

Intestine with spiral valve
Completes the digestion process

Duodenum
Extracts nutrients from food

Liver
Processes nutrients and helps with buoyancy

WARMING TO THE CHASE
Most sharks, rays, and other fishes have body temperatures that match the water temperature. When the water is warm, they are active and speedy. When it is cold, they are sluggish and slow. But big, fast hunters such as great whites and threshers don't have to slow down when it's cold. They can warm their blood by using special networks of blood vessels and outswim coldwater prey.

HANDS ON
Oil and Water

Try this simple experiment and you'll see just how well a shark's oil-filled liver helps with buoyancy.

Take a 12-ounce (350-ml) clear glass jar and pour about 6 ounces (175 ml) of water into it. Then slowly add about 3 ounces (90 ml) of any type of vegetable oil to the jar. Wait for a minute or two to see what happens. Where is the oil now?

Greenland shark

UNDERWATER EXISTENCE
The Greenland shark lives in the icy depths of Arctic waters, where water pressure can be hundreds of times greater than at the surface.

MAKING A DASH FOR IT
The bramble shark is stout and usually slow-moving, like most sharks that live in deep water, but is capable of short bursts of surprising speed.

Bramble shark

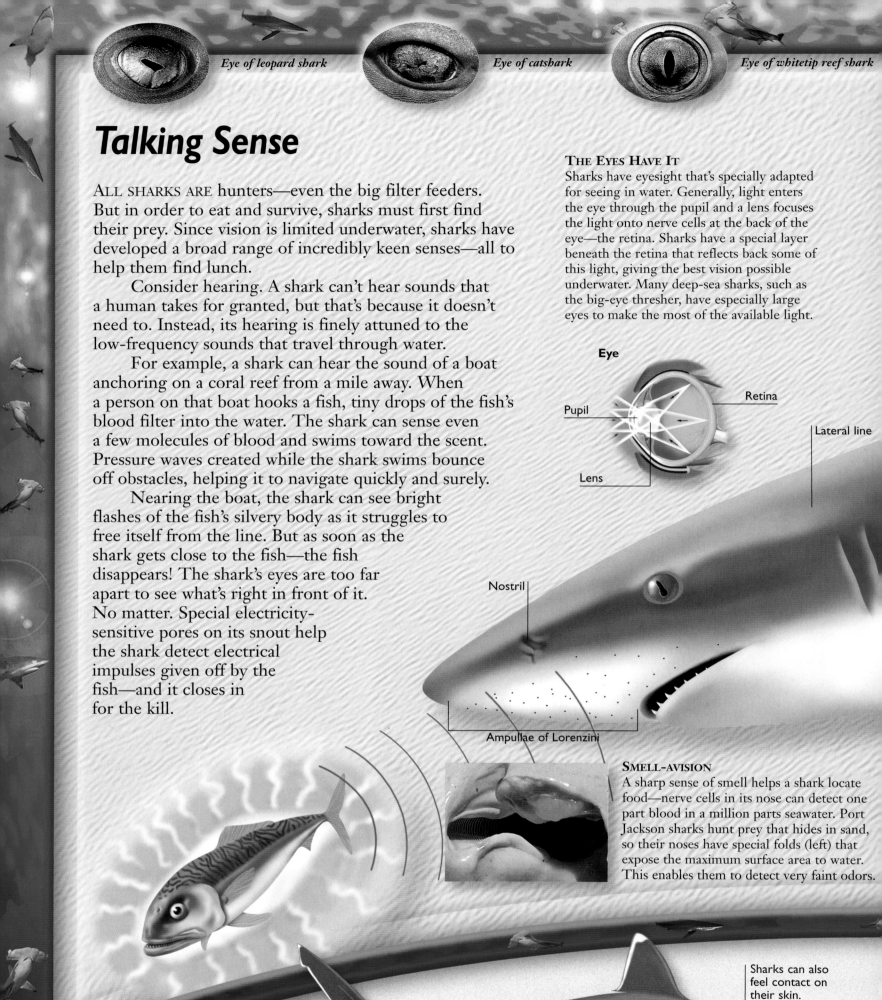

Eye of leopard shark   *Eye of catshark*   *Eye of whitetip reef shark*

Talking Sense

ALL SHARKS ARE hunters—even the big filter feeders. But in order to eat and survive, sharks must first find their prey. Since vision is limited underwater, sharks have developed a broad range of incredibly keen senses—all to help them find lunch.

Consider hearing. A shark can't hear sounds that a human takes for granted, but that's because it doesn't need to. Instead, its hearing is finely attuned to the low-frequency sounds that travel through water.

For example, a shark can hear the sound of a boat anchoring on a coral reef from a mile away. When a person on that boat hooks a fish, tiny drops of the fish's blood filter into the water. The shark can sense even a few molecules of blood and swims toward the scent. Pressure waves created while the shark swims bounce off obstacles, helping it to navigate quickly and surely.

Nearing the boat, the shark can see bright flashes of the fish's silvery body as it struggles to free itself from the line. But as soon as the shark gets close to the fish—the fish disappears! The shark's eyes are too far apart to see what's right in front of it. No matter. Special electricity-sensitive pores on its snout help the shark detect electrical impulses given off by the fish—and it closes in for the kill.

THE EYES HAVE IT

Sharks have eyesight that's specially adapted for seeing in water. Generally, light enters the eye through the pupil and a lens focuses the light onto nerve cells at the back of the eye—the retina. Sharks have a special layer beneath the retina that reflects back some of this light, giving the best vision possible underwater. Many deep-sea sharks, such as the big-eye thresher, have especially large eyes to make the most of the available light.

Eye

Pupil   Retina   Lens   Lateral line

Nostril

Ampullae of Lorenzini

SMELL-AVISION

A sharp sense of smell helps a shark locate food—nerve cells in its nose can detect one part blood in a million parts seawater. Port Jackson sharks hunt prey that hides in sand, so their noses have special folds (left) that expose the maximum surface area to water. This enables them to detect very faint odors.

Sharks can also feel contact on their skin.

GOOD VIBRATIONS

A shark feels touch in two ways. One way is through bodily contact. The other is through sensing vibrations. A swimming shark makes pressure waves that bounce off creatures and objects. Nerves along the shark's body detect the vibrations caused by the returning waves.

Vibration-sensitive nerve cells, arranged in a series called the lateral line, run along a shark's sides. They help the shark to "feel" objects several feet away.

More nerve cells in the lateral line continue around the shark's eyes and head.

Word Builders

• From the Latin word *rete*, meaning "net," the **retina** is the layer of nerve cells at the back of the eye.
• **Lateral** means on the side of something—for example, the lateral line is on a shark's side. The word comes from *lateralis*, Latin for "side."
• *Ampullae* is Latin for "small tubes." The shark's **ampullae of Lorenzini** are tubelike sensory organs that detect weak electrical signals.

That's Amazing!

• Ampullae of Lorenzini are named for Stefano Lorenzini, an Italian scientist who discovered them in the 1600s. It took another 300 years for experts to realize that these sensory organs detect electricity.
• The spiny lobster grinds parts of its shell together to communicate with other lobsters. Nearby tiger sharks have learned that this sound means lunch is just around the corner.

Pathfinder

• When designing tanks for captive sharks, aquarists have to make allowance for their electrosense systems. Find out why on page 72.
• How is a hammerhead shark's strange head shape related to its senses? Go to pages 82–83.
• There's no light to see by in the deepest layers of the ocean, so some creatures make their own. See page 120.

SCENT-SATIONAL!

For many years, people incorrectly called sharks "swimming noses" because they thought they mainly used their sense of smell to find food. Now we know that, while they can smell very well, they are also able to detect electricity, see colors, sense distant vibrations, and hear well through their watery environment.

Lateral line

Silvertip shark

Skin

Macula neglecta

Semicircular canal

Ear

SWIMMER'S EARS

A shark looks as though it has no ears—all that is visible are tiny openings on the top of its head. But sharks actually have very sensitive hearing (even though the hearing is tuned to a different frequency than ours). A shark has inner ears—organs inside the brain case—called macula neglecta. Fluid-filled tubes near the macula neglecta, called semicircular canals, regulate balance.

INSIDE STORY

How Smart Are Sharks?

When biologist Michelle Jeffries set out to test shark electrosense, she also discovered how clever sharks can be. Her experiment involved two nurse sharks swimming in a y-shaped maze. Each of the maze's two exits had a magnetic pole that was switched on and off at random. The sharks were given some food if they chose the exit with the active pole. But as the strength of the charge was reduced, it got harder for the sharks to sense it, and sometimes they would make mistakes. "But they soon realized that this meant missing out on a treat," said Jeffries. "One time I even caught a shark clambering over the barrier into the other exit lane just to get at the food."

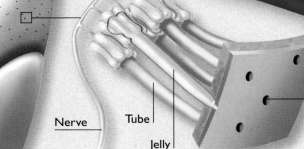

THE BODY ELECTRIC

Sharks have an extra sense that humans don't have—they can actually detect electricity in seawater. A network of jelly-filled pores (called ampullae of Lorenzini) spread across its snout helps a shark detect weak electrical fields created by a fish when it moves. Hammerhead sharks, with their widened heads, have a long series of such cells. They can find prey in the sand and in crevices, and perhaps even navigate, with the electrical signals they receive.

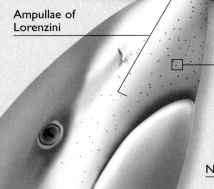

Ampullae of Lorenzini

Nerve

Tube

Jelly

Surface pore

Close-up of ampullae of Lorenzini

Leopard shark
(a fivegill shark)

Bluntnose sixgill
(a sixgill shark)

Broadnose sevengill
(a sevengill shark)

Deep Breathing

TAKE A BREATH. There. When you're human, getting life-giving oxygen is that easy. Getting oxygen is pretty simple for a shark, too. It's just how they get it that's different, because they must breathe underwater.

Sharks and other fishes have developed special organs called gills for getting oxygen from water. A shark breathes by taking in water through its mouth much as we take in air. The water flows over the gills (which remove the oxygen) before passing out through the gill slits. When sharks swim, water is forced over the gills so they get oxygen. The faster they swim, the more oxygen they get. But not all sharks have to swim to breathe. Some bottom dwellers have learned to pump water over their gills while keeping still.

As all animals do, sharks need oxygen for survival. Inside the body's cells, oxygen combines with nutrients from food to create energy. Since blood carries oxygen to the rest of the body, the gills contain many blood vessels. Blood also carries wastes like carbon dioxide from the cells to the gills, where they pass into the water.

BREATHING WITH GILLS

Sharks are not the only animals with gills. Most creatures that live in water use them. All fishes have gills, as do octopuses, squids, shrimps, and all other shellfishes. Most sharks have five pairs of gills, but two families—the sixgill and sevengill sharks—have more.

Caribbean reef shark

Gill opening

RAMMING IN OXYGEN
Large, fast-swimming sharks such as makos and great whites (above) need plenty of oxygen in order to push their muscles harder. This means they must force large volumes of water over their gills. By swimming fast with their mouths barely open, they can force oxygen-containing water over their gills. This process is called ram ventilation.

HOW GILLS WORK

Gills are a series of blood-filled structures in the shark's throat that help it to breathe in water. Each gill has hundreds of feathery gill filaments that are filled with oxygen-absorbing blood. Gill filaments are supported by part of the shark's skeleton called the gill arches. By swimming forward and using throat muscles to pump, a shark pushes water over the gills and out through gill slits. Big arteries bring blood to the gills, and this blood gives the gills their red color.

HOLD STILL AND BREATHE
A scientist uses a special dye to study the flow of water through a nurse shark's gills. When at rest, these sharks use their gill and throat muscles to pump water over their gills.

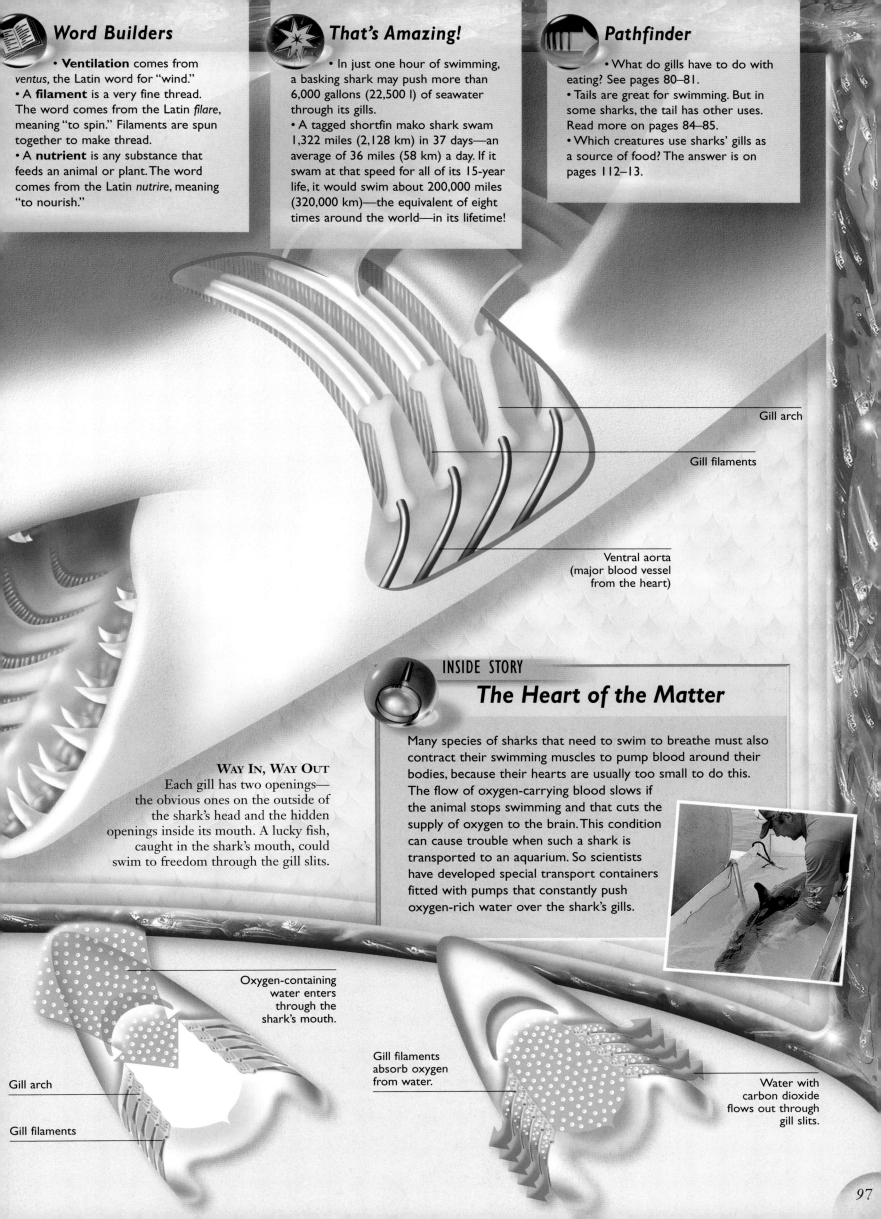

Word Builders

- **Ventilation** comes from *ventus*, the Latin word for "wind."
- A **filament** is a very fine thread. The word comes from the Latin *filare*, meaning "to spin." Filaments are spun together to make thread.
- A **nutrient** is any substance that feeds an animal or plant. The word comes from the Latin *nutrire*, meaning "to nourish."

That's Amazing!

- In just one hour of swimming, a basking shark may push more than 6,000 gallons (22,500 l) of seawater through its gills.
- A tagged shortfin mako shark swam 1,322 miles (2,128 km) in 37 days—an average of 36 miles (58 km) a day. If it swam at that speed for all of its 15-year life, it would swim about 200,000 miles (320,000 km)—the equivalent of eight times around the world—in its lifetime!

Pathfinder

- What do gills have to do with eating? See pages 80–81.
- Tails are great for swimming. But in some sharks, the tail has other uses. Read more on pages 84–85.
- Which creatures use sharks' gills as a source of food? The answer is on pages 112–13.

Gill arch

Gill filaments

Ventral aorta (major blood vessel from the heart)

WAY IN, WAY OUT

Each gill has two openings—the obvious ones on the outside of the shark's head and the hidden openings inside its mouth. A lucky fish, caught in the shark's mouth, could swim to freedom through the gill slits.

INSIDE STORY

The Heart of the Matter

Many species of sharks that need to swim to breathe must also contract their swimming muscles to pump blood around their bodies, because their hearts are usually too small to do this. The flow of oxygen-carrying blood slows if the animal stops swimming and that cuts the supply of oxygen to the brain. This condition can cause trouble when such a shark is transported to an aquarium. So scientists have developed special transport containers fitted with pumps that constantly push oxygen-rich water over the shark's gills.

Gill arch

Gill filaments

Oxygen-containing water enters through the shark's mouth.

Gill filaments absorb oxygen from water.

Water with carbon dioxide flows out through gill slits.

The salmon shark is 10 feet (3 m) long from nose to tail

The Atlantic devil ray has a 5-foot (1.5-m) wingspan

Swimming Lessons

COMPARED TO FLYING in air, "flying" in water is a cinch. Water is 800 times as heavy as air and holds up much more weight. But in many other ways swimming through water is like flying through air. Think of the shark's tail as an airplane propeller, but set at the back. The power of the tail drives the shark forward, and the pectoral fins—like an airplane's wings and flaps—help the shark climb or dive.

If a broad, powerful tail is so important, how do skates and rays, which have slender, whiplike tails, manage to "fly" through the water? These relatives of sharks get their power from their big pectoral fins. Some, such as manta rays and bat rays, swim along in open water, flapping their pectoral fins like wings, much as birds do. Stingrays, however, do not flap their fins. They use their strong pectoral muscles to ripple along the bottom.

Birds can overcome gravity because they don't weigh much for their size. The same is true of sharks and their relatives. Cartilage is lighter than bone, and this allows cartilaginous fishes—even the larger ones—to slice through the water with a minimum of effort. Large livers filled with fatty, lighter-than-water oils also enable sharks to stay buoyant easily.

Bat ray

GOING INTO HIDING
Well-developed pectorals are good for more than just swimming. Rays and skates use their pectoral fins to cover themselves with sand in order to hide from predators.

Thornback ray

DOUBLE WHAMMY
When you see a swimming ray, you might think it has two faces! That's because it has eyes on its upperside and its mouth and gills on its underside, and both can be seen when the fish is on the move.

HOW THEY SWIM
Sharks and rays swim differently. Rays flap their pectoral fins as if they were flying. Sharks move their tails from side to side to push themselves forward. A shark's pectoral fins merely control its direction.

98

Word Builders

• **Buoyancy** is the ability to float. It comes from the Spanish word for "float"—*boyar*.
• **Pectoral** fins are on either side of a fish, about where the chest might be. In Latin, the word *pector* means "breast" or "chest."
• **Gravity** is the force that draws an object or living thing downwards. The word comes from the Latin *gravis*, meaning "heavy."

That's Amazing!

• Shark babies can swim—and hunt—as soon as they are born. The great white shark swims nonstop its entire life.
• One of the fastest-swimming sharks is the mako. It has a streamlined, torpedo-shaped body that is ideal for cruising and for sudden bursts of very high speed. Speeds of 22 miles per hour (35 km/h) have been recorded.

Pathfinder

• Most sharks swim alone, but some hammerheads prefer company. Find out why on page 83.
• Different tails for different sharks? Learn more on pages 84–85.
• Swimming takes a lot of oxygen. How does underwater breathing work, anyway? Find out on pages 96–97.

WINGING IT

Stingrays and skates stay near the seafloor, but eagle rays, cownose rays, and manta rays seem to fly through the water, far above the bottom. Mantas can be found a long way offshore, near the surface but in very deep water.

Blue shark

ROCK CLIMBER

The nurse shark is a sluggish bottom dweller that sometimes uses its specially adapted pectoral fins for clambering rather than swimming. The fins help it to move across the rocky seabed. The nurse shark doesn't need to swim to breathe, an ideal adaptation for a creature that is often seen resting on the reefs and rocks of its habitat.

THEY GET AROUND

Some sharks can swim rapidly only for short distances, while other species have the stamina of marathon runners. Blue sharks caught, tagged, and released off Massachusetts were caught again near Spain 40 days and 2,000 miles (3,220 km) later. Tag returns show that blue sharks regularly swim back and forth across the Atlantic Ocean. These trips require strong muscles, stamina, and the ability to navigate. Just how sharks find their way is something scientists are still studying.

INSIDE STORY

The Problem with Pecs

All sharks have pectoral fins. These fins can bend and tilt to help the shark maneuver and brake. They also steady the shark's body as it swims. In many sharks, the pectoral fins are shaped like a shallow upside-down bowl, providing lift as the shark moves forward. The size and shape of the pectorals vary between species. Those of the fastest sharks, such as the mako (below), are short with a small surface area to reduce drag. They are also stiff, helping the shark to turn sharply at high speed. Other sharks, such as hammerheads, have small pectorals that don't give much lift, too. However, the hammerheads' broad head shape compensates for this, giving them that extra lift. Sluggish bottom dwellers such as angel sharks don't need speed, so they've developed pectoral fins that are large and broad.

The Cutting Edge

WHEN YOU THINK of sharks, you automatically think of teeth. All sharks have teeth, even the big filter feeders who no longer use them. But for all their amazing teeth, there's one thing that sharks can't do—chew their food. While different sharks have developed specialized teeth for tackling different food items, the end result is the same: sharks use those teeth to cut food up into chunks small enough to swallow. If food is swallowed whole, then the shark uses its teeth for holding or disabling the prey.

Sharks usually have only one kind of tooth, depending on what they eat. Makos have stabbing teeth for grabbing hold of fast prey. Wobbegongs have small, sharp teeth for crushing shellfish. Great whites have slicing teeth for cutting large prey into smaller pieces. Horn sharks are an exception. They have both stabbing and crushing teeth—perfect for grabbing spiny sea urchins and crunching them up. This mixture of teeth is called heterodonty, and it gives this order of sharks—the Heterodontiformes—its name.

Although sharks can go through thousands of teeth in a lifetime, they generally only have one row or band of teeth in biting position. As teeth are broken or wear out, new ones move up and out to take their place.

JUTTING JAWS

People used to think that sharks had to turn over to bite, because their noses got in the way. Now we know that the shark has muscles that lift the snout up and out of the way. Protrusile jaws—jaws that can be pushed out and forward then drawn back in again—increase the power of the shark's bite and let it grab relatively large prey easily.

With one big bite, a great white can take a 22-pound (10-kg) chunk out of a dolphin or a seal.

NONE TOO SHARP

How did the gummy shark, a type of smooth dogfish, get its name? Without sharp teeth to slice up its food, this shark appears to gum it instead. Its flat teeth can crush bottom-dwelling creatures such as octopuses, fishes, and shrimps.

INSIDE STORY

Close Call

In 1985, Joe Thomson was bodyboard surfing off the Kauai coast in Hawaii when he found himself eyeball to eyeball with a tiger shark—and his hands were actually inside the shark's mouth! He was able to free one hand and repeatedly socked the shark in the eye until it released its grip. He managed to escape, but with only one of his hands. He made it to the beach and hitched a ride to a hospital. But he sent his friends back to retrieve the surfboard.

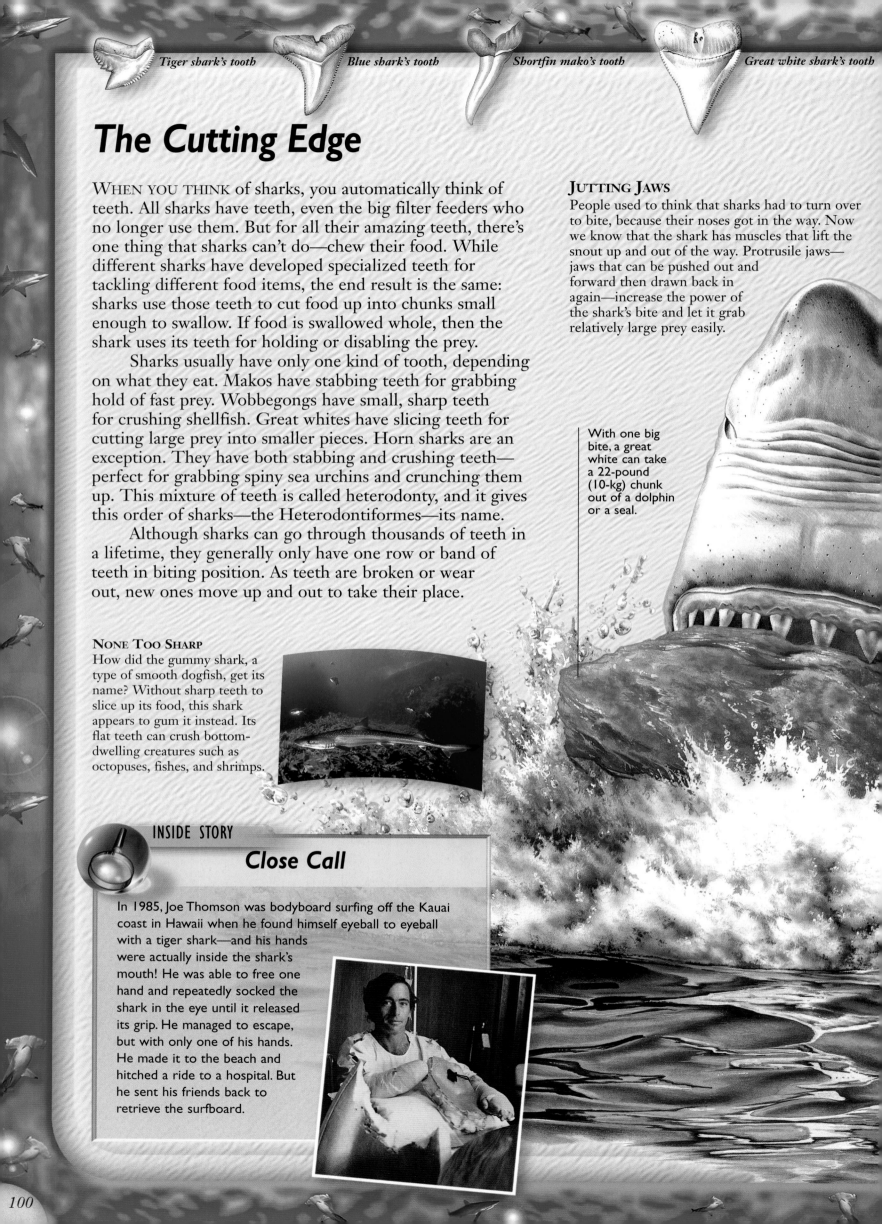

• **Heterodonty** comes from the Greek words *hetero,* meaning "other" or "different," and *odon,* meaning "teeth."
• **Protrusile** comes from the Latin words *pro,* meaning "in front of," and *trudere,* meaning "to thrust."

• A shark may use more than 30,000 teeth in its lifetime. It can have up to 3,000 teeth in its mouth at once.
• In medieval times, sharks' teeth were used to detect poison in drinks. The brew was thought to be deadly if it fizzed when the tooth was dropped into the liquid.

• How big were the teeth and jaws of Megalodon, an extinct cousin of the great white? Find out on pages 74–75.
• How do tiny toothlike structures, called denticles, on a shark's skin help it to swim fast? Go to page 92.
• Do sharks use their teeth during courtship? See pages 102–03.

SAY "AAAAH!"

A great white's powerful jaws are made of light and flexible cartilage. The two bumps on the top of the upper jaw show where it was loosely connected to the bottom of the shark's brain case, allowing the jaws to detach from the brain case when the shark attacked. The teeth in the back of the jaw are much smaller than the teeth in the front.

OPEN WIDE

Jaws that slide out of the mouth sound like something out of a science fiction movie! But slow-motion footage of feeding sharks confirms the truth. Protrusile jaws give the shark a better grip on its prey—and absorb some of the force of its powerful bite.

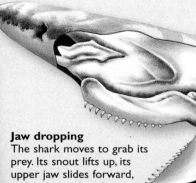

At rest
In its resting or crunching position, the shark's jaw lies just under its brain case.

Jaw dropping
The shark moves to grab its prey. Its snout lifts up, its upper jaw slides forward, and its lower jaw drops.

Extra bite
Once the jaw is fully open, muscle contractions force it away from the brain case and out of the shark's mouth.

CONVEYER-BELT TEETH

A shark's teeth are always sharp. The rate of replacement is unknown for most species, but experiments with captive lemon sharks and horn sharks show that each tooth lasts from one month to about a year. The thousands of teeth lost during a shark's life fall to the seafloor and may eventually become fossils.

Generation Next

HAVING BABIES IS the ultimate goal of all animals. After all, producing young is vital for the survival of any species. And sharks are no exception.

But sharks do reproduce differently from most of the sea creatures that surround them. Most marine animals release sperm and eggs into the water at the same time, and when sperm joins with egg, fertilized eggs are the result. With sharks, however, fertilization takes place inside the female's body, just as in mammals. Male sharks transfer sperm to the females with organs called claspers.

Depending on the shark, fertilized eggs develop in one of three ways. Some sharks lay egg cases that attach to surfaces. Others keep their eggs inside them, where pups develop and hatch before being born into the water. Several species bear live young without benefit of egg cases at all. These sharks have placentas with umbilical cords that nourish the young as they develop. It usually takes them six to 12 months to produce their pups. That's why many shark population numbers are low. They are being fished faster than they can reproduce.

MALE VERSUS FEMALE
All male sharks and rays have a pair of claspers between their pelvic fins for fertilizing the females' eggs.

PRE-MATING BALLET
Before mating, a male and female shark swim gracefully around each other like ballet dancers. The male signals his intentions by nipping his mate on her back. She stops swimming, and together they spiral down toward the seafloor.

INSIDE STORY

Living Under Glass

Scientists have learned much about shark reproduction from sharks that have given birth in large aquariums. One of the world's most successful shark breeders is Senzu Uchida of the Okinawa Expo Aquarium in Japan. He was the first person to catch and display the world's largest fish—the whale shark. In a one-million-gallon (3,785,000-l) tank, Uchida has studied mothers and pups of seven kinds of rays and seven kinds of sharks, including whitetip and blacktip reef sharks, and bull sharks. Uchida says, "We have to be careful about including bull sharks in displays. They will eat pups, mantas, and even tiger sharks. If bull sharks are included, they must be fed all the time."

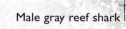
Male gray reef shark

Word Builders

• The **placenta** is a flattened, spongy organ inside a pregnant animal. The word comes from the Greek for "flat cake"—*plakoeis*. The placenta nourishes the baby, which is attached to it by the umbilical cord.
• *Umbilicus* is Latin for "navel" or "center." The **umbilical cord** is a tube running from the fetus's navel (belly button) to the placenta.

That's Amazing!

• Expectant shark mothers lose their appetite just before giving birth. And a good thing, too—this keeps them from eating their own babies!
• Newborn spined pygmy sharks are less than ½ inch (12 mm) long. Contrast that with newborn basking sharks, which are 66 inches (170 cm) long—as big as an adult human.

Pathfinder

• How fast does a shark pup grow? And how do we know how old a shark is? Turn to pages 104–05.
• Why do pregnant gray reef sharks congregate in warmer waters? The answer is on page 115.

HIDING HER EGGS

Once mother sharks lay their eggs they do not stay around to protect them. However, they do make sure that the egg cases—each containing one baby and one nourishing yolk—rest in a safe place. It may take six to 24 months for a pup to hatch. Shark egg cases have flexible brown covers. They are not fragile like birds' eggshells.

ONCE BITTEN

A quick look at a female shark's back and pectoral fins can confirm whether she's mated. Scars on her back and pectoral fins show that a male has bitten her during mating. A lack of scars suggests she has not yet begun courtship.

ANCHORING AN EGG

Swellsharks and catsharks lay flat, rectangular egg cases called mermaid's purses. All four corners have hooks or long threads which the sharks use to attach the egg cases to rocks, seaweeds, plantlike animals, such as sea whips, and other fixed items.

BABIES ALIVE!

Hammerhead and some requiem sharks have live young with placentas and umbilical cords instead of eggs that hatch outside or inside the body. Placental sharks may have only a few pups or as many as a hundred. Most sharks have two uteri, unlike mammals, which have only one.

Uterus
Developing sharks
Uterus
Ovary

Female gray reef shark

WEDGING EGGS IN CREVICES

Horn sharks lay oval egg cases ringed with screwlike ridges. The mother wedges the egg cases into cracks and crevices, where the ridges hold the egg case firmly and safely. Each species of horn shark lays a slightly different shape of egg case.

Juvenile zebra shark *Adult zebra shark*

Shark Meets World

CAN A SHARK be called a teenager? It may sound strange, but it's not far off the mark. Like all animals—including humans—sharks take time to grow and mature. They even go through a period like human adolescence, where they undergo rapid physical changes that leave them ready to breed. For the males, it means that the claspers grow. For the females, it means that their ovaries begin to develop eggs. At this point, sharks are sexually mature—ready to have babies.

How long a shark takes to become a breeding adult varies with each species. Smaller species, such as bonnetheads and leopard sharks, mature quickly. Larger ones, like dusky sharks and great whites, can take longer.

Sharks go through other physical changes before they hit "adolescence," too. As well as growing larger, species like zebra sharks change their color or skin patterns. Others, like great whites and horn sharks, eat different foods as they mature, so their teeth change shape to cope with the difference.

FASTEST-GROWING SHARK
Shark species that are small at birth tend to grow faster than larger sharks. This smallish (3 feet/1 m) sharpnose shark has a lifespan of 10 or 15 years but may reach maturity within a year of its birth.

A 10-year-old dusky shark is about 5 feet (1.5 m) long.

A one-year-old dusky shark measures just under 4 feet (1.2 m).

TEN YEARS STRONG
A 10-year-old human girl averages 4 feet 8 inches (1.4 m) in height. She is some years away from sexual maturity and is still dependent on her parents. Sexual maturity for a dusky shark of the same age is also some years away.

STARTING OUT
Most human babies weigh about 5–10 pounds (2.5–5 kg) and are between 19–23 inches (48–58 cm) at birth. A newborn dusky shark is almost 3 feet (1 m) long. But a baby dusky has to fend for itself, while the human baby is completely dependent on parents for survival.

IN THE BEGINNING
Just after a shark egg is laid, the yolk is large and clearly visible. But you would need a magnifying glass to see the tiny shark embryo as it rests on top of the yolk.

The young shark gets food from the yolk through a tube connected to its intestine.

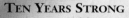

WHAT'S INSIDE...
One swellshark egg case holds one growing shark and a fat-filled yolk that feeds it. Laid in cold water, a shark's egg may take a year to hatch. Young sharks develop more quickly in warmer water.

Eggs are laid in amber-colored cases known as mermaids' purses.

Word Builders

• **Adolescence** is based on two Latin words—*ad-*, a prefix for "toward," and *alescere*, which means "to grow" or "to be nourished."
• Something that grows within—like a baby—is an **embryo**. It comes from the Greek *enbryein*, meaning "to swell."

That's Amazing!

• How do scientists tell the age of a dead shark? Much the same way that botanists count the rings in a tree trunk. Marine scientists stain a shark's vertebrae—the bones of the spinal column—then count the rings in one or more of the largest vertebrae. Most sharks produce one new ring each year.
• Most kinds of sharks live to be about 25 years old, but spiny dogfish have been known to live for 100 years.

Pathfinder

• How do shark young hide in plain sight? Go to page 86.
• Learn how baby sharks are made on pages 102–03.
• Sometimes newborn sharks equal sharkfood. What's a mother to do? Find out on pages 106–07.

At age 20, the dusky shark is about 7½ feet (2.3 m) long. It won't stop growing completely until it dies, at about 40 years of age and a length of around 10 feet (3 m).

INSIDE STORY

In the Nursery

Dr. Samuel Gruber, who directs a summer program to teach young people about sharks, has been studying lemon sharks around Bimini Island in the Bahamas for 30 years. By tagging them, he and his students have learned how fast they grow. "At first we thought lemon sharks grew fast, maturing in two to three years. Now we know that they grow very slowly indeed. After four years in the nursery shallows, they have grown only about 16 inches (40 cm). And they may not mature for 15–20 years." Adult lemon sharks can grow to 11 feet (3.4 m) in length.

TWENTY YEARS AND MORE

By age 20, humans can survive on their own and have reached their full height—around 6 feet (2 m) in males. Most wait until their twenties to start a family, although they've been sexually mature for years. Dusky sharks, in contrast, are just reaching sexual maturity at this age.

NEARLY THERE

As the young shark absorbs the yolk and develops, it gets larger and the yolk gets smaller. The baby shark breathes through well-developed gills.

The newborn shark pup emerges from the splitting egg case.

HATCHING

When the young shark—called a pup—has completely absorbed the yolk and developed into a miniature adult, it hatches from its flexible egg case. The shark is on its own. It must be especially wary of becoming food for larger creatures like groupers and adult sharks.

The Game of Life

LIFE IN THE OCEAN is a continual (and dangerous!) game of hide-and-seek. The simple truth is that sharks eat everything—including other sharks. But many have developed ways to improve their chances of survival in order to pass their genes on to the next generation.

Take tiger sharks, who produce a large number of small young. The bigger the numbers, the greater the chances are that some will survive. The downside is that these defenseless young are likely to become fish food. Great whites make a different kind of gamble. Mother whites produce only a few young, but the young are relatively large. This is an advantage, but their lack of numbers is a risky tradeoff.

Shark mothers provide no care for either live pups or eggs. Instead, they concentrate on finding the safest birthing environment for their young. Live bearers will choose shallow bays—free of large predators—as nurseries. Egg-layers hide their eggs in crevices or seaweed.

Many newborn sharks, such as zebras and whiskery sharks, have protective markings or coloration that keeps them out of sight. Some, like baby whitetip reef sharks, are preyed on by the adults of the species, so the babies hide among the corals, safely out of reach. Even adult whitetips are at risk of being eaten—by larger sharks. So they've learned to hide in caves by day, coming out to hunt at night under cover of darkness.

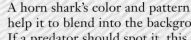

PRICKLY PREY
A horn shark's color and pattern help it to blend into the background. If a predator should spot it, this shark also has two sharp spines on its back to help it survive the encounter. It can wedge itself in a rocky crevice with its back—and spines—pointing outward. Few predators will risk trying to eat that prickly mouthful.

SWELL IDEA
A swellshark resists attack by first wedging itself in a crack and then inflating its stomach with water until it is firmly stuck. Predators find it impossible to pull the balloonlike shark from its hiding place.

INSIDE STORY
A Flash of Terror

American Mike de Gruy is a marine biologist and professional filmmaker. His work has taken him to many places, and one he won't forget in a hurry is Enewetak Atoll in the South Pacific. "I was using my flash camera to take photos of gray reef sharks. I needed a flash because the white bellies of gray reefs blend with the light from above, and you can't see their darker tones. If you're beneath them, looking up, they are almost invisible. I got some good 'looking-up' shots. Then I noticed one smaller shark starting the typical threat posture. 'What a shot!' I thought. I tripped my flash—and bang! The shark grabbed my arm and shook it. I dropped the camera, losing my amazing pictures forever. I made it back to the boat, bleeding from my wound. No pictures, but I've got a great scar to remind me of that two-tone shark!"

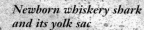

Newborn gray carpetshark and its egg case   *Newborn whiskery shark and its yolk sac*

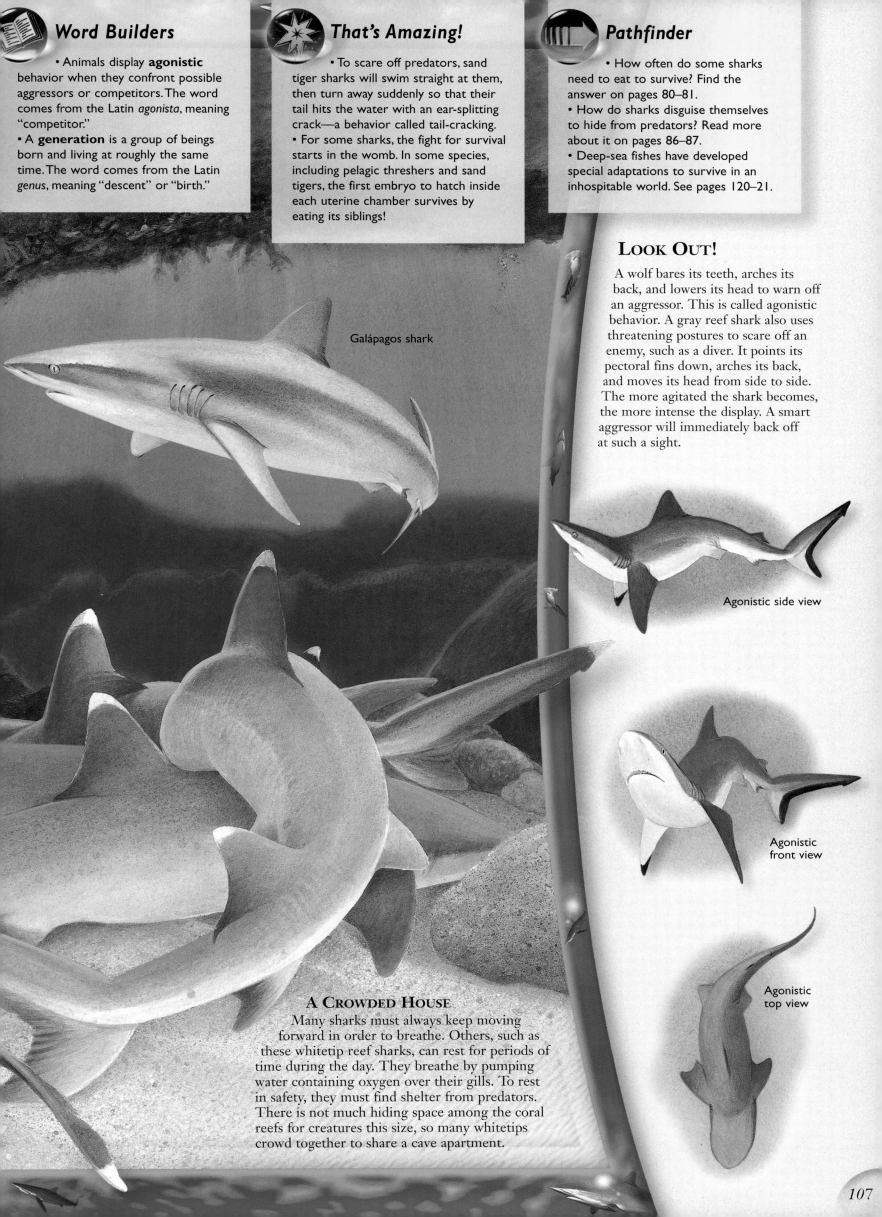

Word Builders

• Animals display **agonistic** behavior when they confront possible aggressors or competitors. The word comes from the Latin *agonista*, meaning "competitor."
• A **generation** is a group of beings born and living at roughly the same time. The word comes from the Latin *genus*, meaning "descent" or "birth."

That's Amazing!

• To scare off predators, sand tiger sharks will swim straight at them, then turn away suddenly so that their tail hits the water with an ear-splitting crack—a behavior called tail-cracking.
• For some sharks, the fight for survival starts in the womb. In some species, including pelagic threshers and sand tigers, the first embryo to hatch inside each uterine chamber survives by eating its siblings!

Pathfinder

• How often do some sharks need to eat to survive? Find the answer on pages 80–81.
• How do sharks disguise themselves to hide from predators? Read more about it on pages 86–87.
• Deep-sea fishes have developed special adaptations to survive in an inhospitable world. See pages 120–21.

Galápagos shark

LOOK OUT!

A wolf bares its teeth, arches its back, and lowers its head to warn off an aggressor. This is called agonistic behavior. A gray reef shark also uses threatening postures to scare off an enemy, such as a diver. It points its pectoral fins down, arches its back, and moves its head from side to side. The more agitated the shark becomes, the more intense the display. A smart aggressor will immediately back off at such a sight.

Agonistic side view

Agonistic front view

Agonistic top view

A CROWDED HOUSE

Many sharks must always keep moving forward in order to breathe. Others, such as these whitetip reef sharks, can rest for periods of time during the day. They breathe by pumping water containing oxygen over their gills. To rest in safety, they must find shelter from predators. There is not much hiding space among the coral reefs for creatures this size, so many whitetips crowd together to share a cave apartment.

Grouper—a danger
to young sharks

Killer whale—a
shark predator

Shark Food

IF IT SWIMS in the sea and it's bigger than the nail on your pinky, chances are it will be food for sharks. Of course, there's the matter of tracking down this prey—and different prey animals have various methods to elude capture. As predators at the top of the food chain, sharks have an arsenal of hunting tools—their senses—for tracking prey. Individual species may also have particular hunting styles, depending on their food choices.

Some sharks, such as the mako and great white, can simply outswim their prey. Others hunt in groups, allowing them to tackle even very large schools of food fishes. The filter feeders generally swim around with mouths agape, scooping up their food. Still other sharks use camouflage to take prey by surprise.

Even though sharks are hunters, they are sometimes the hunted as well. Young and small sharks of many species are eaten by other, larger fishes, such as groupers or adult sharks, and even toothed whales.

SCHOOL'S OUT
Some fishes swim in large schools—there's generally safety in numbers. But this is not true when the predator is a blue shark. Normally unable to catch anything from a swirling mass of schooling fishes, these blue sharks are breaking up the mass into smaller groups. Some fishes will lose their place—becoming easy prey.

WATCH THE BIRDY
Seabirds nest in big colonies on many low, sandy, tropical islands. Young birds, like this albatross fledgling, take off from land and can crash into nearby shallows when they are just learning to fly. If they are lucky, the wind and their paddling feet return them to the beach for another try. If they are unlucky, a cruising tiger shark rushes up from beneath, snatches them, and gulps them down.

Reef sharks swallow fishes such as this harlequin tuskfish whole.

Cephalopods, such as squid, are a favorite food of blue sharks and some kinds of hammerheads.

The hard shells of lobsters and crabs don't protect them from the powerful jaws and teeth of hungry sharks.

WHAT'S ON THE MENU?
Sharks used to be thought of as the garbage cans of the sea, eating whatever they could find. While tiger sharks have been known to eat just about anything—including kangaroos and cows that have washed down flooded rivers, as well as plastic bags and cans of food—other species are more discerning. Most species of sharks eat a variety of animals, allowing them to maintain their food intake as the abundance of each type of prey varies. Others have very individualized diets. The California horn shark, for example, feeds on sea urchins.

Word Builders

- A **predator** is an animal that eats other animals. The word comes from the Latin *praeda*—the same word that gives us the word "prey."
- A **frenzy** is a state of agitation or excitement. The word comes from the Latin *phrensis*, meaning "mind."

That's Amazing!

- What do California sea otters and horn sharks have in common? Pink skeletons! Both feed on purple sea urchins. Pigment from the sea urchins enters the bloodstream. It then combines with calcium in the growing cartilage of sharks or skeletons of sea otters, tinting them pink.
- Some sluggish bottom dwellers, such as swell sharks, have survived for over a year in captivity without eating.

Pathfinder

- Some sharks really use their heads when they hunt for food. Find out about them on pages 82–83.
- Do sharks have special cutlery for special food? Read up on teeth and jaws on pages 100–01.
- What's on the menu for developing shark embryos? Turn to pages 104–05.

STIR CRAZY

The "feeding frenzies" seen in movies have usually been provoked by people throwing bloody bait into the water. Sharks seldom behave this way in the wild. Scavenging tiger sharks, for example, will appear completely calm around a dead whale and tend to avoid one another, even while feeding.

INSIDE STORY

Bite and Spit

Peter Pyle is a biologist with the Point Reyes Bird Observatory in California. On the Farallon Islands west of San Francisco, he has observed the attack and feeding behavior of great white sharks. "From the high cliffs I would see a shark approaching a seal," he reports. "The shark charged, took a bite, and then backed off while the seal died. This is called 'bite and spit' feeding." This feeding method does two things. It lets the shark taste the prey to see if it will make a good meal. It also conserves energy, because blood loss—rather than hard work on the part of the shark—will eventually kill the prey.

Rays are some of the largest fishes in the sea, but that doesn't keep sharks from attacking and eating them.

A tiger shark can munch through a sea turtle's hard shell.

Seals are a favorite food of great whites.

Cookiecutter sharks take cookie-shaped chunks out of dolphins and other large prey.

A Shark's World

NOW THAT YOU'VE learned something about sharks from the inside out, it's time to see them in action on their home turf. First, we'll look at creatures who've managed to find a way to actually live with these fierce ocean predators. Then, after a visit to a reef and some cool water shallows, we'll head out to the open ocean. From there we'll descend through the murky midwaters and into the deepest, darkest layer of the sea. Sharks share their watery world with some of the most fantastic creatures, and you're about to meet them face to face. So get ready to dive right in...

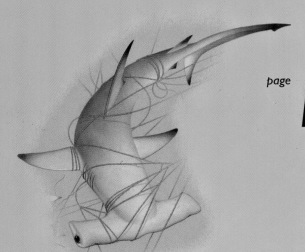

Fish louse

Tapeworm

Leech

Hangers-On

WHILE MOST SHARKS are loners, they never really swim alone. Sharks carry a variety of marine passengers, both inside and outside their bodies. First, there are parasites. Many kinds of worms live inside a shark's intestinal tract, while leeches and crablike copepods live on a shark's outside—leeches near the mouth and cloaca, and copepods near gill slits, fins, and even on the eyes. Parasites such as these actually feed on the shark (or host) itself, but they don't usually weaken the host to the point of death. They must strike a delicate balance so that their host will continue to provide them with food.

Other companions aren't nearly so harmful. Pilot fishes and remoras are a shark's most frequent attendants—pilot fishes riding pressure waves in front of the shark, and remoras attached to the shark itself with suction. Pilot fishes are opportunists who take advantage of the shark's feeding habits to live off the leftovers. Remoras and other caretakers have a symbiotic relationship with sharks, which means that both parties benefit—the sharks get a free cleaning service, and the remoras and other creatures make a good living eating the parasites that live off the sharks.

PAYING THEIR WAY
Remoras, which can attach and detach at will, can be found on the underside or back of their hosts. The eight different species have distinct preferences—some are found with rays and sharks (such as this Caribbean reef shark) and others with whales or sea turtles. But providing sharks with a cleaning service doesn't always guarantee the remoras' safety.

Sandbar shark

Remora

Bow wave

UNDERWATER SURFING
When a streamlined object moves through water, it creates pressure waves in front of it. These waves help push along smaller swimmers ahead of the larger object.

FREE MEALS?
Pilot fishes get protection from their travel buddies, the sharks—not many predators will risk hunting near a shark. The smaller fishes also manage to make some good meals out of the scraps the sharks leave. But they have to watch their backs, or they can become shark food themselves.

Pilot fishes

HELPING HANDS
King angelfishes usually eat sponges, sea squirts, and other animals attached to the rocky bottom. But when a shark swims by, the angelfishes swim up to dine on parasites that live on it. Sharks accept the services of these and many other "cleaners" and stay still as the visitors groom and clean them.

King angelfish

Word Builders

- A **parasite** is an animal that lives by taking substances, such as blood, from other animals. Although parasites don't usually kill their hosts, they don't help them either. The word comes from the Greek for "one who lives at another's expense."
- **Remora** is from the Latin for "delay." These fishes, which attach themselves in large numbers to boats, too, were once thought to slow ships down.

That's Amazing!

- Some kinds of parasitic worms will live in only one species of shark. When the first megamouth shark was discovered, its stomach contained a new species of worm that has never been found in any other kind of shark.
- Do parasites affect shark behavior? Maybe. Makos have been known to leap from the water. Scientists think they do it to shake off irritating parasites.

Pathfinder

- Sharks like some shrimps for their maid service and others for their food value. Learn more on pages 80–81.
- Pilot fishes use hydrodynamics to surf the bow waves in front of sharks. See how hammerheads employ hydrodynamics on pages 82–83.
- Cleaner fishes that are swallowed by sharks sometimes find an ingenious escape route. See page 97.

PERSONAL GROOMING

Copepods, often referred to as sea lice, are small crustaceans that feed on the skin tissue of their hosts. They usually attach themselves to the fins or gills, but one species latches onto the corneas of Greenland sharks' eyes, as pictured.

REEF CARETAKERS

Several kinds of coral reef and kelp bed animals make their living by cleaning larger animals, such as sharks. Sharks visit these "cleaning stations" just as you might go to a dentist. Some cleaners even swim into the shark's mouth looking for parasites to eat.

Cleaner Wrasses
These fishes live on coral reefs and eat copepods and other parasites that live on sharks.

Cobias
Relatives of the remora, cobias hang around larger fishes (including sharks) for protection. They also keep the reef clean by eating scraps from the other fishes' meals.

HANDS ON

All-day Sucker

How does a remora manage to hold on to shark? The answer is suction. That's what allows a cup-shaped object to stick to a smooth surface after the air is removed. This is called a vacuum, and remoras make them with special muscles in ridges (which are actually modified dorsal fins) atop their heads.

You can try this for yourself. Take a rubber suction cup—like the plunger shown here—press it onto a smooth surface such as a refrigerator door, and press out the air. Now pull. It sticks to the door because the weight of the Earth's atmosphere is pressing down on it. In the case of the remora, the weight of the surrounding water presses against it to hold it in place.

Banded Coral Shrimp
Sharks will remain very still while the cleaner shrimp does its job along the gills and in the shark's mouth.

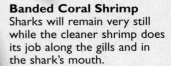

Whitetip reef shark,
5 feet (1.6 m) long

Caribbean reef shark,
10 feet (3 m) long

Blacktip reef shark,
6 feet (2 m)

Riot on the Reef

CORAL POLYPS ARE the architects of the sea. These tiny creatures can transform an underwater desert, nearly devoid of nutrients and inhabitants, into a thriving colony where other plant and animal life abounds.

A new reef is formed when free-floating coral larvae are carried on ocean currents away from their reef of origin. Once they reach shallow water, they take up residence. First they attach themselves to hard surfaces. Then they use a symbiotic algae that lives in their gut to convert chemicals in seawater into stony, exterior skeletons. The skeletons make huge underwater structures—the coral reefs. These reefs provide food and shelter for a riot of plant and animal life, such as seaweeds, algae, shellfishes, sponges, sea urchins, sea stars, and fishes—including sharks.

Indo-Pacific reefs are home to blacktip reef sharks, whitetip reefs, gray reefs, tiger, and Galápagos sharks. Caribbean reefs support Caribbean reef sharks, lemon, bull, sandbar, and tiger sharks. These many types of sharks have developed different feeding habits and tastes to avoid competing with each other for food.

Jellyfishes are related to corals and sea anemones.

The gray reef shark is a top predator of the coral reef.

Octopuses hide in the reef and hunt crabs.

INSIDE STORY

The Living Coral

Dr. Bruce Carlson is a marine biologist who studies corals and coral reefs. He also directs the Waikiki Aquarium in Hawaii where corals are displayed and reared. "Spawning corals are a magical sight! I saw them once on a dive in the Pacific off the Solomon Islands. It was during a full moon in November—species always spawn at the same time every year—and the corals released millions of eggs and clouds of sperm into the water at once. The amazing part is that we were able to predict the exact night of the spawning."

Gray reef shark

FOOD CHAIN GANG

Tiny fishes get eaten by small fishes, and the small fishes get eaten by larger ones. But sometimes the chain of events gets more complicated. In this reef food chain, damselfishes feed snappers, which feed jacks, which feed gray reef sharks. But what feeds the damselfish? The eggs of the jack! This complex food chain is called a food web.

Word Builders

• **Polyps** have many tentacles. They get their name from the Latin *polypus*, for "many-footed."
• The eight-legged **octopus** is named for its shape. *Okto* is Greek for "eight," and *pous* is Greek for "foot."
• **Spawn** is both a verb—to deposit eggs—and a noun—the mass of eggs themselves. It comes from the Old French *spandre*, meaning "to spread out or expand."

That's Amazing!

• Australia's Great Barrier Reef is 1,250 miles (2,012 km) long—the largest coral reef in the world, and the only non-manmade structure that is visible from outer space. It can be seen clearly from the Moon—239,000 miles (384,000 km) above the Earth.
• Extremely efficient filter feeders, sponges can process up to 1,000 times their own bulk of water—per hour!

Pathfinder

• Which shark relatives find their food in the sand? The answer is on pages 88–89.
• Coral and algae are symbionts. Do sharks have symbiotic relationships? See pages 112–13.
• Swim with a Caribbean reef shark? Only if you're careful! Find out more on pages 124–25.

LIFE IN THE CORAL

Tiny coral polyps, each no bigger than a pinhead, can team up to become mighty builders. Other creatures benefit from the stony homes built by coral polyps. Thousands of kinds of animals all find places to hunt and hide. Marine plants grow on the coral structures and provide food for many reef creatures.

Cleaner wrasses pick parasites off bigger fishes.

KEEPING WARM

In the warmer months of the year, crowds of pregnant gray reef sharks come into shallow water and mill around. Marine scientists think that the warmer water helps the shark fetuses to develop at a faster rate inside their mothers.

Parrotfish

Yellow tang

Clownfishes find protection from predators by living among the stinging tentacles of sea anemones (but they don't get stung themselves).

Colorful reef fishes like this double-saddled butterflyfish use their markings to hide themselves among the brightly colored corals.

Sponges attach themselves to the reef and feed on tiny particles, including coral polyp eggs, that they filter from the water.

Damselfish

Jack

Snapper

Jack eggs

Sand tiger shark, 8½ feet (2.6 m) long

Bonnethead shark, 3 feet (1 m) long

Sandbar shark 6½ feet (2 m) long

Living the Shallows Life

SUNLIGHT HELPS TO make shallow coastal waters areas of high biodiversity—places where many kinds of organisms live. Marine plants of all types use sunlight to make food. But plants need nutrients to grow best. The richest plant growth thrives along coastlines, where natural substances, such as silt, wash from the land to nourish the plants. Many different kinds of animals live in these shallows, feeding off these very plants—or off one another. A swim through the turtle grass beds growing in the warm waters of Florida or the kelp forests of a cool California sea reveals an amazing richness of life. And as usual, sharks are at the top of the connected food chains.

A swimmer in the cool waters of the Pacific Ocean kelp beds may see the most dangerous shark of all—the great white. But it's far more likely that he or she will see smaller, harmless sharks, such as horn sharks, leopard sharks, swellsharks, angel sharks, guitarfishes, and torpedo rays.

The warm shallows of the Atlantic Ocean are home to a greater number of larger sharks—bull sharks, tigers, sandbars, lemons, and Caribbean reef sharks. Here they can feed on fishes such as menhaden and herrings, and even sea turtles.

SHALLOWS VERSUS REEF

Coral reefs often form in shallow water—so what's the difference between reefs and shallows? Corals need clear water to establish themselves, and the clearest waters are far from coastlines. The habitats known as shallows are those along continental coasts. Nutrient-rich waters such as these are usually green and sometimes murky, like the waters off California. Shallows habitats can be found in all the world's temperature zones, from tropical to polar.

Bull shark
This shark favors shallow water and will swim far up rivers in search of prey.

Nudibranchs
Colorful sea slugs, called nudibranchs, live in the zone between high and low tide. They feed on invertebrates. When they meet others of their species, they often fight, biting and eating chunks of each other.

Purple shore crab
This crab mainly eats algae, but also scavenges dead animals.

COOL CUSTOMERS

The sheltered rocks and bottoms of a cool-water kelp forest are home to many creatures, both mobile and otherwise. All have relatives in the warm shallows of turtle grass beds and on coral reefs. Mobile animals, such as crabs, nudibranchs, and sea stars, move around and hunt for food. Animals such as sea anemones, sea squirts, and sponges can't move. They are attached to surfaces and must wait for ocean currents to float food, in the form of plankton, to them. To protect themselves, many of these animals have spines or protective armor. Others can sting or inject their enemies with poison.

Word Builders

- **Biodiversity** is a new word formed from *bios*, Greek for "life," and diversity, from Latin *divergere*, "to turn aside" or "to take different paths."
- **Spine** has two meanings—a sharp-tipped spike, and the backbone of an animal. It comes from the Latin *spina*, meaning both "thorn" and "backbone."
- **Nudibranchs** are so called because of their external gills. Their name is a combination of the Latin words *nudus*, "naked," and *branchia*, "gills."

That's Amazing!

- Some sharks can poison people. The meat of whitetip reef sharks can cause ciguatera, a type of food poisoning that involves severe stomach cramps.
- Some nudibranchs "borrow" the stinging tentacles of the sea anemones that they feed off of. Somehow, these tentacles aren't digested by the nudibranch, but become part of the animal's own appendages. And they work, too. When a predator attacks a nudibranch, it gets a stinging mouthful.

Pathfinder

- Horn sharks lay unusual eggs. Read about them on pages 102–03.
- The sea's largest structures are built by some of its smallest animals. Find out more on pages 114–15.
- Not all shallows are frequented by sharks, but it's useful to know how to avoid a shark attack just in case. Turn to pages 124–25.

A sea turtle in the shallows may be unaware of a bull shark approaching.

A SHARK WITH HORNS

The California horn shark is one of nine living species of horn sharks. These sharks usually grow to 2 feet (60 cm) long, but can reach twice that size. A large spine in front of each dorsal fin gives them their name. They live among large rocks at the base of cool-water kelp beds. Their strange, screwlike egg cases and distinctive looks make them popular exhibits in public aquariums. Fossil records show that this family of sharks has remained virtually unchanged for 160 million years.

DANGER IN THE SHALLOWS

Shallow waters—like the warm waters of the Florida turtle grass beds pictured here—are rich with food. But for a shark's prey eating can mean danger. If an animal, such as a turtle, lets down its guard for a minute, it runs the risk of being gobbled up as it feeds. When clear, shallow waters mean easy hunting for sharks, since they generally have good vision. However, their prey can also see them sooner than in dimmer light in deep water and has more chance of avoiding being a shark's dinner.

HANDS ON

Getting in Touch

Most aquariums have "touch-tanks" where you can learn what some sea creatures—such as small sharks and rays, sea stars, and sea urchins—feel like. You can touch the denticles on sharks, the spines of sea urchins, and the skeletons of coral. Some animals have surprising textures. For example, some sea stars look soft, but are actually rock hard. And the egg cases of horn sharks feel so much like flexible plastic that most people can't believe they're real!

Sea anemones
These bowl-shaped animals have stinging tentacles. Some anemones reproduce by splitting themselves in pieces. Each piece forms a new individual.

Sea stars
Known to eat shellfishes and coral polyps, sea stars push their stomachs out of their mouths to surround prey. Once digested, the food is then sucked up into the sea star's digestive glands.

Sea squirts
These animals attach themselves to rocks and are sometimes mistaken for plants. A large sea squirt can pump 4–5 gallons (18–22 l) of seawater a day to filter its food, obtain oxygen, and pass waste products.

Crocodile shark,
3 feet (90 cm) long

Prickly dogfish,
2½ feet (75 cm) long

Necklace carpetshark,
3 feet (90 cm) long

Making It in the Midwaters

THE OPEN OCEAN is a vast expanse of water. To make it easier to study, scientists have divided it into layers. The first layer is the one we can see—the upper waters near the surface. The bottom of the deep sea, or the abyss, is another layer. But the biggest layer by far is the midwaters—1,000 feet (300 m) below the surface yet far above the abyss, which can be 35,425 feet (10,900 m) deep. The farther down you go, the darker it is. Seawater is so dense that it filters out the sunlight. And this is the key to life in the midwater layer—somehow the animals that live there have learned to cope with little or no sunlight.

Tiny plants called phytoplankton form the basis of the ocean's food chain. To make food, they need light. Tiny animals—zooplankton—live near the surface to feed on these plants, as do fishes and other sea creatures. Since there's plenty of food in this upper layer, some midwater sharks such as cookiecutters and megamouths migrate upward just to feed. Others, such as catsharks and sleeper sharks, stay put and dine on their deep-living neighbors.

STRUGGLE IN THE DEPTHS

In the life-or-death struggle to survive in the midwaters layer, the small get eaten by the large—and the sharks usually eat them all. Pictured below is a confrontation between two large midwater predators—a frill shark and a giant squid. Because they live hidden in the deep, we know very little about either species. In fact, no one has ever seen a living giant squid and it is quite possible that the shark is the prey and the squid is the predator. The deep midwaters hide many large creatures, so that some may still remain undiscovered, and others, like the megamouth shark, are scarcely known.

PRIMITIVE SPECIMEN

The ruffled edges of its large gill slits give the frill shark its name. Frill sharks grow to 6½ feet (2 m) long and feed on squids, fishes, and other sharks. These sharks resemble fossilized sharks that lived on Earth 200 million years ago.

HIDDEN PREDATOR

Named for its ability to take bite-size plugs out of the flesh of its prey, the cookiecutter shark stays hidden in deep midwaters below 2,000 feet (600 m) by day. At night, it migrates up to the surface to stalk swordfish, tuna, dolphins, other sharks, and even large whales.

Bramble shark,
7¼ feet (2.2 m) long

Word Builders

Names for the layers of the sea come from Greek words. **Pelagios** means "open sea," **epi** means "upper," **meso** means "middle," and **abyss** means "deeper than you can imagine." **Epipelagic** is surface to 1,000 feet (300 m) deep, **mesopelagic** is 1,000–5,000 feet (300–1,500 m) deep, and **abysso-pelagic** is more than 5,000 feet (1,500 m) down.

That's Amazing!

• Cookiecutter sharks don't just attack other fishes. One has even been known to take a bite out of the rubber dome of a nuclear submarine.
• Large eyes absorb more light—a handy adaptation in deep, dark waters. A giant squid's eye is 16 inches (40 cm) across—the size of a large pizza!

Pathfinder

• To learn more about sharks that feed exclusively on plankton, see pages 80–81.
• Do sharks need to see to find food? Find out on pages 94–95.
• Do sharks live in the deepest waters of all? Go to page 120.

TENTACLED TERROR

Giant squid are the largest invertebrates in the world. With tentacles outstretched, they can be as long as 60 feet (18 m). A squid might release a large ink cloud to confuse predators—or prey.

IN DEEP MIDWATERS

Sharks are not the only creatures in the deep middle layers of the open sea. Many of the world's strangest fishes live there, too. Prey is scarce and hard to find in the dark, and so are mates, so deep-sea dwellers need special features to help them survive and breed.

Bristlemouth
Light organs on their belly help them to see prey and to find potential mates.

DEEP-SEA GOBLIN

The bizarre-looking, pinkish-grey goblin shark grows to 12¾ feet (3.9 m) and is the only member of its family. It is rarely seen and little is known of it. Its long snout is packed with electrosense organs that help it locate and catch prey.

Dragonfish
A movable, glowing lure on the chin attracts prey and is thought to help these fishes signal to others of their species.

INSIDE STORY

The Wonder of Sharks

Gil van Dykhuizen loves his job at the Monterey Bay Aquarium in California. "I go fishing for small midwater sharks and then try to bring them back alive to display at the aquarium in our new deep-sea exhibit," he says. For these sharks to survive in captivity, the darkness and extreme cold of their natural environment must be replicated. Because deep-living sharks are sensitive to light, van Dykhuizen and other keepers are experimenting with different wavelengths of light, such as infrared, so that people can observe the sharks while the sharks remain safely in the dark.

Lanternfish
Tiny lights on their chest and belly attract mates and provide camouflage through counter-shading in upper waters.

Cross-toothed Perch
This fish can open its mouth very wide, enabling it to swallow prey larger than itself.

False catshark, 8¼ feet (2.5 m) long

In Total Darkness

IN THE DARKEST depths of the ocean, more than 3,000 feet (1,000 m) below the surface, lies a strange and mysterious world. At depths three times the height of the Empire State Building, the water is freezing, it is completely dark, and the pressure is hundreds of times greater than at the surface. Still, a variety of fishes and other sea creatures have adapted to these harsh conditions—and where there's a steady supply of fishes for food, there are bound to be sharks.

Although divers can't go this deep, scientists can—as long as they travel in submarines or deep-water submersibles. Through the windows of these special vessels, they've photographed the false catshark at 700–5,000 feet (200–1,500 m), the tiny spined pygmy shark at 6,000 feet (1,800 m), and the bluntnose sixgill at 6,500 feet (2,000 m). We also know about some deep-sea sharks from fishers with deep-sea dragnets. The Portuguese shark, caught at a depth of 12,000 feet (3,660 m), was identified this way.

Some scientists have visited depths even greater than 12,000 feet (3,660 m). There they found fishes, including shark cousins like the skate and chimaera—but no sharks. Scientists aren't sure why, but they think it's most likely due to lack of food. After all, sharks have adapted to just about every other environment— as long as there's enough food to support them.

GLOW-IN-THE-DARK SHARK
No sunlight reaches the very deep sea, but many deep-sea animals produce their own light—they are bioluminescent. This spined pygmy shark's belly is covered with tiny organs that produce just enough light to equal the faint glow that filters down from the surface when it swims to upper waters to feed. This is called counter-shading and helps the shark merge with the ocean so it can't be seen by predators.

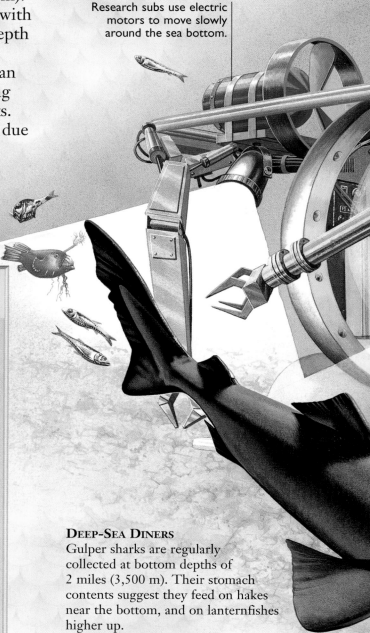

Research subs use electric motors to move slowly around the sea bottom.

INSIDE STORY

A Trip Down Under

"Our sub, the *Pisces VI*, was just about to settle on the bottom, 2,000 feet (600 m) deep off the island of Bermuda. I thought, 'Gosh, I hope I can see something.' Then, this huge, broad head came from underneath the sub, and the green eye of a shark was peering in as if looking at me."

This is how scientist Eugenie Clark described an incident on one of more than 100 dives that she and deep-sea photographer Emory Kristof made in submersibles worldwide. These two Americans have added greatly to our knowledge of sharks. Kristof was a pioneer of direct deep-sea observation, and Clark catalogued the pair's discoveries. On a typical dive they took their vessel to the bottom and waited up to 17 hours for sharks and other creatures to come along.

DEEP-SEA DINERS
Gulper sharks are regularly collected at bottom depths of 2 miles (3,500 m). Their stomach contents suggest they feed on hakes near the bottom, and on lanternfishes higher up.

Bluntnose sixgill shark, 15¾ feet (4.8 m) long

Portuguese shark, 3 feet (1 m) long

Word Builders

- **Bioluminescence** means light produced by a living animal, such as a firefly or a deep-sea fish. It comes from the Latin *bios*, meaning "life," and *lumen*, meaning "light."
- **Bathyscaphe** is from the Greek word *bathys*, for "deep," and *skaphe*, meaning "a small boat or skiff."

That's Amazing!

The seafloor in the deepest parts of the ocean is a virtual desert. No light ever reaches these depths, so there are no plants. Yet in some places, volcanic activity has created hot water vents. Here, a host of creatures like mussels, clams, and huge tubeworms thrive. What do they eat if there are no plants around? Bacteria! This was the first clue scientists had that not all food chains are plant-based.

Pathfinder

- How does a shark see in the darkest waters? Go to pages 94–95.
- How deep are the layers of the ocean? Find out on pages 118–19.
- What could possibly threaten the deep sea's top predators? Learn more on pages 122–25.

SMALL BUT VALUABLE
Fishers use deep-bottom trawls to catch little gulper sharks off the coast of western Africa. A component in their oil-rich livers, and those of some other deep-water sharks, is used in cosmetics and medicinal drugs.

At 8 inches (20 cm) long, the spined pygmy shark is one of the smallest sharks.

DEEP-SEA DENIZENS

Deep-sea fishes have developed some strange adaptations to attract prey and elude predators. These include special lures, large teeth, big mouths, and stomachs that can expand to make the most of a rare meal—whatever the size. Some deep-sea fishes have light organs on their bodies. These attract prey and also camouflage the fishes when they migrate to upper levels of the sea to feed.

Gulper Eel
This eel's jaws are nearly one-fourth of its body length. A flashing pinkish light on its tail attracts prey.

Hatchetfish
Lights on their bellies camouflage these fishes in the dimly-lighted midwaters where they migrate each night to feed. Predators looking down see blackness. Those looking up see light—but no fish.

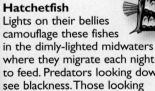

Viperfish
When this fish eats prey with light organs, a special black stomach lining keeps the light from shining through the viperfish's flesh and exposing it to predators.

DEEPER THAN YOU CAN IMAGINE

A late 19th century scientific expedition proved that the ocean is full of life at all depths. Since then we've learned that creatures such as sponges, sea cucumbers, glowing octopuses, shrimps that puff clouds, and fishes with lighted fishing poles live in very deep waters. Scientists view the ocean world from submersibles (once called bathyspheres and bathyscaphes). These vessels are made of steel and are designed to withstand tremendous water pressure. In 1960, the U.S. Navy bathyscaphe *Trieste* dived a record 35,770 feet (10,910 m)—about 7 miles (11 km) down—into the Marianas Trench, the deepest known place on Earth.

Lives on the Line

SHARKS MAY BE the ocean's top predator, but they are more than matched by that two-legged land creature known as man. Fact: People kill millions of sharks every year. Fact: Sharks take a long time to produce fewer young than most fishes. Fact: As top predators, sharks play a vital role in the maintenance of healthy fish populations, much as wolves do in North America's woodlands, or lions on Africa's plains. Fact: We don't know what will happen to the balance of life in the sea without sharks to keep it all in check.

People kill sharks for a number of reasons. Many feel threatened by these large, mysterious predators and want to get rid of them for safety's sake. In Asia, an entire industry known as finning has emerged just to meet the huge demand for shark fins to make soup. Fishers catch the shark, cut off its fins, then throw it back into the sea to starve or drown. In addition, plenty of sharks die after becoming trapped in fishing nets. Some fishers will let the sharks go, but many simply keep their catch. Such accidental captures are called bycatches.

Another threat to shark numbers is overfishing in general. Today's technologically savvy fishers are catching more fishes all the time—and that cuts into the sharks' food supply.

TRAPPED!

We all know that fishing nets can accidentally kill dolphins. The same goes for many other sea creatures—sharks included. The nets, which are miles long, hopelessly entangle any creature, such as these hammerheads, that comes into contact with them. Worse, when the nets are lost or left behind, they can continue to do damage for years to come.

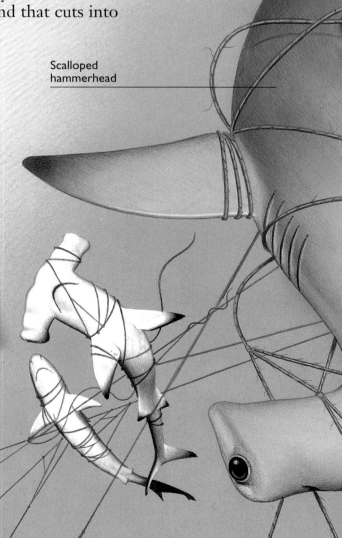

Scalloped
hammerhead

SAVE A SHARK—CLEAN A BEACH

Ever walk on the beach and trip over an empty jug of bleach or get your leg caught in a discarded fishing line? This kind of careless litter can destroy habitats and the creatures and plants that live in them. One way to help save all ocean animals (including sharks) is to join a volunteer beach cleanup crew like the one pictured. A little effort goes a long way.

Word Builders

• A **volunteer** is a person who willingly does something for the good of others, generally without any payment or other reward. The word comes from the Latin *voluntas*—"will."
• **Conservation** is the protection and careful management of natural resources such as plants, animals, and the environment. It comes from the Latin *conservare*, "to keep safe."
• The Old English word for "sheltered place"—*haefen*—is the origin of **haven**.

That's Amazing!

• More than 60,000 sharks were caught in Central and Western Pacific fisheries in 1998. Ninety-eight percent of them were killed for their fins.
• For every single human killed by a shark, two million sharks are destroyed by humans. Twelve million sharks are killed by people each year, compared to six humans killed by sharks.

Pathfinder

• What are the facts and figures about shark attacks on humans? Find out on pages 78–79.
• Just how many babies *can* a mother shark produce at one time? Go to pages 102–03.
• Can we live in harmony with dangerous predators such as sharks? Turn to pages 124–25 and read on.

PARKS FOR SHARKS

Marine parks—such as Australia's Great Barrier Reef Park (above) and Ningaloo Reef Park—were set up to protect and observe life in reef waters. Balancing conservation and tourism, the parks provide a safe haven for many types of sharks. Divers from all over the world travel to these parks to swim with sharks—such as the gentle whale shark—in their own environment.

Caribbean reef shark

INSIDE STORY

Protecting Sharks

Dr. Merry Camhi is working hard to stop careless finning and overfishing. She is the Senior Scientist of the National Audubon Society's Living Oceans Program. "Our job is to convince the U.S. Congress and coastal state legislatures, as well as foreign governments, that sharks, rays and other large ocean fishes are in real danger. We must work and act to save shark populations—and that means limiting catches to more reasonable levels."
The program is also involved in protecting sharks' nursery grounds, as well as limiting recreational catches of sharks—or, for some particularly vulnerable species, allowing only catch-and-release recreational fishing.

TO DIE FOR

Some products from sharks are important—nutrient sources or medical products that improve human lives. Other shark products are luxuries that can be replaced with synthetic substitutes.

Food
Shark fins are an expensive delicacy, especially when the rest of the shark is thrown away. But some kinds of shark are sold for their meat as well as fins.

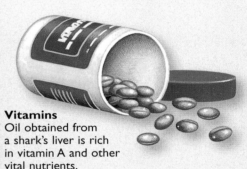

Vitamins
Oil obtained from a shark's liver is rich in vitamin A and other vital nutrients.

Cosmetics
Shark oil is also used in creams, lotions, and lipsticks.

Medical uses
Shark corneas (the transparent covering of the eye) can be transplanted into humans to repair damaged eyes.

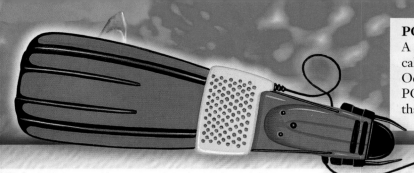

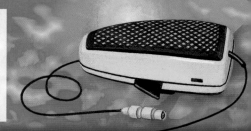

POD
A new invention to ward off sharks is called the POD—short for Protective Oceanic Device. Using a battery, the POD creates a strong electrical field that repels sharks.

Sharing the Water

SHARKS HAVE BEEN around for millions of years. They were swimming the world's oceans long before people arrived on the scene, and with luck, sharks will still be around millions of years from now—but only if we humans learn to play fair and share the water.

Although many people throughout history feared sharks, some people did not feel this way. In places such as Hawaii, Tahiti, and Fiji, people lived close to the sea and knew their local sharks well. They realized that some sharks were dangerous, but that most were not. Some people even believed in the power of sharks to help and protect their human neighbors.

Today we are beginning to understand sharks better all the time. As undersea technology improves, new species are being identified and more is being learned about the species we already know. Now that we know more about sharks, perhaps we can learn to treat them with the respect they deserve.

TAKE CARE
A confused shark is a dangerous shark, so never swim or dive in an area where a shark, such as this tiger shark, could mistake you for food or an enemy. Avoid rough or murky water and water that is polluted or has blood in it. Never swim alone.

Divers keep their arms folded so that they don't appear threatening to sharks.

PLAYING TAG
The best way to learn about sharks such as this lemon shark is to observe them in their habitat. But biologists also learn a lot by catching and tagging them and tracking them down later. Many things about sharks have been learned this way—including how fast they grow and how far they swim.

KEEPING SHARKS AT BAY
Generally, people feel more comfortable using protective gear around sharks. Chemicals, barriers, and special suits are just a few of the ways (not all of them equally successful) in which humans try to stay safe in the water.

Lifejacket with chemical repellent for shipwreck and air crash survivors at sea

U.S. Navy shark bag for survivors at sea

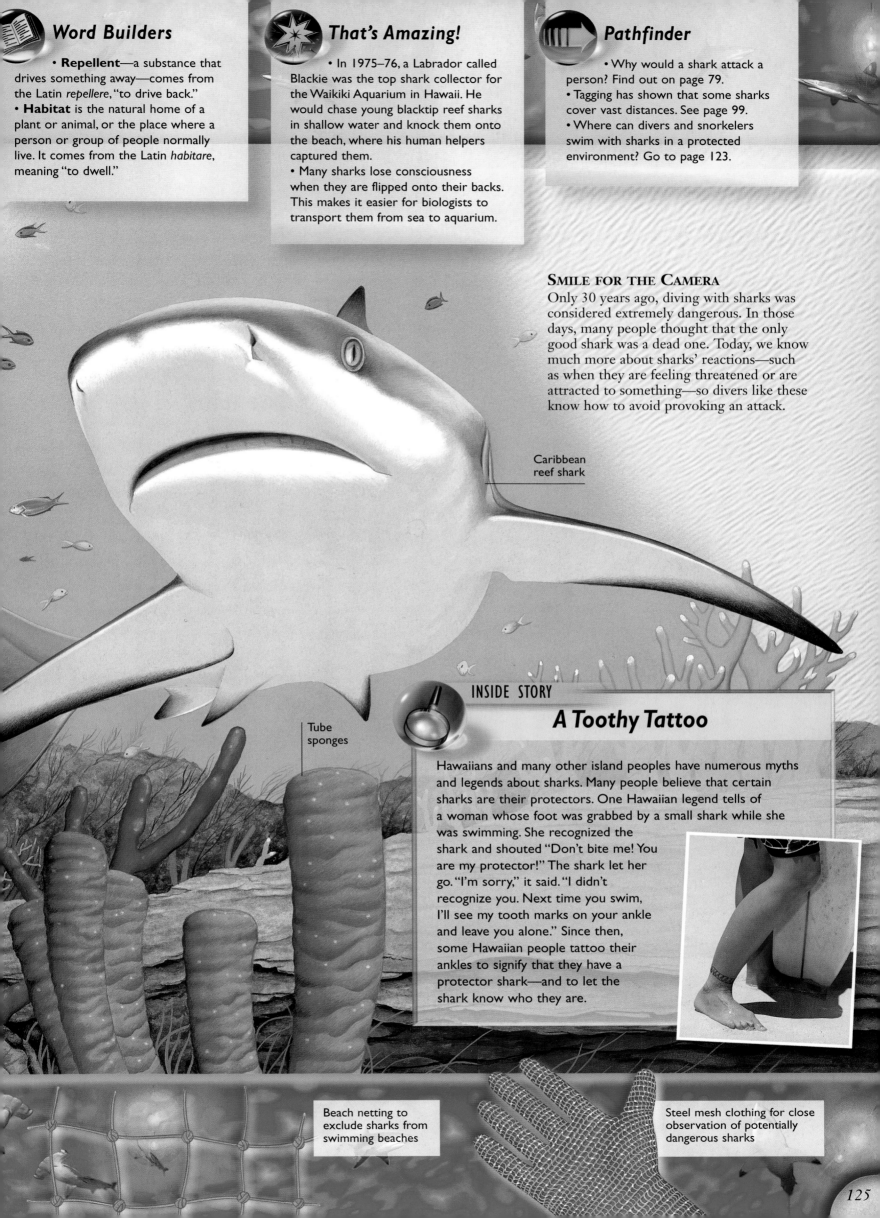

Word Builders

• **Repellent**—a substance that drives something away—comes from the Latin *repellere*, "to drive back."
• **Habitat** is the natural home of a plant or animal, or the place where a person or group of people normally live. It comes from the Latin *habitare*, meaning "to dwell."

That's Amazing!

• In 1975–76, a Labrador called Blackie was the top shark collector for the Waikiki Aquarium in Hawaii. He would chase young blacktip reef sharks in shallow water and knock them onto the beach, where his human helpers captured them.
• Many sharks lose consciousness when they are flipped onto their backs. This makes it easier for biologists to transport them from sea to aquarium.

Pathfinder

• Why would a shark attack a person? Find out on page 79.
• Tagging has shown that some sharks cover vast distances. See page 99.
• Where can divers and snorkelers swim with sharks in a protected environment? Go to page 123.

SMILE FOR THE CAMERA

Only 30 years ago, diving with sharks was considered extremely dangerous. In those days, many people thought that the only good shark was a dead one. Today, we know much more about sharks' reactions—such as when they are feeling threatened or are attracted to something—so divers like these know how to avoid provoking an attack.

Caribbean reef shark

Tube sponges

INSIDE STORY

A Toothy Tattoo

Hawaiians and many other island peoples have numerous myths and legends about sharks. Many people believe that certain sharks are their protectors. One Hawaiian legend tells of a woman whose foot was grabbed by a small shark while she was swimming. She recognized the shark and shouted "Don't bite me! You are my protector!" The shark let her go. "I'm sorry," it said. "I didn't recognize you. Next time you swim, I'll see my tooth marks on your ankle and leave you alone." Since then, some Hawaiian people tattoo their ankles to signify that they have a protector shark—and to let the shark know who they are.

Beach netting to exclude sharks from swimming beaches

Steel mesh clothing for close observation of potentially dangerous sharks

batoid *caudal fin* *embryo*

Glossary

absorb To soak up; a shark's intestines absorb the nutrients from its food.

adaptation A genetic characteristic of an animal that helps it to survive. Gills are an adaptation for breathing in water.

anal Relating to the area around an animal's anus. Most sharks have a single anal fin.

aquarium A container of fresh or salt water in which living plants and animals are kept. Also, a large institution, similar to a museum, where living ocean plants and animals are displayed and where scientists and students can study them.

basking Sun-bathing; lounging in sunlight.

batoid A member of the group of fishes that includes all rays and skates.

camouflage A special color or pattern on an animal's skin or fur that helps it blend into its surroundings, making it harder for predators or prey to see it.

carnivorous Meat-eating. Sharks, seals, cats, bears, and dogs are all carnivorous animals.

cartilage A tough, flexible tissue that forms the skeleton in sharks and rays, and the outer ear and nose tip in humans.

caudal Relating to the area around an animal's tail. "Caudal fin" is another term for a fish's tail.

cavity A chamber within an animal that can contain some of the animal's organs.

cloaca A common opening for the digestive, excretory, and reproductive tracts.

cold-blooded Having a body temperature matching that of the surrounding air or water. Most fishes (sharks included) are cold-blooded.

copepod A tiny relative of shrimps and crabs that makes up most of the world's zooplankton. Some copepods are parasitic.

courtship The complex behavior of two or more mature animals that leads to mating.

denticle A "scale" on a shark's skin that is very similar to a tiny tooth.

documentary A factual film or television program, such as a film about a historical event or the life and natural behavior of a particular animal.

dorsal Relating to the area on an animal's back. Most sharks have two dorsal fins.

electrical field A space filled with electricity.

embyro An unborn animal or human in the first stages of development.

enamel A hard, glossy, white coating that protects teeth.

environment All the physical and biological circumstances that surround an animal or group of animals.

exterior The outside of something.

fertilization The act of combining a sperm and egg to begin the development of a new individual.

fetus An unborn animal or human in the later stages of development.

filament A fine, thread-like fiber.

filter feeding To eat by removing tiny food particles or creatures from a large volume of seawater. Whale sharks are filter feeders.

finning The act of catching sharks (usually on a long-line), cutting off and selling their fins, and discarding the dead bodies.

food web A complex interrelationship of different species of animals that eat and are eaten by others.

fossil The ancient mineralized remains or traces of an animal or plant embedded within a rock.

gills Special blood-filled structures that remove dissolved oxygen from water. Sharks, other fishes, baby frogs, and shellfish all use gills to breathe.

habitat The area in which a plant or animal lives.

horizontal In a side-to-side direction.

hydrodynamics The study of the way water moves.

interior The inside of something.

invertebrate An animal with no backbone. Sea urchins, sea stars, shellfish, and worms are all invertebrates.

lateral line A series of sensory organs along a shark's side that enables it to detect vibrations in the water.

lobe A protruding section of a larger organ or body part. Ears have lobes; so do livers. A shark's tail is divided into an upper lobe and a lower lobe.

long-line A way to catch large ocean animals by setting a line that is miles long and that bears a series of baited hooks.

lure A decoy to attract an animal.

microscopic Something so small that it can only be seen with a microscope.

midwaters A layer of the ocean that is some distance below the surface yet also far above the seafloor.

food web *hydrodynamics*

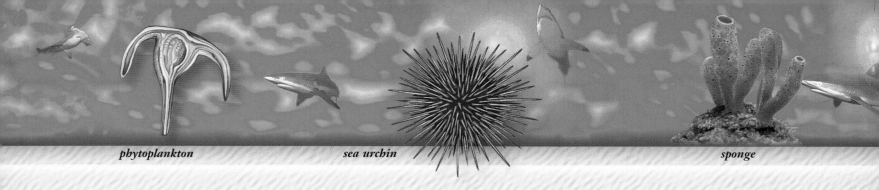

phytoplankton   *sea urchin*   *sponge*

migration Seasonal movement of a group of animals from one place to another, often for breeding purposes or in search of food.

muscle Tissue made of elastic fibers that pull and relax to make a creature or human move.

nerve A bundle of energy-conducting fibers that connect the nervous system to muscles and organs.

omnivorous Eating a wide variety of plants and animals. Humans are omnivorous; sharks are carnivorous (meat-eaters).

order A category used by biologists who classify animals. An order contains families which in turn contain genera and then species.

organ A complex of tissues that performs a specific function in an animal, such as the heart, brain, or liver.

organism Any living thing, either plant or animal, of any size.

oxygen A chemical element vital for life; its most common form is as a gas in air. Oxygen dissolves in water.

parasite An organism that benefits from the life of another creature and usually harms the creature in the process. Tapeworms, lice, and fleas are all parasites.

pectoral Relating to the area around an animal's chest. All sharks have a pair of pectoral fins.

pelagic Relating to the wide open sea.

pelvic Relating to the area near the hips (or pelvis), or to the skeletal complex near the anus. Humans have a pelvic bone. Sharks have a pair of pelvic fins.

phytoplankton Tiny plants that form the basis of all ocean food chains.

placenta A spongy organ inside the uterus of a female human or animal that nourishes an embryo or fetus.

plankton Tiny plants and animals that drift with the ocean's currents.

pollution The contamination of air, water, or land with harmful substances.

predator An animal—such as a mako shark, lion, or wolf—that eats other living animals and usually stalks or hunts them.

pressure A force that is exerted equally in all directions and that is due to the weight of a gas (such as air) or a liquid (such as water).

prey Animals eaten by predators.

propulsion The process of driving or moving something in one direction.

remora A kind of fish that attaches itself to sharks and other large ocean creatures with suction via a modified dorsal fin.

sea urchin A round invertebrate animal, usually covered with stiff spines; a relative of sea stars and sea cucumbers.

seamount An underwater mountain.

serrated Evenly and sharply notched along an edge. Many knives and some shark teeth have serrated edges.

skeleton The bony structure that supports an animal's body.

species All of the biologically similar animals that can mate with one another.

spiracle A small hole behind the eye of a shark or ray, sometimes used for breathing.

sponge A simple, aquatic, plant-like animal with a soft body wall.

streamlined Shaped to offer the least resistance to movement.

submersible An underwater vehicle used in ocean research; also called a research sub.

symbiotic relationship A situation in which plants and/or animals of different species live together in a way that benefits both parties.

tissue An organized mass of similar cells.

trawl A large net that is dragged along the seafloor, scraping up and catching everything that lives there.

umbilical cord A long, flexible tube filled with blood vessels that connects a fetus to the placenta. This cord provides nourishment to a developing animal. Your navel, or belly button, marks the spot where the umbilical cord attached you to your mother's placenta when you were growing in her uterus.

uterus An organ inside a female animal's body in which a fetus develops. Also called the womb. Most sharks have two uteri. Mammals (including humans) have only one.

vertebrae The series of interlocking bones that make up the backbone or spine. One such bone is a vertebra; two or more are vertebrae.

vertebrate An animal with a backbone, such as an eagle, snake, shark, dolphin, or dog.

warm-blooded Having a body temperature that is unaffected by the temperature of the surrounding air or water. Humans and mammals are all warm-blooded. Some sharks are also able to raise their body temperatures.

wingspan The straight distance from the tip of one wing to the tip of the other wing.

zooplankton Tiny animals that live in the ocean's surface layers.

submersible   *wingspan*   *zooplankton*

Index

Whales, Dolphins, and Porpoises

Contents

Introducing...Whales 132

Life as a Whale 152

Whales and People 174

Pick Your Path!

DIVE DEEP into the world of *Whales, Dolphins, and Porpoises* and unearth the secrets of these mysterious mammals. Begin with the gentle giants, then learn to sort out the porpoises from the dolphins. Or go straight for a poolside seat in "Captured Creatures."

You'll find plenty of other discovery paths to choose from in the special features sections. Read about real-life whale watchers in "Inside Story," or get creative with "Hands On" activities. Delve into words with "Word Builders," or amaze your friends with fascinating facts from "That's Amazing!" You can choose a new path with every reading—this book will take you wherever *you* want to go.

INSIDE STORY
An In-Depth Look

Feel the frustration and hope of rescuers as they attempt to save stranded pilot whales at Farewell Spit, New Zealand. Read about a bottlenose dolphin called Percy who showed a diver how to untangle some fishing lines. Join Mike Noad as he discovers the new song of the humpback. INSIDE STORY introduces you to the men, women, and whales who have shaped our understanding of these amazing creatures.

HANDS ON
Create and Make

Make up the length of a humpback whale with your friends and see how big these beasts really are. Create your own baleen and discover how the great whales skim and swallow their tiny prey, or feel the cold as you plunge into the polar seas of the beluga. The HANDS ON features offer projects and activities that will help you to appreciate the watery world of whales.

Word Builders
What a strange word!
What does it mean?
Where did it come from?
Find out by reading
Word Builders.

That's Amazing!
Awesome facts, amazing records, fascinating figures—you'll find them all in *That's Amazing!*

Pathfinder
Use the *Pathfinder* section to find your way from one subject to another. It's all up to you.

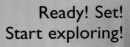

Ready! Set!
Start exploring!

Introducing... Whales

WHALES, DOLPHINS, and porpoises come in a mesmerizing array of shapes and sizes. And now's your chance to get to know some of them. First meet the whale ancestors and explore the origins of modern cetaceans. Then cruise alongside some of today's whales, from the tiny vaquita to the hefty blue whale—larger than any dinosaur that ever lived. You'll find blunt-snouted porpoises, leaping dolphins, and little-known beaked whales with lopsided skulls. So what are you waiting for? Jump in...

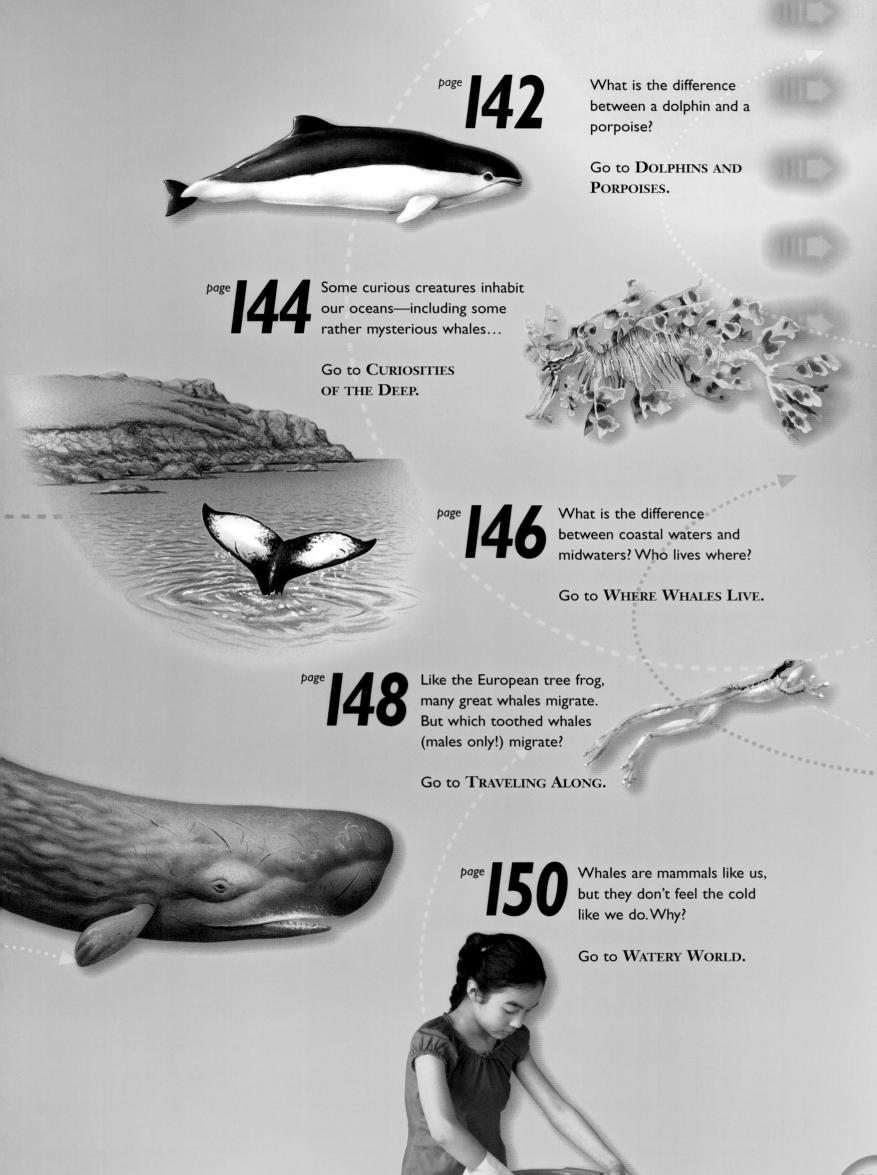

Orca   Humpback whale   Gray whale   Common dolphin

What Is a Whale?

WHAT'S HUGE, GRAY, lives in water, and is a mammal, not a fish? And what's petite (in comparison), pink, also lives in water, and is also a mammal, not a fish?

The answer to both these questions is a whale. Scientists call whales, including dolphins and porpoises, cetaceans. There are more than 80 different species, or types, of cetacean, in a huge range of shapes, colors, and sizes (not just extra-extra-large!). And, although they spend their whole life in water and have fins, flippers, and tails, they are mammals, not fishes. In fact, they have more in common with you than with your pet goldfish.

To begin with, whales are warm-blooded. They have smooth skin, a little hair, ears (small holes just behind the eyes) and they breathe in air through their nostrils, which are called blowholes. Whales give birth to live young which they suckle with milk and look after for a year or more. Fishes, on the other hand, are cold-blooded, covered in scales, and get their oxygen from the water, which they breathe in through their gills. They usually lay eggs and don't look after their young. Another way to tell a whale from a fish is to watch the tail action: A whale tail moves up and down but a fish tail goes from side to side.

WHALE OR SHARK?
A whale shark has a body shaped like a whale, but it's a shark—and that makes it a fish. Its tail is upright, not flat, and its huge gills breathe in water. Yet, like the big whales, this big fish feeds on tiny floating food, or plankton.

DOLPHIN OR FISH?
These 6-foot (1.8-m), bright blue-green creatures are called dolphins. They are also called dorado or mahimahi. But they are fishes, not mammals. They just have the same name.

Blowhole

Gray whale

Orca

Word Builders

• **Cetacean** comes from the Latin *cetus* and Greek *ketos*. Both mean "large sea animal." *Ology* means "study of." Cetology is the "study of whales."
• **Mammalia** are a class of animals that have a bony skeleton and feed their offspring with milk suckled from the breast. This comes from the Latin *mammalis*, meaning "of the breast."

That's Amazing!

The closest relatives to whales don't have fins and flippers—they have legs with hoofs. Known as ungulates, they include mammals such as cows, sheep, deer, horses, hippopotamuses, and rhinoceroses.

Pathfinder

• What were the ancient whales like and how similar are they to the whales of today? Turn to pages 136–37.
• Whales come in all sizes, but just how big do the record holders get? Turn to pages 138–39 to find out.
• Discover the true colors of the Amazon River dolphin on page 144.

MORE MARINE MAMMALS

Other mammals live in the water, as well as whales. There are two other groups of animals: the sirenians, which include dugongs and manatees (sea cows), and pinnipeds, which include walruses, sea lions, and seals. Pinnipeds spend time on land as well as in the sea.

COMING UP FOR AIR

Like all whales, this sei whale spends most of its time underwater. But, unlike a fish, it has to come up for air eventually. That's because if a whale took a breath with its head underwater, like a fish does, it would drown. A whale pokes its head above the surface, and breathes in air through the blowholes on top of its head.

Sei whale

The sea lion hunts in the sea and lives on land. Yet when it uses its four flippers to walk, a sea lion can look clumsy to us.

INSIDE STORY

Now You See Them...

After almost 20 years of studying whales, Peter Gill says, "If they don't want to be found, you won't find them, and if you do find them, but they don't want to stay around, they won't." Studying whales, which spend 70 to 90 percent of their time underwater, is hard work. Many whales live in remote areas and dive to great depths. Also, when a whale surfaces most of its body remains hidden, and weather and ocean swell can make them even harder to see. So imagine how this would have felt for Peter Gill: "A blue whale feeding about 330 feet (100 m) away suddenly began swimming toward our yacht. When it was about 50 feet (15 m) from us, it dived and we watched as this huge, glowing, blue-green, shimmering thing passed slowly beneath us. It seemed to take forever."

The seal powers through the ocean after its food—fishes. Then, like all pinnipeds, it climbs out when it needs to take a rest, breed, or shed its thick fur coat.

Southern right whale

Blue whale

The dugong spends all its life in warm, shallow water, where it swims around slowly, feeding on sea grass.

135

EARLY EVIDENCE
Mesonyx could be the oldest known mammalian relative to cetaceans. The *Protocetus* skull (far right) shows clearly the lengthening of the upper jaw, typical of the early aquatic relatives—the archaic whales.

Mesonyx *skull*   Protocetus *skull*

The Ancient Ones

FOR ABOUT 180 MILLION years, dinosaurs ruled the Earth and swimming reptiles dominated the oceans. But all the dinosaurs, many reptiles, and other creatures suddenly became extinct about 65 million years ago. That made way for another group of animals—the mammals.

In this dinosaur-free environment, mammals evolved quickly into many sizes and shapes. They made homes everywhere. Some burrowed underground. Others lived on mountains and in treetops. A few developed webbed feet about 50 million years ago and made water their part-time home. These first whale ancestors, known as archaic whales, were probably about dolphin-size and fed in warm, shallow seas. Between 50 and 35 million years ago, their bodies became smoother and their back legs disappeared. Their front legs became flippers and their tails flattened into flukes for up-and-down, tail-powered swimming.

Two types of whales evolved between 35 and 30 million years ago—toothed and baleen whales. Toothed whales had acute hearing and a sound system called echolocation. Baleen whales had a new feeding style. They filtered food through comb-like filters called baleen. From these two types of whale came today's variety of cetaceans.

THE LANDLUBBERS
Until 65 million years ago, mammals were rat- and mouse-sized. The oldest known relatives of cetaceans lived 55 million years ago. They were meat-eating mammals that lived on land—probably dog-size like *Mesonyx*.

DOLPHINLIKE DEVELOPMENTS
Dorudon, which lived about 25 million years ago, looked more like today's dolphins with its streamlined shape and dorsal fin. Its nostrils were more toward the top of its head.

FIRST FILTER FEEDERS
Toothed filter-feeding whales like 23-million-year-old *Mammalodon* came before baleen whales. It probably had fringes between its teeth to filter its food.

WHALES IN TIME
The history of Earth is divided into eras, periods, and epochs, which are based on layers of rock and the fossils they contain. Archaic whale fossils appear in the Tertiary period.

Triassic	Jurassic		Cretaceous	Tertiary	Q er
		Mesozoic		Cenozoic	
248 mya	208 mya	144 mya		65 mya	2 mya

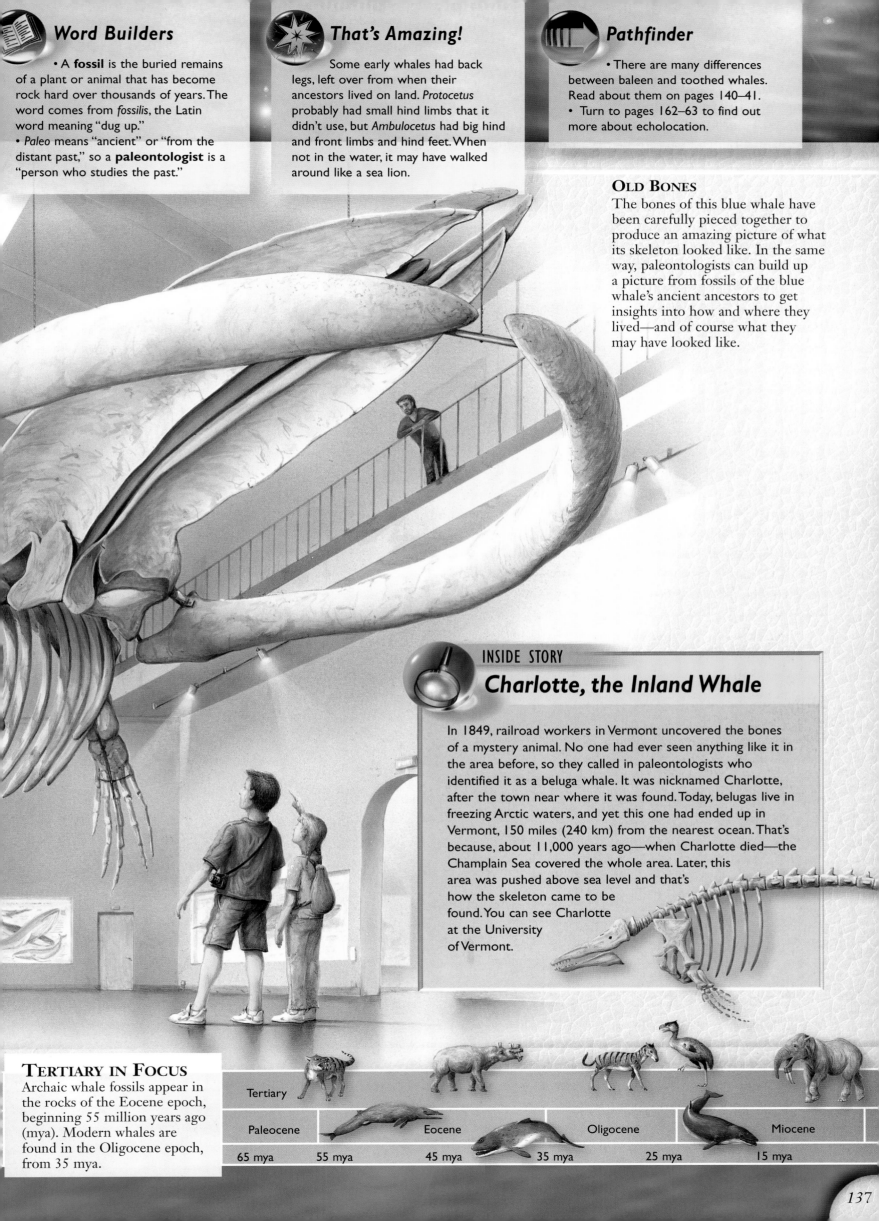

Word Builders

• A **fossil** is the buried remains of a plant or animal that has become rock hard over thousands of years. The word comes from *fossilis*, the Latin word meaning "dug up."
• *Paleo* means "ancient" or "from the distant past," so a **paleontologist** is a "person who studies the past."

That's Amazing!

Some early whales had back legs, left over from when their ancestors lived on land. *Protocetus* probably had small hind limbs that it didn't use, but *Ambulocetus* had big hind and front limbs and hind feet. When not in the water, it may have walked around like a sea lion.

Pathfinder

• There are many differences between baleen and toothed whales. Read about them on pages 140–41.
• Turn to pages 162–63 to find out more about echolocation.

OLD BONES

The bones of this blue whale have been carefully pieced together to produce an amazing picture of what its skeleton looked like. In the same way, paleontologists can build up a picture from fossils of the blue whale's ancient ancestors to get insights into how and where they lived—and of course what they may have looked like.

INSIDE STORY

Charlotte, the Inland Whale

In 1849, railroad workers in Vermont uncovered the bones of a mystery animal. No one had ever seen anything like it in the area before, so they called in paleontologists who identified it as a beluga whale. It was nicknamed Charlotte, after the town near where it was found. Today, belugas live in freezing Arctic waters, and yet this one had ended up in Vermont, 150 miles (240 km) from the nearest ocean. That's because, about 11,000 years ago—when Charlotte died—the Champlain Sea covered the whole area. Later, this area was pushed above sea level and that's how the skeleton came to be found. You can see Charlotte at the University of Vermont.

TERTIARY IN FOCUS

Archaic whale fossils appear in the rocks of the Eocene epoch, beginning 55 million years ago (mya). Modern whales are found in the Oligocene epoch, from 35 mya.

Tertiary

Paleocene	Eocene	Oligocene	Miocene
65 mya	55 mya	45 mya	35 mya	25 mya	15 mya

Giants of the Sea

NOT ALL WHALES are *that* big, but the ones that are. . .well, they're enormous. No matter what their size, though, all whales have features in common. Their bodies are smooth and streamlined. They have a layer of blubber, or fat, which stores energy and heat. Most whales have a dorsal fin on their back, which keeps them stable in the water, though some have a few ridges or humps instead of a fin. Pectoral fins—the flattened fins on either side—are used for steering. In all cases, powerful tail flukes beat up and down to push the whale—big or small, fast or slow—along.

As for the whale giants, the only reason they can grow so huge is because their bodies are supported by water. On land—where the animals are surrounded by air—the weight of these colossal creatures would be too much for their skeleton to hold up. In the ocean, however, their weight is supported by water, so they become almost weightless. They don't need big, heavy bones or a complex skeleton with four legs and a long neck like land mammals do. They get by with a relatively simple skeleton of softer, lighter bones. This skeleton holds the same organs (except an appendix and gall bladder) that all mammals have and helps power a body perfectly designed for life in the water.

FAMILY DIFFERENCES
It's easy to see the amazing size difference between this southern right whale and the bottlenose dolphins swimming beside it. Yet dolphins are a type of small whale. Both animals are cetaceans.

BIG BLUE
The blue whale is the biggest animal on Earth. It is up to 26 times as heavy as an African elephant, with a heart the size of a small car. And the biggest blue whale of them all is female—female baleen whales are always bigger than males.

 HANDS ON

How Big?

A humpback whale can reach 62½ feet (19 m) in length. Can you imagine how long that is? To help get a picture for yourself, gather some friends together and measure everybody's height with a tape measure. Add up all the measurements. Do you have enough people to make up the length of the longest humpback? If not, make up a 29½-foot (9-m) orca instead.

When you work out what whale length you and your friends can make, get everybody to lie down, end to end, in a park—your backyard will probably be too small—to see how big your whale is. A blue whale can be up to twice as long as a humpback. How many friends would you need to make up the length of a blue whale?

Sperm whale:
65½ feet (20 m)

Humpback whale:
62½ feet (19 m)

Word Builders

When is a whale a whale and when is it a dolphin? Or a porpoise? **Whale** is usually used for the biggest cetaceans, the ones more than 10 feet (3 m) long. **Dolphin** tends to be used for cetaceans that are smaller than that, and **porpoise** for the ones that are smaller again. Even so, there are at least three whales that are less than 10 feet long, and one or two porpoises are bigger than some dolphins.

That's Amazing!

If an elephant had a skeleton of bone as light as a whale's, it would not be able to stand up. Its legs would break under its weight. And, if a whale, especially one of the great whales, had to spend time on land (for example, if it became stranded), it would be crushed by the weight of its own body.

Pathfinder

• Want to learn more about the little cetaceans? Turn to pages 142–43.
• Whales have adapted to a watery life, but how can these giants swim so gracefully? Find out on pages 158–59.
• Some of the great whales were once thought to be ferocious sea monsters. Find out more on pages 176–77.

ON THE INSIDE

Every cetacean has organs found in all mammals, such as a heart, lungs, liver, and stomach. But the tall spine bones and enlarged melon above the skull of this common dolphin are adaptations for life underwater.

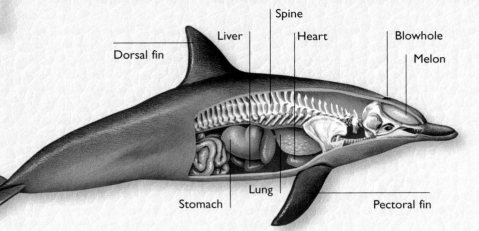

Spine
Liver
Heart
Blowhole
Melon
Dorsal fin
Stomach
Lung
Pectoral fin

Bowhead whale: 49 feet (15 m)

Orca: 29½ feet (9 m)

Human: 6 feet (1.8 m)

Minke whale: 33 feet (10 m)

Vaquita: 5 feet (1.5 m)

SIZE UP

Cetaceans come in all sizes, from small to extra-large. The smallest, the vaquita, is about shoulder-high on a six-foot man. The largest, the blue whale, is about 18 times as long as the man. Here's how the record-holders in each species size up against each other.

Narwhal tusk   Harbor porpoise tooth   Ganges River dolphin tooth

Teeth or Combs?

THERE ARE TWO types of whales—baleen whales and toothed whales (known to scientists as mysticeti and odontoceti). The best way to tell them apart is to take a look inside their mouths. The baleen whales don't have teeth. They have baleen instead. Baleen are bristly plates made from a material called keratin—the same stuff as our fingernails. The plates hang down from the upper jaw and form combs, which act as a kind of strainer, or filter. When the whale sucks in mouthfuls of water and tiny food, it squirts the water back out and the food gets trapped. It is by swallowing huge amounts of this tiny food that the 11 baleen whale species grow to be the giants of the whale world—like the rights, rorquals, bowheads, and grays.

Toothed whales tend to be much smaller—they range from dolphins and porpoises, to the narwhal and beluga, and to the beaked, bottlenose, and sperm whales. Their teeth come in many shapes and sizes—from 2 to a whole set of 252. Using a special sense called echolocation (which scientists believe only toothed whales possess), they hunt fishes and squid, gulping them down whole. Another difference between the two whale types is the blowhole. Toothed whales have one and baleen whales have two, with a raised "splashguard" in front to keep water out.

FROM TRIANGLES TO CONES
Fossils of ancient toothed whales show that they had triangular teeth. Today, most have teeth shaped like pointy cones, running along their upper and lower jaws.

HANDS ON
Whale Baleen at Work

Put a handful each of dried peas or beans, rice, sand and salt in a large bowl and cover them with water. Stir them together for a few minutes and you've got food you can use to test your baleen. Place a colander (ask an adult if you can borrow one from the kitchen) in a sink or basin. Imagine that the top of the colander is the whale's mouth and the strainer part is the baleen. Now watch what happens when you tip the bowl full of "food" into the colander. The water filters through the baleen and gushes out. Most of the dried peas and rice get caught, ready to be swallowed. This is how whale baleen works. But what happens to the sand and salt?

Strap-toothed whale   Sperm whale

140

Word Builders

• **Odontoceti** comes from the Greek *odont*, which means "tooth," and the Latin *cetus*, which means "large sea animal." **Mysticeti** comes from the Greek *mistak*, which means "upper lip or mustache." It refers to the whales with a "mustache" of baleen.
• **Baleen** is sometimes referred to as **whalebone**, but that's confusing—baleen is flexible and nothing like bone.

That's Amazing!

The fin whale's bottom lip and baleen plates are gray on the left side and white on the right. Scientists cannot explain why the fin whale has this two-tone mouth. Maybe the bright-white, right side startles prey in the dimly lit water so the whale can scoop it up more easily.

Pathfinder

• When are bubbles a deadly weapon? Learn how the humpback creates a net of bubbles to snare its prey. See pages 156–57.
• How does a dolphin catch the food it can't see? Find out more about echolocation on pages 162–63.

SKIM AND SWALLOW

The bowhead whale has the longest baleen of all whales. It keeps its massive mouth slightly open as it swims. Water streams through the baleen while its food—tiny crustaceans called copepods, each the size of a grain of rice—gets caught. Bowheads can eat up to 50,000 copepods per minute.

WART HEAD

The bumpy, warty-looking things on this right whale's head are called callosities. The patterns formed by these growths of hardened skin help scientists identify one right whale from another.

BALEEN VERSUS TEETH

Baleen and toothed whales have different hunting and eating habits. But there are many other ways to tell the two types of whales apart. Their external shapes and sizes vary and so do their skeletons.

TAPERING DOLPHIN

The Atlantic white-sided dolphin needs to swim fast to catch fast-moving prey. Its tapering body helps it do that.

STOCKY WHALE

The pygmy right whale is more stocky—like all baleen whales—because it can go slower to catch its prey. It needs a very arched upper jaw to fit in all those baleen plates.

Dolphins and Porpoises

THE POPULAR IMAGE of a dolphin is a "smiling" bottlenose dolphin. These are the ones most seen bodysurfing at the beach or doing tricks for fish at the zoo. But the dolphin family, known as the Delphinidae, includes many different types, shapes, and sizes. For example there is the orca (also called the killer whale), other oversized dolphins like the pilot whales, and 26 more ocean-dwelling dolphins.

The classic dolphin shape is long and slim with a rounded melon on the head and a beak (or rostrum) that sticks out. But there are also dolphins that have stockier bodies and blunt, rounded beaks. All but two have a dorsal fin, which may be tall or short, round or pointy. Many have body markings—spots, stripes, or shapes in black and white—and a few are plain gray or brown. Dolphins like living in groups and are found in tropical waters, ice floes, close to shore, or out to sea.

Porpoises aren't dolphins, although people do refer to dolphins as porpoises. All of them—and there are six species in the Phocoenidae, or porpoise, family—have a small, rounded head with a blunt snout, small flippers, and spade-shaped, slicing teeth. They are smaller and more chunky than most dolphins and tend to live near the coast. But, like dolphins, they are social animals and, also like the dolphins, they are toothed whales.

BATTLE SCARS
Dolphins live in groups but they do sometimes fight. These Risso's dolphins show the scars from fights or mating rituals, where dolphins rip at each other's skin with their teeth.

INSIDE STORY

Dolphin Rescue!

Some scuba-divers were trying to practice their life-saving skills off the Cornish coast, in England. A local dolphin called Donald thought this was a great game. He kept butting in and pushing the divers apart, so eventually they had to stop.

Later, the divers went for a dive around a nearby shipwreck. One of them got into trouble. He made it to the surface and signalled to the person on look-out duty in the boat, but then he sank. The look-out started swimming to the rescue, and so did Donald. Somehow, this time, Donald knew it wasn't a game. He gently supported the diver to keep him afloat and helped the rescuer get him back to the boat by towing him along. He even watched with his head out of the water until the diver was aboard. Donald was one of many dolphins that has helped drowning humans.

Long-beaked common dolphin

Word Builders

Dolphin comes from the Greek for dolphin, *delphinos*. **Porpoise** comes from the Latin *porcus*, for "pig," and *piscis*, for "fish." The porpoise got the name "pig fish" because of the shape of its snout, which is blunt like a pig's. Porpoise is also the word for a style of speedy swimming used by porpoises and dolphins.

That's Amazing!

Dolphins and porpoises often look like they are smiling for the camera. But what they are doing is listening. They push out their lower jawbone, which acts as a super-sensitive ear. So when they look like they are smiling, they are trying to pick up the sounds made by other dolphins and porpoises. They detect these sounds from more than a mile (1.6 km) away.

Pathfinder

• They moan, groan, belch, bellow, and even sing. To find out how different cetaceans communicate, turn to pages 164–65.
• How intelligent are dolphins, and how do we measure their intelligence? Check out how their brains measure up to ours on pages 166–67.

TAKE A LEAP

The Pacific white-sided dolphin (below) is one of the many that leap into the air. Dolphins appear to leap when they are excited and having fun. They also leap to communicate. The dusky dolphin, for example, leaps when it comes across a school of fishes, possibly as a signal to others that there is food around.

PORPOISE SPOTTING

The six porpoise species include the smallest cetacean, the vaquita, as well as the speediest, the Dall's porpoise. The spectacled porpoise is rarely seen, and so are the finless and Burmeister's porpoises. In contrast, the harbor porpoise is seen throughout Northern Hemisphere harbors.

DALL'S PORPOISE
Dall's porpoise, found in the north Pacific, is the strongest swimmer of all cetaceans.

SPECTACLED PORPOISE
This south Atlantic porpoise got its name from its black eye patch, outlined in white.

FINLESS PORPOISE
Coastal waters, rivers, and estuaries of Asia are where you will spot this porpoise.

SWIMMING WITH DOLPHINS
In the Bahamas, Atlantic spotted dolphins often swim with people. They are a small dolphin, but at up to 7½ feet (2.3 m) long, they are still more than a foot (30 cm) longer than the average man is tall.

White-beaked dolphin

HARBOR PORPOISE
The harbor porpoise is so named because it is seen most often in harbors and bays.

Curiosities of the Deep

SOME STRANGE AND mysterious cetaceans live in the world's waterways. Perhaps the most intriguing of all are the tusked narwhal and the beluga. These whales live in the icy waters of the Arctic Circle, around the North Pole. They are similar to each other in size and shape, neither has a dorsal fin, and they often swim together. But belugas are pale gray when they are born and turn pure white as they get older. They have mobile heads padded with blubber which makes them look like they're smiling, frowning, or even whistling. Narwhals, on the other hand, are born gray and turn mottled black or dark brown with age. Males have two teeth and the left tooth pushes through the top lip and grows to a spiraling tusk 6–10 feet (2–3 m) long.

The group of cetaceans that scientists know the least about is the beaked whales. These little-known whales are hard to find. They often live far out to sea, dive deep for an hour or more at a time, and disappear when humans are around. They have lopsided skulls, long, narrow beaks, and most males have two to four bottom teeth.

The last unusual cetaceans are the five species of river dolphins. These small dolphins have tiny eyes and are almost blind. They find food with their long beaks lined with rows of teeth. The extra-long beaks can snap shut fast on the fish in the muddy rivers of Asia and South America.

ALWAYS A CROWD
Belugas are very social animals. They spend the summer in herds of 1,000 or more, feeding, nursing their young, and rubbing off dead skin in the shallows. They migrate in smaller groups of 5 to 20 during winter.

DUEL
Two male narwhals fight with crossed tusks. Young males play-fight, but older males can spear each other when competing for females. Occasionally males have been spotted with two tusks.

WRAP-AROUNDS
The male strap-toothed whale has two bottom teeth that grow up and wrap around the top jaw so it can hardly open its mouth. These wrap-around teeth are not for eating—some scientists think they may be for fighting.

THINK PINK
The Amazon River dolphin, or boto, starts life gray, but can turn bluish gray, off-white, or pink. The color change depends on age and individual variation—some botos are more pink than others.

Word Builders

• **Beluga** comes from the Russian words *byelyi*, for "white," and *byelukha*, for "whale." Whalers used to call the beluga "sea canary" because it is one of the noisiest whales.

• The **narwhal** takes its name from an old Norse word, *nahvalr*, meaning "corpse whale." This refers to its belly, which is pale and white, like a corpse.

That's Amazing!

Every time the Amazon River floods, the boto leaves the river and goes looking for food among the trees and grasses of the flooded rain forest. Its flexible neck and its flippers help it swim between the branches. It often swims upside down, because its cheeks bulge out so much that it is hard for the boto to see over them when it is right-side up.

Pathfinder

• Some whales like to live alone. Others, like belugas, are very social, living in groups of hundreds or even thousands. Find out how different whales live together on pages 170–71.

• Narwhals are not the only cetaceans to fight. Discover others on page 172.

INSIDE STORY

On the Trail of the Beaked Whales

Beaked whales are the least known of all cetaceans, and many have never been seen alive. Dr. Graham Ross has studied cetaceans in the Indian Ocean for over 30 years. He describes these whales as "enigmas that bug you gently." Until recently, Longman's beaked whale was known from just two skulls—one from an Australian beach and the other from a garbage dump in Somalia. When a newborn calf washed ashore in South Africa in 1976, Dr. Ross identified it as a bottlenose whale. Then a researcher, Merel Dalebout, analyzed the whale's DNA and saw that it was a Longman's beaked whale—the first complete specimen discovered. She realized that Longman's beaked whale and the tropical bottlenose whale were the same species! There are still mysteries to be solved as new whales are found.

STRANGE SEA CREATURES

The oceans are full of strange creatures—not just mammals—that have unusual adaptations for survival in special situations.

THE ANGLERFISH

Anglerfish live in the gloomy depths of the oceans. The female has a bright light on a lure attached to her head, which she uses to attract prey.

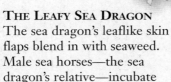

THE LEAFY SEA DRAGON

The sea dragon's leaflike skin flaps blend in with seaweed. Male sea horses—the sea dragon's relative—incubate babies in a special pouch, but male sea dragons do not.

THE LONGHORNED COWFISH

This fluorescent fish is slow and shy. But the cowfish—armed with spikes, poisonous flesh, and a toxin that kills on contact when released—can take care of itself.

 *Northern right whale range*

 *Dall's porpoise range*

 *Bryde's whale range*

Where Whales Live

OCEANS COVER MORE than 70 percent of Earth's surface—and cetaceans are found in almost every part of the world's oceans. Depending on the species, they could be diving deep for fish in the Atlantic, riding the waves off an African beach, dodging icebergs near Alaska, or mating in warm tropical waters.

The ocean world is made up of many different habitats, from the surface to the pitch-black bottom, and from the equator to the poles. The depth changes from relatively shallow continental shelves, to steep drops down the continental slopes and, finally, the ocean floor, which is at least 2½ miles (4 km) below the surface. The temperature changes too—from warm and tropical, through cool and temperate, to cold and freezing.

Some whales live almost anywhere. The orca and the minke whale, for example, are found in all oceans, at all temperatures. A bottlenose dolphin can surface either in a sheltered bay or miles from land. But some whales prefer one special spot. The Hector's dolphin inhabits the shoreline around New Zealand. The vaquita is found only in the northern Gulf of California off Mexico. River dolphins hardly bother with oceans at all. And there are whales that like to travel between two different habitats for feeding and breeding.

WARM-WATER WHALES
Baleen whales are the travelers of the whale world. They migrate between icy cold and warm tropical waters. But Bryde's whales only make short migrations, if any. They stay in warm tropical and subtropical waters.

ORCAS ALL OVER
Orcas are easily satisfied when it comes to picking a place to live. They are found close to the shoreline and far out in the open ocean—from the equator to the North and South Poles. These two polar-dwellers have poked their heads up to spyhop. Spyhopping is a method of looking around—whales raise their head vertically out of the water and silently submerge again.

MOTHER WHALES UP CLOSE
Southern right whales breed close to shore. At certain times, from May to November, you can stand on clifftops in Chile, Argentina, South Africa, and southern Australia and look down on mothers swimming in the water below with their new calves.

 *Orca range*

📖 Word Builders

• **Ocean** comes from *okeanos*, the Greek word for "river." The ancient Greeks thought Earth was surrounded by a vast river.
• *Habitare* is the Latin word for "to possess or inhabit." It's the basis of the word **habitat**, the place where an animal or plant lives.

✳ That's Amazing!

Minke whales in the Antarctic have been seen balancing blocks of ice on their heads. Belugas and bowheads can survive under the pack ice. They can swim for more than a mile (1.6 km) under the thick frozen crust and, if they don't find a hole or crack to breathe through, they make their own. Belugas can use their backs to smash layers of ice 3 inches (7.5 cm) thick.

Pathfinder

• Some whales feed in one area and give birth in another. Read on— check out pages 148–49.
• Did you know that a sperm whale can dive to 10,000 feet (3,000 m) for food? Read more on pages 150–51.
• Some whales never get to swim free in the open sea. Find out about whales in captivity on pages 184–85.
• Discover how you can see whales for yourself by reading pages 186–87.

HANDS ON
Make Your Own Polar Sea

Collect five or six strong plastic bags, each about the size of a sandwich bag. Fill some of them half full with water and the others a third full. Tie the ends in a double knot or seal the bag to make sure that no water leaks out. Place the bags in a freezer between other frozen foods so they freeze in interesting shapes. Leave them overnight. The next day, take them out of the plastic bags and throw the bags away. Fill a basin three-quarters full with water, add salt to the water, then put your "icebergs" in. Look at how they float, how much ice is above the water, and how much is below. Imagine being a whale in the Arctic, trying to move around without bashing into huge ice chunks all over the place. How would you do it, especially if it was too murky to see underwater?

OCEAN ENVIRONMENTS

The oceans contain many habitats: mud flats, sandy beaches, rock platforms, estuaries, swamps, coral reefs, shallow waters, and cold, dark midwaters (1,000 feet/ 300 m below the surface).

KELP FOREST
This is a jungle of giant seaweed. It grows in cold, sunlit waters along the coast. Both whales and dolphins hunt here for food.

ROCKY COAST
Shallow, blue-green, coastal waters are full of plankton and fishes. A rocky coast offers whales food and protection.

TWILIGHT ZONE
The midwaters are cold, dark, and full of see-through fish, big-mouthed eels, and giant squid—favorite foods of the deep-diving sperm whale.

147

Traveling Along

SOME WHALES SPEND their summers in the Arctic or Antarctic, gorging on their favorite food. They move to warmer waters when the weather cools. Like the creatures illustrated on the border of this page, these whales make a long-distance journey, or a migration. Heading off in pods, they swim every day for two to three months, stopping to rest or socialize—but hardly ever to eat—until they reach their destination: the tropics. There they stop for the winter, mating, or giving birth and caring for young. When the warm weather returns, they head back to the ice.

Almost all the great whales (baleen whales) make these incredible journeys. The longest is the humpback's round trip from Antarctica to Costa Rica and Colombia. The gray whale's journey from Alaska to Mexico and back is also impressive. Most travel slowly, between 1 and 5 miles (1.6 and 8 km) an hour, but a fin whale was recorded at 10½ miles (17 km) per hour over 2,300 miles (3,700 km).

A few of the toothed whales also migrate. Sperm whales (males only!) make the polar-to-tropics round-trip every year. And belugas are known to migrate across the Arctic Circle.

MINKE MOVES
Although many minke whales head for the hot spots for winter breeding, others stay behind in the cold. They are usually the whales that are not ready to breed, so they eat lots of food and save their strength for the next year.

FOLLOW THAT FOOD
The long-finned pilot whale is a nomad, not a migrator. Nomads cover much shorter distances than the migratory whales and usually travel in response to the movement of their food—in this case, squid—as it travels with the currents.

THE GREAT MIGRATORS
The rights, humpbacks, and grays are the whale marathon swimmers. Every year, gray whales swim 12,400 miles (20,000 km) from Mexico to Alaska and back (a gray whale with her calf is pictured above right). They begin this journey as two-month-olds. If they live to be 40, they will have swum as far as the moon and back.

Humpback whale breeding area	Right whale feeding area
Humpback whale feeding area	Gray whale breeding area
Right whale breeding area	Gray whale feeding area
Migration route	

Sockeye salmon

Word Builders

• **Migrate** comes from the Latin word *migrare,* which means "to move from one place to another, to change."
• **Nomad** comes from the Greek *nomas,* for "roaming about the pasture." Nomad whales are ones that do not migrate, or travel along a particular route. They appear to go where the food takes them!

That's Amazing!

The great whales can double their weight during the feeding season. But during migration they may not eat for eight months. They survive on the energy stored in their blubber but they sometimes snack on the return to their feeding grounds.

Pathfinder

• Find out what makes whales perfectly adapted to life in the water by turning to pages 150–51.
• Whales use echoes to help them navigate. Find out more on page 162.
• Some whales sing songs as they swim. Find out more on page 164.

INSIDE STORY

Counting Whales

Counting whales is tricky. After all, they spend most of their time underwater and it can be very easy to count the same whale twice. The solution is aerial surveys. Researchers from the Canadian Department of Fisheries and Oceans have been using this technique to count the belugas of St. Lawrence, in Canada. They go up in a small airplane and fly over the area in an exact route. A camera attached underneath the plane takes photos. At the lab, researchers count all the belugas they see in the photos and make an estimate, which includes the belugas that missed the photo opportunity because they were underwater at the time. At the last count, there were about 1,000 belugas living in the area. While that's still only about 20 percent of what there were 100 years ago, their numbers seem to be stable—good news.

WHALES FROM SPACE

Scientists got help from space to find out where the belugas of northeastern Canada went on their winter migration. They attached a radio transmitter to a beluga, which sent signals to a satellite, revealing the beluga's location. They picked up the signals and mapped out the journey. Since belugas travel in groups, they only needed to track one to know where they all go: Greenland.

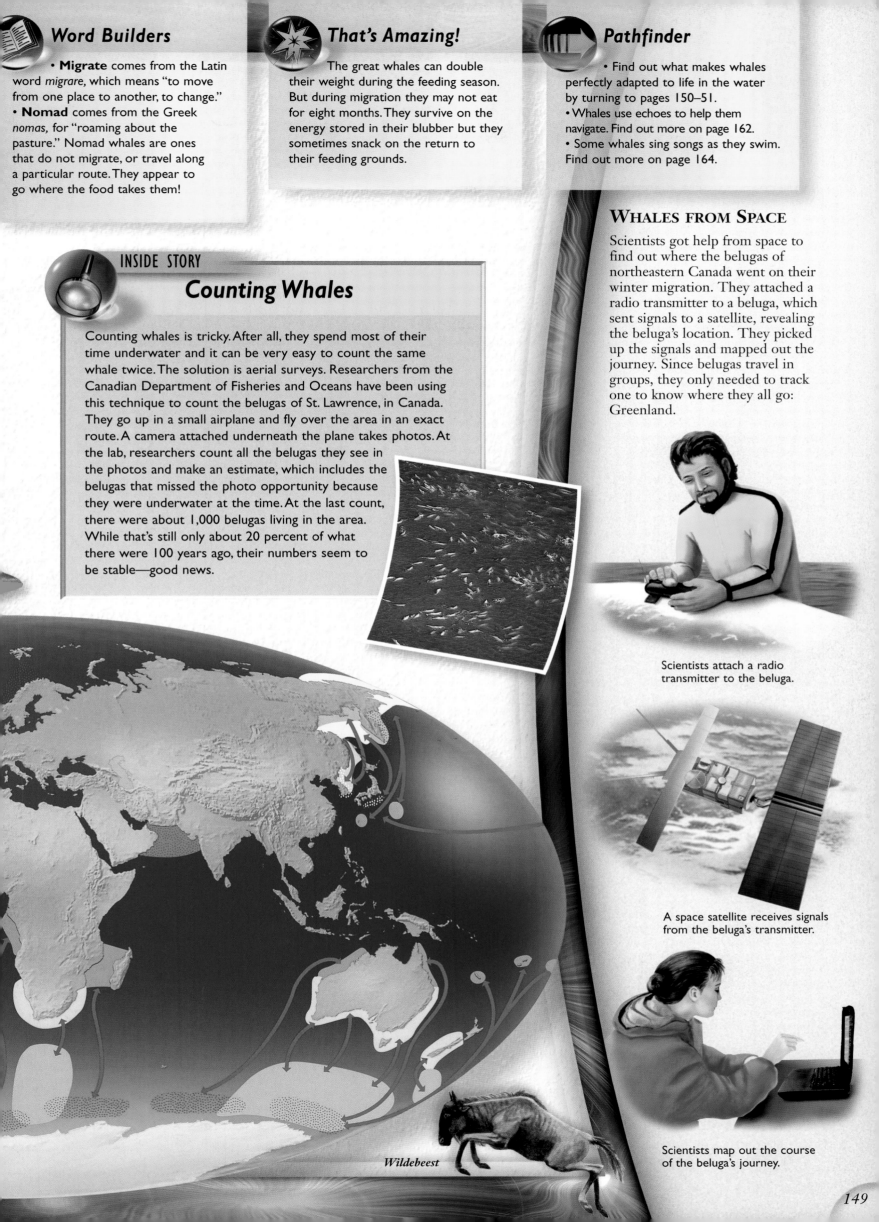

Scientists attach a radio transmitter to the beluga.

A space satellite receives signals from the beluga's transmitter.

Scientists map out the course of the beluga's journey.

Wildebeest

Watery World

IF YOU SPENT just a few hours in the ocean, you would end up wrinkly, burnt by the sun and wind, crusted with salt, and very, very cold. But whales, who spend their entire lives in water, have none of these problems. That is because they have adapted, over millions of years, to living in the water.

Their bodies are streamlined and their skin is silky smooth and flexible, without wrinkles and virtually without hair. This ultra-smoothness makes it easier to swim through water, which is much thicker and more difficult to move through than air (try walking in a swimming pool compared with walking on the sidewalk). Whale skin has oily substances that keep it moisturized and protected, while just underneath, a layer of blubber keeps them warm in cold water and acts as an energy store.

Whale skeletons are light, so they can grow big and still be supported by water. Yet they would sink if their bodies hadn't developed buoyancy to float. They can also dive very deep, slowing their heartbeat to save oxygen, and never be affected by the increasing water pressure that gives humans "the bends." And they have excellent hearing and echolocation, senses that make the most of the best way to communicate underwater—via sound. All these adaptations make whales the only mammals, apart from manatees (sea cows) and dugongs, that can live full-time in a watery world.

TUCUXI TYPES ONE AND TWO
Some tucuxi like fresh water and some like salty. The first type lives in the rivers of South America, the Amazon and the Orinoco. The second lives just off the coast, in the Atlantic Ocean—they're bigger and darker than the river tucuxi.

IN THE SHALLOWS
The Indo-Pacific hump-backed dolphin keeps to the coast, all the way from southern Africa up and across Asia then down to northern Australia. It spends its time looking for fish and shellfish in the warm, shallow waters of mangrove swamps, lagoons, and estuaries. Occasionally, it swims a little way upriver.

HANDS ON

Feel the Cold

To experience how whales keep from feeling the cold, fill a basin with cold water. Now put your hand in. How long can you keep your hand there before it starts feeling too cold? Tip out half the water and add lots of ice cubes. Put your hand back in. How long can you keep your hand in this time? Dry your hand well, then pull on a rubber glove or a plastic bag. Put your hand in the water and check if it takes less or more time to feel icy. Try on a wool glove under the rubber glove or plastic bag. Put your hand back in the water. Is the cold more bearable now? You'll probably find it is. And that's how whales keep warm, even in icy waters. But layers of blubber works even better than layers of wool and rubber.

Word Builders

The bends causes excruciating muscle and joint pain. Sudden changes in pressure make bubbles of nitrogen form in the bloodstream. These days, it is divers who get the bends, but the phrase was originally coined by miners, who were frequently left bent over and stiff by the disorder.

That's Amazing!

Even though they often live in freezing cold water, whales can get hot from exercising too hard. To prevent overheating, warm blood is pumped through arteries to the flippers, fins, and tail flukes. These areas are thin and have no blubber, so the heat is quickly lost into the water and the cooled blood flows back into the body.

Pathfinder

• Their slip-through-the-water bodies make swimming look easy. Find out how whales make their graceful moves—turn to pages 158–59.
• Hard to imagine a whale out of water? Discover what happens when whales get stranded on pages 182–83.

skin
blubber
arteries
muscle

UNDER THE SKIN

Just under the skin of every cetacean, there's a layer of fat called blubber. Like insulation, it keeps them warm and stores energy. Bowheads have the thickest blubber—20 inches (50 cm) of it all over.

GREASE SLICK

Humans don't have blubber like whales, or a thick coat of hair like most other mammals, so they have to use other ways to insulate themselves. Long-distance swimmers slather their bodies with grease to keep warm in cold water.

SURFACE TO SEA FLOOR

The deeper the ocean, the darker and colder it is. The franciscana likes shallow waters. The short-beaked common dolphin swims between the surface and 330 feet (100 m) down, while the short-finned pilot whale goes three times deeper for krill. And the sperm whale sucks up giant squid from the depths of the ocean.

Franciscana, to 30 feet (9 m)

Short-beaked common dolphin, to 330 feet (100 m)

Short-finned pilot whale, to 990 feet (300 m)

Sperm whale, to 10,000 feet (3,000 m)

Life as a Whale

FROM MUDDY RIVERS to vast deep oceans and polar seas, the waters of the world are home to all whales. And like every other water creature, whales have their own special way of swimming. Because they breathe air, whales spend a lot of time swimming near the surface, but they are expert at diving for food, and their senses are highly tuned. They can sense, hunt, and capture prey without ever seeing it. But how do they do all these things? Read on and find out.

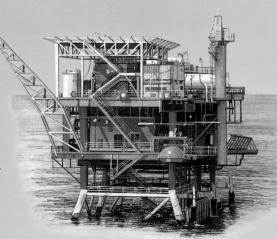

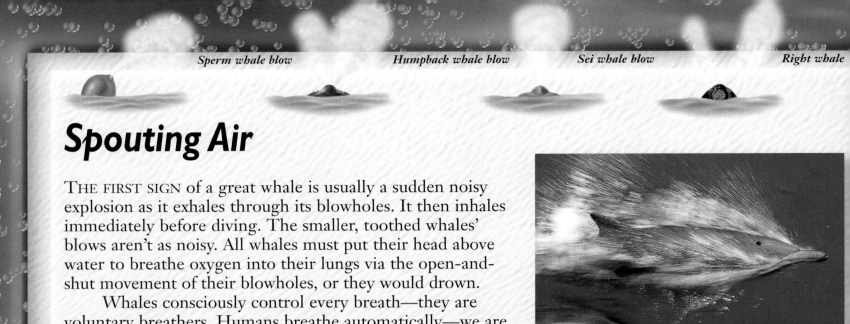

Spouting Air

THE FIRST SIGN of a great whale is usually a sudden noisy explosion as it exhales through its blowholes. It then inhales immediately before diving. The smaller, toothed whales' blows aren't as noisy. All whales must put their head above water to breathe oxygen into their lungs via the open-and-shut movement of their blowholes, or they would drown.

Whales consciously control every breath—they are voluntary breathers. Humans breathe automatically—we are involuntary breathers. A rorqual resting at the surface blows slowly, and a porpoise speeding through the waves breathes quickly. When whales are operated on, they are never put to sleep completely, because they may stop breathing.

Once underwater, whales hold their breath—from 10 seconds for a dolphin in the shallows, to 2 hours for a sperm whale headed for the ocean depths. You would expect them to have a huge lung to enable this, but their lungs are small for their body size. Yet their breathing is efficient—each time whales breathe, they replace 80 percent of the stale air in their lungs with fresh air (we replace about 25 percent). Their blood also stores more oxygen than ours.

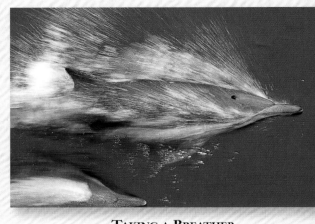

TAKING A BREATHER
Cetaceans breathe out and then in very fast. When dolphins and porpoises are swimming at speed, they leave the water altogether as they take a quick breath—it's easier traveling through air than water.

Gills

BREATHING SHARK-STYLE
Like any fish, a shark uses gills, not lungs, to breathe. Water, rich in oxygen, rushes into its mouth and across its gills, where the oxygen enters the shark's blood. The water exits via the gill slits.

INSIDE STORY

Half-asleep

If dolphins went to sleep like we do, they'd drown. They need to stay in contact with each other plus make sure they're safe and still breathing all the time, even when they're asleep. So they sleep with one eye open and only half their brain in deep-sleep mode. The other half is wide awake. Dolphins swim round and round in a tight group with their open eye looking into the circle, checking up on the other group members. After a while, they swap eyes and let the other half of the brain sleep. This is how their whole brain gets the rest it needs while they continue swimming, breathing, and keeping an eye on what's going on around them.

Common dolphin

Fin whale

Sperm whale

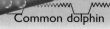
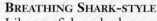

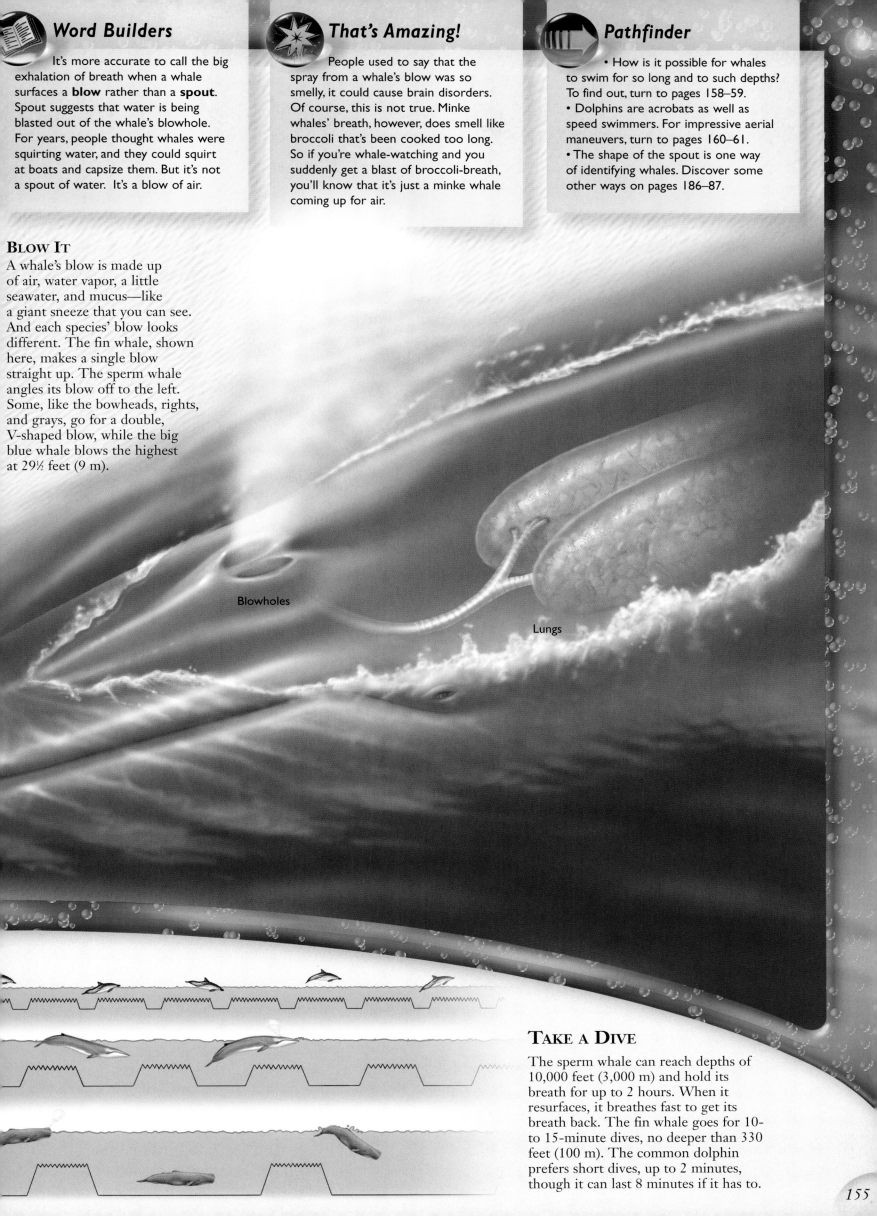

Word Builders

It's more accurate to call the big exhalation of breath when a whale surfaces a **blow** rather than a **spout**. Spout suggests that water is being blasted out of the whale's blowhole. For years, people thought whales were squirting water, and they could squirt at boats and capsize them. But it's not a spout of water. It's a blow of air.

That's Amazing!

People used to say that the spray from a whale's blow was so smelly, it could cause brain disorders. Of course, this is not true. Minke whales' breath, however, does smell like broccoli that's been cooked too long. So if you're whale-watching and you suddenly get a blast of broccoli-breath, you'll know that it's just a minke whale coming up for air.

Pathfinder

• How is it possible for whales to swim for so long and to such depths? To find out, turn to pages 158–59.
• Dolphins are acrobats as well as speed swimmers. For impressive aerial maneuvers, turn to pages 160–61.
• The shape of the spout is one way of identifying whales. Discover some other ways on pages 186–87.

Blow It

A whale's blow is made up of air, water vapor, a little seawater, and mucus—like a giant sneeze that you can see. And each species' blow looks different. The fin whale, shown here, makes a single blow straight up. The sperm whale angles its blow off to the left. Some, like the bowheads, rights, and grays, go for a double, V-shaped blow, while the big blue whale blows the highest at 29½ feet (9 m).

Blowholes

Lungs

Take a Dive

The sperm whale can reach depths of 10,000 feet (3,000 m) and hold its breath for up to 2 hours. When it resurfaces, it breathes fast to get its breath back. The fin whale goes for 10- to 15-minute dives, no deeper than 330 feet (100 m). The common dolphin prefers short dives, up to 2 minutes, though it can last 8 minutes if it has to.

SMALL FRY
Baleen whales eat zooplankton (far right), which is made up of minute crustaceans and larvae. Small crustaceans such as krill (right), copepods, and amphipods are also found among zooplankton.

Strain, Suck, Slice

ALL WHALES ARE meat-eaters. But the baleen whales and the toothed whales eat very different food in very different ways.

Baleen whales are some of the biggest sea creatures and yet they eat some of the smallest sea creatures. They swallow swarms of tiny zooplankton, krill and slightly larger mollusks. Schools of smallish fish can also be on the menu. The rorquals use a gulping technique that makes the most of their expanding throat pouches, while the right whales swim at the the water's surface and skim food as they go. Some baleen whales gulp and skim, while gray whales feed on the sea floor.

Toothed whales, on the other hand, hunt and grab their prey one at a time. While a few slice or chew their food before swallowing, most only use their teeth in the capture, then just suck their food straight down. This could explain how whales with deformed jaws or damaged teeth manage to survive—they probably suction their food down like a vacuum cleaner.

Different toothed whales eat particular types of fish, shellfish or squid. While beaked whales deep-dive for deepwater squid, orcas take anything from seabirds and seals to baleen whales. Orcas, like many toothed whales, hunt in groups.

BOTTOM FEEDERS
When feeding, gray whales roll onto their sides and stir up mud and sediment on the sea floor with their snouts. They capture small crustaceans and worms this way. Most gray whales feed on their right side and show wear and tear on that side of their mouth. But a few favor the left side.

BIG BABY
A blue whale eats 6 to 8 tons of shrimplike krill every day. A baby blue whale drinks 100 liters (176 pints) of milk a day.

INSIDE STORY
A Big Bubble Encounter

We were in Alaska to see humpback whales…Suddenly, a bubble broke the surface, no more than 30 feet (9 m) away… It was roughly the size of a dinner plate and was quickly followed by others…Within a few moments, a huge circle of bubbles had formed. Then it happened.

A mind-boggling 14 humpback whales suddenly erupted from the water in one great foaming mass…With water gushing down extended throat pleats, and clouds of leaping herring, the whales rose to nearly 20 feet (6 m) before sinking back. By the time the water had settled…the whales had disappeared, leaving no trace of their spectacular performance.

Diary extract, July 1995, Mark Carwardine, cetologist

DOING THE FOOD DIVE
A fin whale takes a deep breath before rolling into a steep dive. Hearing and other senses help it find a swarm of zooplankton. It gulps the swarm in with water. After filtering and swallowing, the whale surfaces.

Word Builders

Krill is a Norwegian word that means "whale food." **Rorqual** comes from an Old Norse word meaning "groove throat." This refers to the grooves, or pleats, under the throats of all the rorqual whales—the blue, fin, sei, humpback, Bryde's, and minke whales. The grooves allow their throats to expand so they can gulp in more water and more prey.

That's Amazing!

When working as part of a pack, an orca takes on just about anything in the sea, even a blue whale more than three times its size. Each orca has a particular task to perform in the hunt. Some will herd the blue whale, some will keep it from diving, and some even throw themselves across its blowhole so it can't breathe.

Pathfinder

• Where whales live often depends on the types of food they eat. Read more on pages 146–47.
• How do whales hunt for prey in deep, dark, and murky waters? Find out on pages 162–63.

BUBBLENETTING

By swimming in a slow, spiraling circle—blowing bubbles as it goes—a humpback creates a "net" of bubbles around a school of fish. As the fish become trapped, they cluster closer and closer together—and that's when the other humpbacks move in with their mouths wide open.

Down, Down, Down

WHALES MAKE SWIMMING look easy. But moving such bulk through dense water takes enormous energy. Whales minimize the water's drag by maximizing what's called "laminar flow." This is the smooth, streamlined flow of the layer of water surrounding the whale's body, which is traveling at a different speed than the water around it. So whales make the most of a smooth body, an amazing, shape-changing skin, and two powerful tail flukes to travel with minimum effort. The tail action is crucial. It beats up and down, creates laminar flow, and powers the whale along.

All whales are graceful in water, whether stopping or starting, rolling or speeding—even swimming upside-down. The pectoral fins steer and the dorsal fins create stability. Whales usually cruise along to save energy but if they need to go faster the lower body arches further and the tail beats harder. And when whales aren't near the surface, they're diving into deeper water for food. They may dive for ten seconds or two hours, depending on the whale. They might go straight down or travel at an angle, covering great distances and depths, all while holding their breath, and pushed along by that powerful up-and-down tail action.

GOING STRAIGHT DOWN!
The sperm and beaked whales dive the deepest of all the whales. The sperm whale descends vertically, usually to about 1,300 feet (396 m), though the largest males may get to 10,000 feet (3,000 m). The whale searches in almost total darkness for deepwater dwellers such as jumbo flying squid and giant squid.

LIFE IN THE SLIP-STREAM
A calf that stays close to its mother is well-protected. And by swimming beside her, it can "slip-stream" and use its mother's laminar flow to move quickly through the water.

Sei whale: 23.5 mph (38 km/b)

Human: 23 mph (37 km/b)

Word Builders

- **Fluke** comes from the Old Norse, *floke*, meaning "flat." The flukes are the two broad, flat lobes of a whale's tail. **Fluking** is what some whales and dolphins do at the start of a deep dive. They lift their tails high to help them descend at a steeper angle.
- The **hourglass dolphin** is named for the black and white pattern on the side of its body, which looks a little like the shape of an hourglass.

That's Amazing!

The fastest cetaceans are Dall's porpoises. They can skim along just beneath the surface at up to 35 miles per hour (56 km/h). The sei whale is the fastest great whale, with short bursts at 24 miles per hour (38 km/h). But great whales usually only average between 1–5 miles per hour (1.6–8 km/h) over long distances.

Pathfinder

- Some whales travel enormous distances for months at a time. Read more on pages 148–49.
- How do whales, such as the sperm whale, dive down so far without drowning? Find out on pages 154–55.

HANDS ON

How Do You Compare?

Your normal walking speed is probably about 3 miles (5 km) an hour. That equals the fastest speed ever recorded for a migrating humpback—one of the very slow cetaceans. How does your fastest speed (running) stack up against the fastest swimming speed of different whales? To find out, get someone to time you with a stopwatch when you sprint 100 yards (100 m). Now multiply your time in seconds by 17.6 (or 10 for metric)—this will tell you how long you would take to run 1 mile (1 km). Now divide 3,600 by that time and you will get how far you'd run in one hour. Compare your speed with the whales on this spread.

DOLPHIN PROPULSION

The up and down movement of an hourglass dolphin's lower body and tail flukes pushes against the water and propels it along. The upstrokes and the downstrokes are equally important.

159

Up, Up, and Away!

IMAGINE A 28 TON, 56-foot (17-m) humpback whale suddenly rising up out of the water. It turns 180 degrees in midair, then lands with an ear-splitting thwack on its back and disappears from view. This spectacular aerial display is called "breaching," and most cetaceans do it. The great whales usually get about two-thirds out of the water and do either a belly or a back flop. Most porpoises and dolphins leap clear of the water, and spinner, dusky, and striped dolphins twist, turn, somersault, and spin while they leap. But dolphins and porpoises don't just leap high. They also "porpoise," leaping long and low, in and out of the water.

No one is quite sure why whales breach, but scientists do know that it is a form of communication. It could be to warn intruders away, to signal distress to companions, to show excitement, a sense of fun, or to let other whales know of their presence. It may help keep the group organized and together. It may also get rid of skin parasites.

Great whales also use lobtailing and "pec-slapping" to send a message. A loud crack of the tail or pectoral fin means they are irritated or aggressive, and is a threat or warning to stay away, as well as a defense against attacking orcas. But a gentle "pec-slap" could be a caress for courting whales, while leisurely lobtailing is a form of socializing.

ALL TOGETHER NOW
Orcas live, travel, and feed in tight-knit family groups. They can be very active when socializing and playing together, as seen in this display of synchronized breaching.

HIGH-FLYING DOLPHINS
Dusky dolphins are one of the most acrobatic dolphins. Their slim, light bodies enable them to make quite extraordinary leaps and somersaults. Once one dusky dolphin starts to leap, others often follow.

Word Builders

The **humpback** gets its common name from the hump on its back. Its scientific name, *Megaptera novaeangliae*, means "big-winged New Englander." A regular visitor to the New England coast of North America, the humpback is often seen breaching, when its very long flippers can look a little like a pair of big wings.

That's Amazing!

The striped dolphin can leap up to 23 feet (7 m) out of the water—three times its body length. It can also do tailspins and backward somersaults and has been seen porpoising upside-down. A 6-foot (1.8-m) man who could jump three times his height would leap to 18 feet (5.5 m), but he'd need a pole vault to do it.

Pathfinder

• Find out how whales move along underwater on pages 158–59.
• Whales are not only clever communicators. Read about other ways in which they demonstrate how smart they are on pages 166–67.

ALL ON THE SURFACE

Great whales use their tail flukes, pectoral fins, and heads to get messages across. While we don't understand precisely what they're saying, we have some theories.

SPYHOPPING
A gray whale pops its head up to see what's going on—the view is probably better above water.

PEC-SLAPPING
The loud, hard slap of a pectoral fin on the water may signal "Stay away!"

LOBTAILING
Many whales smack their tail flukes hard on the water. It's loud, obvious, and has smashed small whaling boats.

WHALE OUT OF WATER

They may be slow and stocky, but humpbacks get airborne more than any other great whale. They can breach up to 100 times in a row and almost jump clear of the water.

INSIDE STORY

In a Spin

Every morning, large schools of spinner dolphins arrive in Kealake'akua Bay, Hawaii, after spending the night feeding offshore. They rest in the middle of the day then get active, zig-zagging across the bay. They do head, back, and body slaps, arching leaps, salmon-like leaps, tail-over-head leaps, and, of course, spins.

Spins are usually done four to five in a row, but sequences of up to 20 have been seen. Each dolphin has a unique spin and all ages do it. A spin starts with a loud bark and finishes with a loud tail slap that leaves a plume of bubbles. Scientists think the spins act like sound markers. The bark, slap, and bubbles let other dolphins know the size and shape of their school as they swim along. The spins and leaps may also be social. They certainly seem to be contagious.

Using the Senses

WHALES MAY HAVE THE SAME SENSES we do, but underwater living has changed the way these senses are used. Many species have good sight, useful for hunting and close-up vision. Little is known for certain about how whales use taste and smell. Now scientists think they can use taste to navigate and distinguish types of food. Baleen whales may use smell above water to sniff krill on the wind. But touch and hearing are the senses that work best in water, so it is these senses that whales rely on most to communicate, socialize, and explore.

Whales also have senses that we don't, such as a sensitivity to Earth's magnetic field, and echolocation—a sound production and reception system used for navigation and identification. An echolocating dolphin sends out high-pitched clicks. These hit an object, bounce off it, and return to the dolphin as an echo. The dolphin builds an audio image, like a sound X-ray, from the returning echoes to determine where and even what the object is. It's like seeing with your ears. Toothed whales use it constantly. Baleen whales lack the physical features that would allow them to echolocate. Scientists think they make do with their excellent hearing.

SILKY TOUCH
Whale skin is incredibly soft and sensitive, so it's a good tool for touching and understanding things in the whale environment. These young spotted dolphins are getting a feel for seaweed.

EYES WIDE OPEN
Water is 800 times thicker than air but most whales can still navigate well underwater, even when it's dark and gloomy. It's only the dolphins living in muddy rivers that don't have good eyesight.

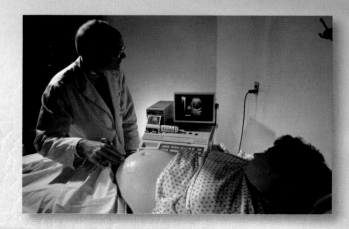

SOUNDS AND PICTURE
This pregnant woman is getting an ultrasound—a visual image of the baby inside her, made from sound waves. Ultrasound technology is how humans use echolocation.

Word Builders

• Echo was the name of a Greek nymph who wasted away for love of a handsome man, Narcissus. All that was left of her was her voice, repeating calls. That's where we get our word "echo." When combined with "location," from the Latin *locare* (to place), you get the word **echolocation.**

That's Amazing!

Good all-round vision is vital when avoiding predators. Pygmy sperm whales have eyes that turn backward. Bottlenose dolphins can move each eye in a different direction—looking straight ahead and to the right. Sperm whales float upside-down so they can see what's above them.

Pathfinder

• Turn to pages 140–41 to find out some other differences between toothed and baleen whales.
• Whales also give out signals to other whales and sea creatures. Go to pages 160–61 to read more.

INSIDE STORY

Stun Beam

Echolocation is used for finding food but toothed whales may also use it like a stun beam, to immobilize or maybe even kill their prey. This is done with a massive burst of intense, high-frequency sound. Such a burst of sound would put the prey off balance or damage its sensory system, making it much easier to catch. And, given that fish and squid are often faster than toothed whales, the whales probably need some kind of secret weapon like this to help them get enough to eat.

Bottlenose dolphins make bursts of intense sound when hunting mullet in the wild and orcas do it when tracking salmon. Narwhals make the loudest echolocation clicks ever recorded, so maybe they do it, too.

MAKING SENSE

There are some senses that humans don't have, but other animals do. Echolocation is one such sense. Magnetic sensing— being able to detect changes in Earth's magnetic field—is another.

BAT
Many bats live in dark caves and hunt at night. They use their excellent hearing, and echolocate with very high-pitched sound, to detect obstacles and prey.

TRACKING WITH A MELON
Belugas use low echolocation clicks, spaced well apart, to scan the ice-filled seas where they live. Once they pick up the presence of a fish and start moving in on the target, the clicks come faster and higher, and end in a long creak.

TURTLE
Every year, green turtles return to Ascension Island in the South Atlantic, where they were born. They find their way over 1,250 miles (2,000 km) of ocean by navigating with magnetic sensing.

OILBIRD
The oilbird uses echolocation to feed at night and navigate the caves where it nests. Even we can hear the rapid clicks it makes when it echolocates.

Talking in Song

SOUND TRAVELS MUCH faster and farther in water than in air, and whales have excellent hearing to take advantage of this. They can pick up very distant sounds—up to hundreds of miles away for baleen whales—and they can also tell from what direction the sounds are coming. Scientists are still unsure how whales do this. They think baleen whales have wax in their ear holes that transmits sound to the inner ear. Toothed whales probably hear via their lower jaw, which is filled with fat that may relay sound to the inner ear.

As a result of this good hearing, whales have learned to make a variety of sounds for communication and more. Porpoises and sperm whales use clicks to communicate and to echolocate. Other species make many different noises. Belugas yelp, squeak, croak, and whistle. Dolphins jaw-clap at conflict and whistle a lot, especially when angry, frightened, or excited. They also squawk. Each bottlenose dolphin has a "signature whistle," a type of individual identification that others recognize. Their complex vocalizations may be a way of sharing information about prey or predators.

Baleen whales make lower-pitched sounds such as moans, snorts, belches, and grunts, which may be arranged as songs. They probably produce sounds in the larynx, the same way we do, while toothed whales use the air passages, lips, and melon in their forehead to make noise.

DUSKY DOLPHIN
Cetaceans don't always use sound to communicate. Visual signals such as breaching may be used by dusky dolphins when they find large schools of fish. This signals distant groups to come and help herd and eat the fish.

INSIDE STORY
Humpbacks Switch Songs

All male humpbacks in the same population sing the same song, usually while migrating or on their breeding grounds. The song changes gradually over the years. But in 1995 and 1996, Michael Noad and his team from the Australian Marine Mammal Research Centre heard something unusual: two whales on the Australian east coast were singing a different song than the others in the area. It was the same as the song of the Australian west coast humpbacks. In 1997, more east coast whales were singing the new song, while some sang a combination of the old and new. By 1998 every whale was singing the new song. Michael Noad thinks that song changes may help attract mates: "If you are a female and suddenly there's a male singing something different, then he will stand out from the crowd."

MELON MAKING MUSIC
Belugas move air in and out of their nasal air sacs and passages, which is then released through a pair of fat-filled "lips." These vibrate and produce sounds, which the oil-filled melon directs outward.

"Lips" Nasal air sacs and passages
Melon
Oil

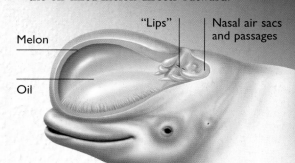
Spotted hyenas laugh

Word Builders

• *Hydor* is the Greek word for "water" and *phone* is Greek for "sound" or "voice." A **hydrophone** is a device that detects sound in water.
• **Sonogram** comes from *sonor*, the Latin word for "sound," combined with the Greek word *gramma*, meaning "what is written, drawn, or recorded." So a sonogram is a "written sound," or "sound recording."

That's Amazing!

Blue whales are the loudest animals on Earth. Their calls travel at least 62 miles (100 km) underwater, maybe as far as 625 miles (1,000 km), and reach up to 188 decibels. A human shout just hits the 70-decibel mark. Sound louder than 120–130 decibels actually hurts human ears.

Pathfinder

• To read about other ways in which whales communicate, turn to pages 160–61.
• Whales use all the senses that humans do—and more besides. Turn to pages 162–63 to find out more.

SONOGRAMS AND SOUND

These sonograms are visual printouts of the soundwaves made when different creatures sing. They show whether the sounds are high or low in pitch and frequency, and how long they last.

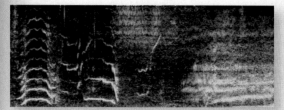

A nine-second segment of a humpback's song includes noises that sound a little like purring and the trumpeting of an elephant.

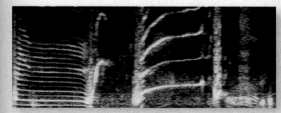

This orca's song lasts three seconds and consists of three sounds—a short boingy moan, a short boingy squeal, then a longer moan.

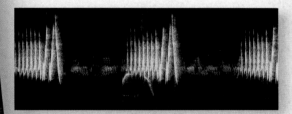

The chestnut-sided warbler whistles two high-pitched notes over and over, very fast, then a slower final note.

This is a woman's voice, singing a single note and then holding it for about four seconds.

HUMPBACK SONG

Male humpbacks are famous for their complex songs. Underwater, it's possible to hear them moan, grunt, chirp, whistle, and wail different themes (like verses) in a special order. This lasts for about 7 to 15 minutes. Then they start the same song again.

LISTENING TO WHALES

Scientists use a hydrophone (an underwater microphone) to listen to whales. Some whale sounds are too high or too low for humans to hear without special equipment, but it's possible to feel their echolocating clicks when they are swimming nearby.

Frogs croak

165

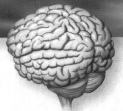
Human brain

Bottlenose dolphin brain

Clever Cetaceans

PEOPLE OFTEN DESCRIBE cetaceans as "intelligent." But it is very difficult to measure intelligence—even in humans. For humans, signs of intelligence include being able to reason and work things through, solve problems, learn from experience and pass on learning, and deal with new situations.

Many cetaceans are very fast learners. Dolphins master complex routines in captivity, and bottlenose dolphins have even learned enough human language to know the difference between "take the Frisbee to the surfboard" and "take the surfboard to the Frisbee." Mother orcas pass on seal-catching techniques to their young, with lessons in how to strand on beaches, then get free again.

Bottlenose dolphins, rough-toothed dolphins, and orcas appear to be the most intelligent cetaceans. Other toothed whales are, in turn, more advanced than baleen whales, which have smaller brains for their body size. But it's difficult for us to know how intelligent cetaceans are— how much of their behavior is learned and reasoned (and therefore a sign of intelligence) and how much is instinctive. We understand so little about them. Their intelligence may be totally different from ours.

PROBLEM SOLVING
Being able to solve problems is thought to be a sign of intelligence. Another sign of intelligence may be the size and complexity of the brain. Cetaceans have large brains for their size, with a complex structure, just like humans.

INSIDE STORY
Percy from Cornwall

Percy was a bottlenose dolphin that lived off the coast of Cornwall, England. He became friendly with the locals and often accompanied fishing boats to check the lobster pots. He seemed to know which pots belonged to which boat, and sometimes swam ahead of a boat to its particular pots. He also played with the pots and entangled their lines. Once, he got some pots in

such a mess, the fisherman had to ask a local diver for help. The diver and Percy were friends and Percy showed the diver how to untangle the pots by pointing to the lines with his beak, in the reverse order to which he'd tangled them. The diver untangled the lines without cutting a single one.

OTHER CLEVER ANIMALS

After humans, chimpanzees and bonobos are probably the smartest animals. They have language skills, can solve problems, use tools, and teach their young. Many other animals can learn complicated tricks.

CHIMPANZEE
Some chimpanzees use sticks to get at termites. Others make a hammer and anvil with wood or stone for cracking nuts.

HORSE
Horses develop a strong bond with a rider and learn to respond to body language, voice commands, and hand signals.

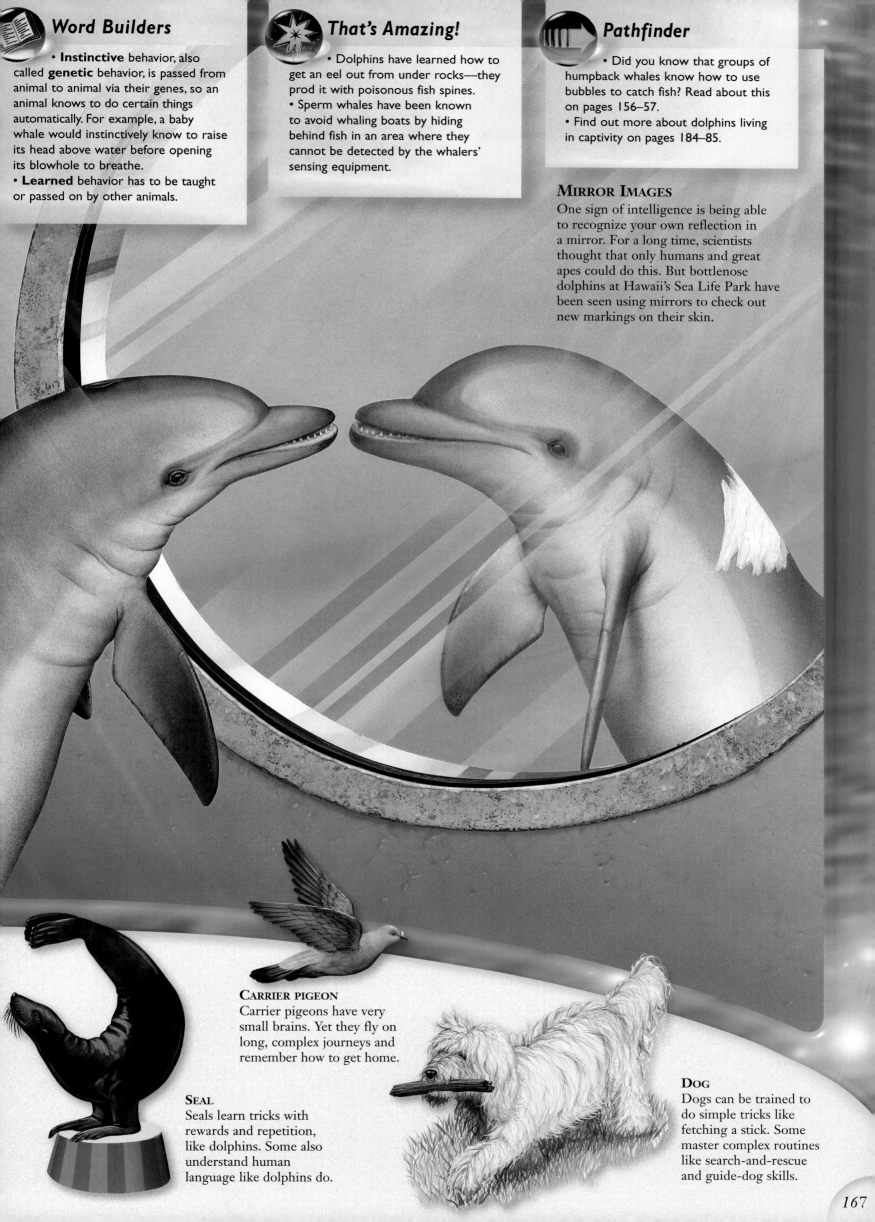

Word Builders

- **Instinctive** behavior, also called **genetic** behavior, is passed from animal to animal via their genes, so an animal knows to do certain things automatically. For example, a baby whale would instinctively know to raise its head above water before opening its blowhole to breathe.
- **Learned** behavior has to be taught or passed on by other animals.

That's Amazing!

- Dolphins have learned how to get an eel out from under rocks—they prod it with poisonous fish spines.
- Sperm whales have been known to avoid whaling boats by hiding behind fish in an area where they cannot be detected by the whalers' sensing equipment.

Pathfinder

- Did you know that groups of humpback whales know how to use bubbles to catch fish? Read about this on pages 156–57.
- Find out more about dolphins living in captivity on pages 184–85.

MIRROR IMAGES

One sign of intelligence is being able to recognize your own reflection in a mirror. For a long time, scientists thought that only humans and great apes could do this. But bottlenose dolphins at Hawaii's Sea Life Park have been seen using mirrors to check out new markings on their skin.

CARRIER PIGEON
Carrier pigeons have very small brains. Yet they fly on long, complex journeys and remember how to get home.

SEAL
Seals learn tricks with rewards and repetition, like dolphins. Some also understand human language like dolphins do.

DOG
Dogs can be trained to do simple tricks like fetching a stick. Some master complex routines like search-and-rescue and guide-dog skills.

The Beginning of Life

WHEN IT'S TIME for whales to mate, the males try to attract a female in many different ways. Humpbacks sing and compete in courtship rituals. Right whales stroke and nuzzle the female, while dolphins push and bite and are often quite rough. Male sperm whales, narwhals, and beaked whales will fight each other, as shown by their scars.

Whales don't mate for life. They have many different partners, or at least the males do. Like all mammals, a whale develops inside its mother's uterus. It takes months for this process, called gestation: 9 to 12 for smaller porpoises and dolphins, 11 to 12 for most great whales, and 16 to 18 for larger toothed whales. After birth, the mother helps the newborn to the surface for its first breath. Then the calf starts suckling her milk. The whale calf can survive the cold water, swim with its mother and vocalize. The mother is usually extremely protective, especially until the calf stops suckling and can look after itself. This is at 4 to 11 months for a baleen whale, or at 1, 2, or even 4 years for a toothed whale.

Bearing and caring for a calf takes a lot of time and energy. Females usually have only one at a time and many species wait at least two years—bottlenose dolphins wait five—before they start the breeding cycle all over again.

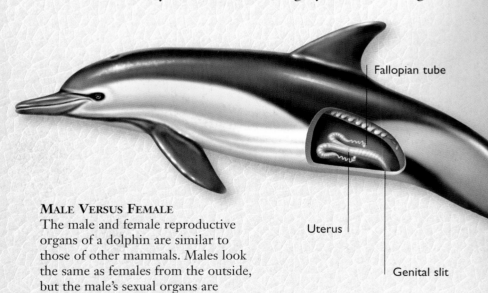

Fallopian tube

Uterus

Genital slit

MALE VERSUS FEMALE
The male and female reproductive organs of a dolphin are similar to those of other mammals. Males look the same as females from the outside, but the male's sexual organs are usually held inside his body to keep him streamlined.

18- to 19-year-old

Word Builders

• **Gestation** comes from the Latin *gestare*, which means "to carry or bear." Gestation is the time when young are carried in the mother's uterus, growing from a newly fertilized egg to a baby that is ready to be born.
• Whales and cattle share the same names to describe their life stages. A baby is called a **calf**, while a mature female is a **cow**, and a male a **bull**.

That's Amazing!

Baby whales have tantrums. Researchers have seen calves let their mothers know they're not happy after the mothers refused them milk by rolling on their sides to stop the suckling. If the calves didn't like this, they slapped down their flukes and head-butted their mother. Sometimes, the cow held her calf with her pectoral fin until it calmed down again.

Pathfinder

• For cetaceans, rearing calves is usually instinctive. Find out about instinctive behavior on pages 166–67.
• Family ties are very important to the survival of young calves. Find out more about families and other groups of whales on pages 170–71.

INSIDE STORY

Whale Age

To find out how old a toothed whale is, scientists examine a cross-section of one of its teeth. Whale teeth grow in layers, with one layer added for every year a whale is alive. Baleen whales don't have teeth, so a cross-section of their waxy earplug is used. As with whale teeth, the earplug grows a layer (of wax and shed skin) every year.

These methods don't give a whale's exact age and can only be used when whales have died. But today, because many individual whales have been photo-identified from their markings, scientists have a new method. They can now identify a whale and follow it through its whole life to know just how old it is. Small porpoises live for 12 to 15 years, bottlenose dolphins to about 50, and blue whales to age 70. Other great whales may make it to 100.

SHOW AND TELL
Male humpbacks don't just sing to win a mate. They also put on a display of rolling, pec-slapping, lobtailing, and breaching. Some males lunge at and sideswipe other males for the position closest to the female.

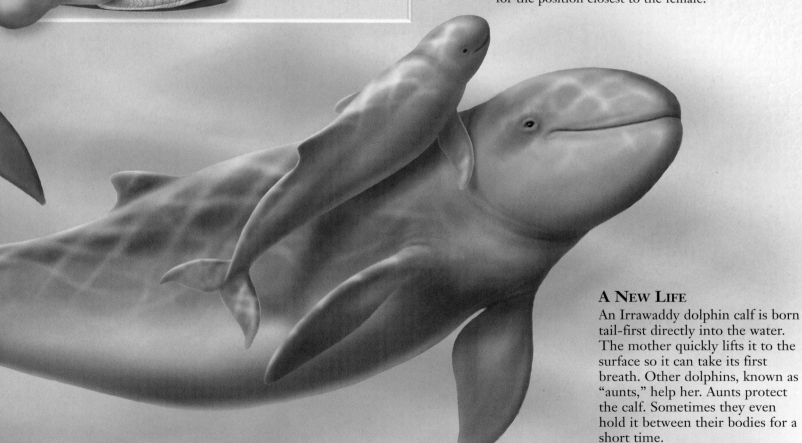

27-year-old

A NEW LIFE
An Irrawaddy dolphin calf is born tail-first directly into the water. The mother quickly lifts it to the surface so it can take its first breath. Other dolphins, known as "aunts," help her. Aunts protect the calf. Sometimes they even hold it between their bodies for a short time.

MAKING IT ON HIS OWN
A male sperm whale becomes sexually mature at about 18 or 19. But he is not socially mature until about 27. At that age, the whale is fully grown, ready to travel alone, and mate.

Living in groups
encourages dolphins to
engage in physical contact.

Family and Friends

SOME WHALES, SUCH as minkes and river dolphins, tend to be loners. But many whales are social animals that live in groups. This gives them protection from predators and helps with mating, giving birth, and raising young. Groups are also important for successful feeding, and the amount of food available usually determines the size of the group.

Baleen whale groups have two to ten members. They feed on scattered krill and small fish. Mothers abandon their calves by the age of one. This may be why many great whale groups are loose and changeable, though humpbacks and southern right males can form long-term relationships.

Toothed whales form larger groups. Coastal dolphins, in groups of 6 to 20, look for fish in bays and along beaches, while oceanic dolphins, or pilot whales, form supergroups of hundreds—even thousands—in search of huge schools of fish. Toothed whale groups are also more stable and closely related, with adult females at their center. Most calves are suckled for one to four years and stay with their mothers until puberty, when the males must leave to join other groups. The most powerful group members (usually adult males) use sound, body language, and teeth to make sure they get the best mate and the best food.

CLOSE FAMILIES
Short-finned pilot whale calves are very close to their mother. They suckle for 2 to 6 years, and up to 15 years if the mother is over 20. They will remain in the same group with her for life.

OLD FRIENDS AND NEW
Close to the coast, spotted dolphins form small schools of up to 15. Dolphins join, leave, and rejoin the group, and there are long-term bonds between them. Spotted dolphins that live far out to sea form schools of hundreds, even thousands, sometimes with bottlenose dolphins.

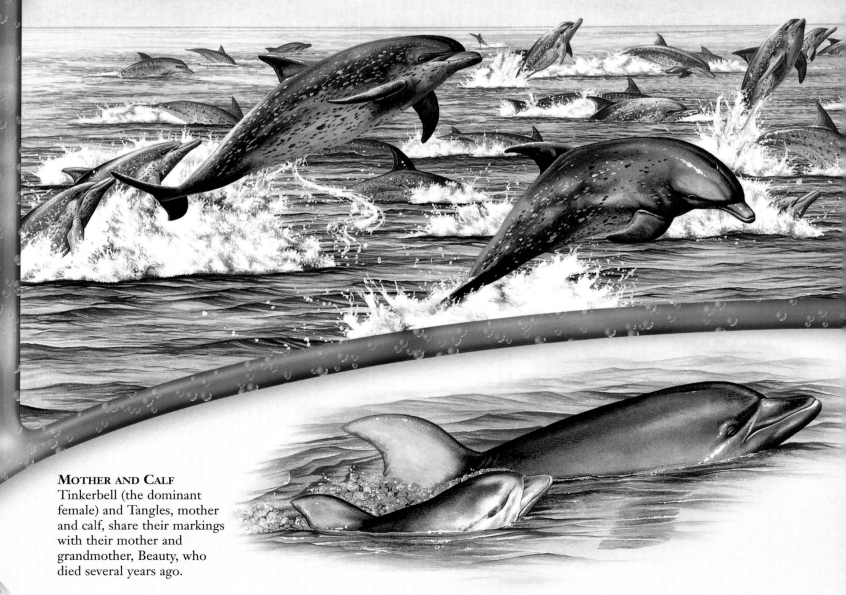

MOTHER AND CALF
Tinkerbell (the dominant female) and Tangles, mother and calf, share their markings with their mother and grandmother, Beauty, who died several years ago.

A **pod** is a small group of animals—and is the term usually used for whales or seals. A **school** is a much larger group of sea creatures. People say "a school of dolphins," but "a pod of dolphins" is also used. Sometimes, a group of whales is called a **herd**—like cattle and antelope, their land relatives.

Many toothed whales are known for their care-giving behavior toward group members. Sometimes they risk their own lives for a close relative. For example, sperm whales will wait beside harpooned companions and even try to defend them and break the harpoon line. This behavior may be a reason for mass strandings among certain species.

• Whales travel in groups or alone. Find out more on pages 148–49.
• Whales communicate in many different ways within groups and with other creatures. But did you know that whales sing to each other? Read more about this on pages 164–65.

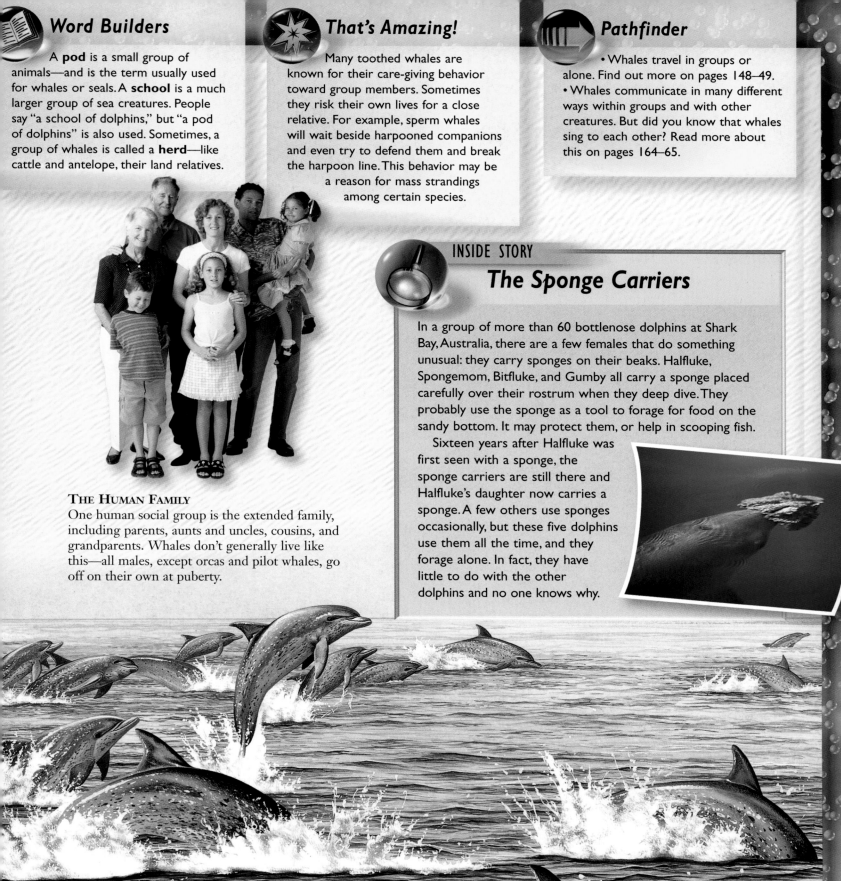

THE HUMAN FAMILY
One human social group is the extended family, including parents, aunts and uncles, cousins, and grandparents. Whales don't generally live like this—all males, except orcas and pilot whales, go off on their own at puberty.

🔍 INSIDE STORY

The Sponge Carriers

In a group of more than 60 bottlenose dolphins at Shark Bay, Australia, there are a few females that do something unusual: they carry sponges on their beaks. Halfluke, Spongemom, Bitfluke, and Gumby all carry a sponge placed carefully over their rostrum when they deep dive. They probably use the sponge as a tool to forage for food on the sandy bottom. It may protect them, or help in scooping fish.

Sixteen years after Halfluke was first seen with a sponge, the sponge carriers are still there and Halfluke's daughter now carries a sponge. A few others use sponges occasionally, but these five dolphins use them all the time, and they forage alone. In fact, they have little to do with the other dolphins and no one knows why.

TANGALOOMA DOLPHINS
Every evening, a group of bottlenose dolphins visits a resort in Tangalooma, Australia. This tight-knit group of dolphins has been coming here for many years. The nightly visits are now a popular resort attraction with the tourists, but they've also provided biologists with an opportunity to observe dolphin families firsthand.

FAMILY RESEMBLANCE
Shadow, Tinkerbell's sister, shares the same physical attributes as her mother and sister. Like humans, these attributes are passed from parents to children.

Danger in the Water

THE WHALE'S BIGGEST natural threat comes from predators such as large sharks and orcas. Not even the huge blue and right whales are safe from orcas working together. The orca's close relatives—the false killer and pygmy killer—sometimes attack, too. In addition, polar bears prey on belugas. Some whales swim away, or dive deep to escape, but others stay and fight, thrashing their tails, charging, and threatening the enemy. Many toothed whales defend the young, sick, or wounded. Some form bands to defend themselves. Groups of thousands of spinner and spotted dolphins have been known to gang up on sharks.

There are other, smaller dangers waiting in the water. External parasites such as whale lice and barnacles feed on the skin and wounds of great whales, but seem to do no real harm. Large numbers of internal parasites can weaken a whale and may even kill it.

But perhaps the greatest danger comes from humans. Cetaceans die in fishing nets. Their coastal and river habitats are being destroyed. The oceans are the dumping ground for huge quantities of sewage, industrial waste, and other pollutants. Ocean pollution could be the biggest threat to cetacean survival.

POLAR BEARS
When belugas get stranded in shallow waters, they stay still and quiet to avoid attracting polar bears. If a polar bear does find a beluga, it bites the beluga's blowhole to disable it. Then it starts eating the beluga's skin and blubber.

DAISIES IN THE SEA
Sperm whales are slow swimmers, so during an orca attack they work as a group. The adults encircle calves and any sick whales, protecting them with their tails pointed outward, lobtailing furiously. This forms a daisy pattern.

Word Builders

- A **parasite** lives and feeds on another plant or animal. Taken from the Greek *parasitos*, parasite means "one who eats at the table of another."
- The Latin *praedari*, which means "to plunder," and *praeda*, which means "prey," give us our word **predator**. A predator captures or preys upon and eats other animals.

That's Amazing!

In a paper published in 1979, author P.F. Major recounts agitated humpbacks off the coast of Hawaii. When one breached he saw two marlin embedded in its side. After one of the whale's twisting leaps, one of the marlin snapped off, leaving the bill embedded in the whale. Marlin do not have teeth, so it is unlikely they were attacking the whale—they probably did it by mistake.

Pathfinder

- Whales also form groups for reasons other than protection. Read all about the different groups they form on pages 170–71.
- There are many people working very hard to save and protect whales. Turn to pages 180–81 to find out more.

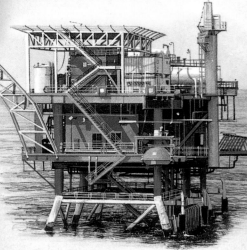

OTHER WHALE TRAPS

The activities of humans are a big health hazard for whales.

WHALE DECOY

The pygmy sperm whale spends most of its time resting near the surface. But if it's surprised it lets out a thick cloud of reddish brown fluid from its intestines. This may act like a cover, or a decoy, as it dives to safety.

NOISE POLLUTION

Increased underwater noise from oil-drilling rigs may make it more difficult for whales to use their sense of hearing to communicate, find prey, and avoid predators.

BOATS

Boats add to underwater noise pollution. Large container ships run into sleeping great whales. Speedboat propellers can wound and cut blubber and fins.

INSIDE STORY

Hangers-on

A whale has many smaller creatures that accompany it on its travels—some are harmful and others harmless, or even beneficial. And the slower the whale, the more it collects. Small cookiecutter sharks, for example, are known to stalk dolphins and whales. With their razor-sharp teeth, they bite deep and then swivel 360 degrees to cut out a circle of flesh, just like a cookiecutter in cookie dough.

Remoras, on the other hand, cling harmlessly to the whale's body to get a free ride. Some barnacles embed themselves on slow-moving great whales, then whale lice infest the barnacles as well as the whale's skin (pictured). It's thought that some lice act like cleaners.

POLLUTION

Whales can get trapped in litter. Swallowed trash can clog digestive tracts. And toxins build up in their bodies and make them sick.

Fishing boat

175

Whales and People

WHALES HAVE ALWAYS captured the human imagination. But our history with whales is a checkered one. In ancient times, sailors viewed them with fear. More recently, we have hunted them, sometimes to the point of extinction. But a greater understanding of these amazing creatures has changed our attitude. Many whales are now protected. Even better, it's possible for you to see them in their natural environments.

page **176** Did you know that whales were once considered to be ferocious sea monsters?

Go to FEARSOME BEASTS.

page **178** Which part of a whale was used to make this corset?

Go to THAR SHE BLOWS!

175

Beast of the deep

Tusked monster

Fearsome Beasts

PEOPLE USED TO THINK that the world was flat. It is understandable, then, that people might also think whales were ferocious sea monsters, given their size. In carvings, paintings, myths, songs, and stories, many cultures depicted whales as tusked or toothed serpents that devoured humans (see the border illustrations on these pages). In the Bible's Book of Jonah, God ordered a whale to swallow Jonah after disobeying him. It then spit him out safely three days later. The Chinese believed a huge creature with the body of a whale and hands and feet of a human ruled the sea. Icelanders feared mythic red-headed whales, which destroyed ships and ate sailors. Yet indigenous peoples who relied upon whales had a different attitude. To the Inuit, for example, whales are children of the sea goddess, Sedna.

Dolphins, on the other hand, have long been viewed with affection. There are many stories of dolphins rescuing people. For the ancient Greeks, killing a dolphin was as bad as killing a person because they believed that dolphins were sailors who had once jumped overboard. Some cultures still believe dolphins have healing powers. Native Americans, Polynesians, and Australian Aborigines see them as messengers of the gods.

Whales have always fascinated people. Some sense a special connection between humans and cetaceans, especially dolphins—the predominant intelligent mammals of land and seaa.

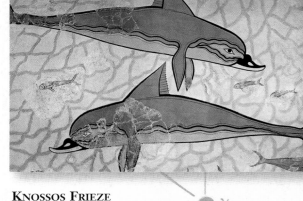

KNOSSOS FRIEZE
These dolphins were painted about 3,400 years ago. You can see them on the wall of the Queen's Room at the Palace of Knossos on the island of Crete.

NAZCA JAR
The Nazca people lived along the South American coast between AD 300 and 800. They would have seen dolphins in the nearby Pacific Ocean, and a Nazca potter has painted one on a jar for storing liquid.

MONSTERS IN THE SKY
Cetus is the name of a group of stars, or constellation, that forms an outline in the shape of a whale. The constellation is named for a terrible sea monster created by Poseidon, the Greek god of the oceans, to represent the power of the sea.

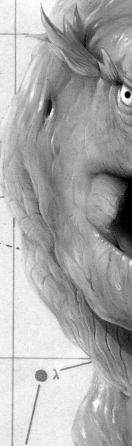

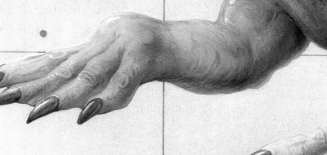

Word Builders

Myth comes from the ancient Greek *mythos*, which means "a word, speech, story, or legend." A myth is an old story that has been developed and told over hundreds of years to try to explain unusual things that happen in the natural world.

That's Amazing!

St. Brendan was an Irish Christian monk who left his home in AD 565 to search for the Promised Land. During his travels, he and his companions landed on what they thought was an island. It was actually a whale, resting in the water—a fact they didn't realize until the whale started to dive. Legend has it that the whale changed into a real island, St. Brendan's Island, which no one has ever found.

Pathfinder

• To learn more about some of the strangest looking and behaving cetaceans, turn to pages 144–45.
• Whales have been feared, revered, and hunted. Turn to pages 178–79 to find out how humans have nearly hunted some whales to extinction.

MYTHICAL MYSTERIES

Sailors have always told stories of mysterious creatures to make sense of the strange or scary things they see in the oceans. Even today, some people believe in the Loch Ness monster.

INSIDE STORY

Special Friends

Stories of a special bond between dolphins and people have been told throughout history. Pliny the Elder, an Ancient Roman senator who wrote down as much as he could about the world around him, told this story nearly 2000 years ago. A boy made friends with a dolphin that was a frequent visitor to his beach. The dolphin and boy regularly played together, and the boy was often seen riding the dolphin's back. One day, though, the boy fell ill and died. His dolphin friend missed the boy so much that the animal was seen searching the nearby beaches and calling for him. At last, the dolphin itself was said to have died from his grief.

UNICORNS

Traders used to sell narwhal tusks, pretending that they came from unicorns—horses with a single horn on their forehead.

MERMAIDS

There are many legends that tell of beautiful mermaids— half-woman, half-fish—who sang to sailors. Dugongs, cousins of seals and sea lions, may be the basis for such legends.

MAKAH CARVING

This 300-year-old rock carving of an orca was found in Washington state. It was made by the Makah people, one of the Native American tribes that hunted whales to survive.

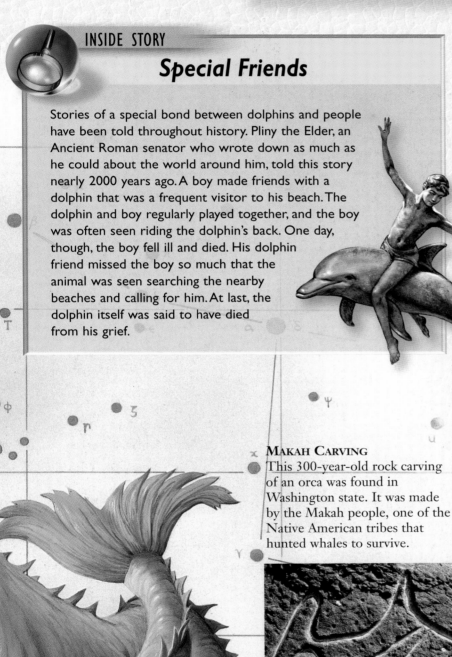

SEA MONSTERS

Oceans were supposedly full of giant sea monsters and serpents. Perhaps these monsters were really great whales and large sharks.

Thar She Blows!

PEOPLE HAVE HUNTED WHALES for food for thousands of years. But whaling didn't become an industry until about a 1,000 years ago, when the Basque people of France and Spain sailed the seas. Nearly every part of a whale had a use—down to the intestines, which were used by Scandinavians to make window panes.

By far the most important whale product was oil for candles and lamps. Before petroleum, whale oil was a major source of energy—and like today, people's appetite for oil was huge. Even after petroleum products knocked whale oil off the market, people discovered uses for baleen, and the technology kept improving so that even more whales could be harvested in less time. Finally, although plastic soon replaced baleen, some countries were so dependent on whaling to feed their people that cutting back seemed an impossibility—until the whales all but disappeared.

Although the bowhead got full protection in the 1930s, it wasn't until 1986 that a worldwide ban on whaling was enforced. Today, only five to ten percent of the original number of great whales remain. Now only limited whaling is allowed, and some species are making a comeback.

INDIGENOUS WHALING
In the past, native peoples of the Arctic and some small island communities survived by hunting whales. Today, they are allowed to kill a set number, or quota, of whales each year.

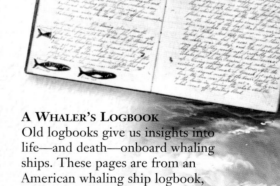

A WHALER'S LOGBOOK
Old logbooks give us insights into life—and death—onboard whaling ships. These pages are from an American whaling ship logbook, dated August 1858.

WHALE MEAT FOR SALE
Slabs of fresh, smoked, or salted whale meat are sold in the Tokyo fish market. It comes from the whales killed by Japan for "scientific research," which is allowed by the ban.

INSIDE STORY
Whales Help Kill Other Whales

From the mid-1850s to 1932, a pack of up to 100 orcas helped whalers in Twofold Bay, Australia, kill the humpbacks that migrated up and down the coast. The orcas worked with the whalers to round up individual humpbacks and received a reward of tongue, lips, and other tender humpback bits. The whalers named the orcas, and the leader was called Tom. Over the years, fewer orcas came—either they were dying or just not returning. One year, only Tom and a few others showed up. When Tom died, his skeleton was hung in the local museum and whaling stopped in the bay.

Gun harpoon

Word Builders

- Whalers used to yell, **"Thar she blows,"** when they saw a whale's blow on the horizon.
- Whalers said **right whales** were the "right" whales to hunt. Being slow and close to shore they were easy targets and had lots of oil, meat, and baleen.

That's Amazing!

Imagine you are away for up to five years. You live on salted meat, hard crackers—perhaps full of maggots—and tea or coffee. You sleep in a dark, filthy cabin with 30 others. There are storms and disease and you might never make it home alive. Welcome to life onboard an American whaling ship in the 1800s!

Pathfinder

- When a whale "blows," it is actually exhaling and spouting air. Find out more about how whales breathe on pages 154–55.
- There are many dangers in the water for cetaceans. Go to pages 172–73.
- To find out what's being done to save whales, turn to pages 180–81.

DEATH OF A SPECIES

A whaling boat rams a northern right whale. Right whales were the first whales to be hunted by whalers. More than 65 years after it became a protected species, the northern right whale remains the rarest great whale in the world—only about 320 exist.

MADE FROM WHALES

It's hard to believe all the different things that were made using whales. The Vikings built chairs out of whale vertebrae, while the Faeroe Islanders built farm walls with skulls. Skin became handbags, shoelaces, and shoes. Tendons made good tennis racket strings.

COSMETICS
Whale oil was used in cosmetic creams, lotions, and lipsticks, as well as in crayons and cooking fat.

FASHION
Baleen plates were turned into corsets and petticoat hoops.

SCRIMSHAW
Bones and teeth were decorated with carvings known as scrimshaw.

Saving Whales

WHALES ARE A VITAL PART of the complex ocean ecosystems. Yet millions of them have died and some species even face extinction—all because of the actions of humans. Centuries of commercial whaling have killed so many great whales that today we are left with just five to ten percent of the original populations. Smaller cetaceans are still hunted, and fishing methods, pollution (chemicals, sewage, and noise), and other environmental problems have reduced populations further.

A whale gives birth to one calf at a time, and only every three to five years. This is why they do not recover as quickly as, say, fishes do. While grays and humpbacks are making a comeback, other species that were never populous, such as bowhead and northern right whales, may not recover.

But there are people and organizations working to save whales and their environment. Researchers and teachers help us to understand whales. Conservationists rescue them, set up whale sanctuaries, encourage cetacean-friendly fishing methods, and try to stop harmful practices. The International Whaling Commission first protected some species from whaling in the 1930s. In 1986, it banned commercial whaling altogether. These are important actions if all the 81 whale species are to continue swimming the oceans.

Seal

Shark

PEACEFUL PROTESTS
These activists have steered their rubber inflatable up to a large whaling ship to protest against whaling. This dangerous action disrupts the whalers as they try to take the whales.

TOXIC DANGERS
Toxins slowly build up in whales' blubber and make them sick and weak. Most animals die at sea, but some, such as this dolphin, are washed ashore covered in sores.

Word Builders

The expression **"to throw a tub to the whale"** was once used to mean making a diversion to escape danger. It comes from an old sailors' custom: If a whale got close to their boat, they used to toss out an empty tub, hoping that it would get interested in the tub and ignore the boat.

That's Amazing!

Even though there's a worldwide ban on hunting great whales, there are some exceptions: Japan hunts minke, Bryde's, and sperm whales in the name of research. Norway and Iceland say they are maintaining cultural rights. Indigenous peoples in the United States, Canada, the Russian Federation, Greenland, and St. Vincent and the Grenadines are allowed to take a small, set number of great whales as well.

Pathfinder

• To find out more about where whales live, go to pages 146–47.
• Read about some of the natural dangers whales face on pages 172–73.
• The history of whaling is fascinating. To learn about this very old industry, turn to pages 178–79.

THE MOST ENDANGERED

Some dolphins and whales are actually in danger of dying out altogether because there are so few of them. The species below are the most endangered today.

FIRSTHAND OBSERVATION

Whale researchers compare their notes and observations. The more we can learn about whales, the better we will understand how they survive in their world and how our actions affect them.

BAIJI

There are less than 100 baiji, or Yangtze River (China) dolphins, left. Even breeding them in reserves may not guarantee their survival.

VAQUITA

The vaquita lives in shallow lagoons in the upper Gulf of California, off Mexico. Most have been killed in gill nets and fewer than 200 are left.

HANDS ON

Store Detective

More dolphins have died in the last 40 years from tuna-fishing than from any other human activity. That's because fishermen were using drift nets and purse-seine nets. These nets catch tuna in addition to many other creatures, like dolphins, seals, and turtles. Some tuna fishermen have changed their methods so they kill few or no dolphins. Their cans of tuna are sold as "dolphin safe" or "dolphin friendly." Next time you're at the supermarket, see for yourself. Look at the cans of tuna and check which ones have a dolphin-friendly logo. Are there any that don't have the logo? What countries are they from? Do the dolphin-friendly cans come from those countries, too? Which brands would you choose?

NORTHERN RIGHT WHALE

This whale was hunted by whalers until it was almost extinct. And despite being protected for 60 years, there are still only about 320.

INDUS RIVER DOLPHIN

Dams on Pakistan's Indus River have split these dolphins into five groups, making breeding difficult. Fewer than 500 survive.

Turtle

Dolphin

181

False killer whale

Pilot whale

High and Dry

ONE OF THE SADDEST sights in the natural world is of whales—perfectly adapted to life in the water—stranded on land. It may be a single whale, too old, sick, or hurt to keep swimming or, more commonly, a small group caught high and dry. Occasionally, a mass stranding occurs. Hundreds of toothed whales, such as pilot whales, false killer whales, sperm whales, and dolphins, have been known to suddenly beach themselves. Why whales do this is a mystery.

Those that strand the most are species that form groups with strong bonds and live far out to sea. Some experts think that they follow prey close to shore and then their navigating ability stops working properly, possibly due to parasite infections, illness, or changes in Earth's magnetic fields. Coastlines with certain features—such as sloping beaches near a sharp headland and sandbars—are particular trouble spots. And if one sick or injured animal strands, others in a close group do not ignore its distress calls. Instead, they stay and end up stranded themselves.

Once a whale strands, its body is no longer supported by water and it can be crushed by its own weight. Rocks or powerful waves may hurt it, sand can block its blowhole, and the sun may burn its sensitive skin. Rescuers can sometimes return stranded whales to the sea but they must be careful not to injure such big, heavy animals when they move them. Despite rescuer efforts, whales frequently strand again.

HELPING STRANDED WHALES
These people are trying to help stranded pilot whales. They have carefully rolled them upright and away from the breaking waves. Here, they are pouring water over the whales (being sure not to get any in an open blowhole) and covering them with wet towels. This keeps their skin moist and protects them from the sun and wind.

MILITARY INTERFERENCE
U.S. Navy ships were using sonar equipment in the Bahamas on the day that seven whales stranded in the area. All whales had ear damage, which would have affected their navigating systems. Scientists think sonar caused the damage.

INSIDE STORY

Double Trouble

In 1994, a group of pilot whales stranded at Farewell Spit, a bay in New Zealand. By the next morning 47 had died and trained volunteers and medics were caring for 45. Battling harsh sun and winds, the rescuers used an excavator to dig a channel to open water. Then they dug carefully under the weaker animals and lifted them onto inflatable pontoons. When the tide rose, the whales were refloated, more than 30 hours after they first stranded. They swam for a while in the shallows, searching for lost pod members, before being escorted by rescue boats, past the dangerous sandbanks in the bay, and out to sea.

It was late in the afternoon, but rescuers had to travel to the other side of the bay where more than 100 pilot whales from another pod had stranded. The rescuers kept them upright and wet through the night and slowly, the next day, the whales headed out to sea.

Sperm whale

Word Builders

Pilot whales get their name from the way one whale acts as a pilot and leads the swimming pod. There is thought to be one leader for each pod. Early whalers used to call these whales potheads because their rounded heads look a bit like an old-fashioned cooking pot, or cauldron.

That's Amazing!

When 80 pilot whales stranded themselves on Tokerau Beach in New Zealand, local people tried to refloat them. Fortunately, a school of dolphins that had been catching fish out to sea arrived in the shallows. They swam around the whales and guided them back out to sea, saving 76 whales.

Pathfinder

• A whale's navigation system allows it to travel great distances. To learn about how and why whales travel, go to pages 148–49.
• To find out more about how whales navigate and find their food, turn to pages 162–63.
• There are many dangers facing whales in the wild—some are natural and some are caused by humans. To find out more, go to pages 172–73.

KEEPING AFLOAT

This stranded whale is being taken back out to sea. New rescue methods involve actually removing whales from where they stranded, rather than just refloating them. This is because experts think the place itself may cause whales to strand.

RESCUE AND RELEASE

Many stranded whales would die if returned to the sea right away. So they are taken to rehabilitation centers. Here, trained people care for them until they are healthy enough to be returned to the wild.

An injured dolphin is carefully moved onto a stretcher and carried to a waiting truck, ready for the trip to the rehabilitation center.

Very young dolphins are bottle-fed milk. Older ones are fed fresh fish by hand. If they are extremely sick, they are given fluids in a tube.

As a dolphin gets stronger in a rehabilitation pool, it tries to swim on its own. Volunteers stay with it and support it if it starts to sink.

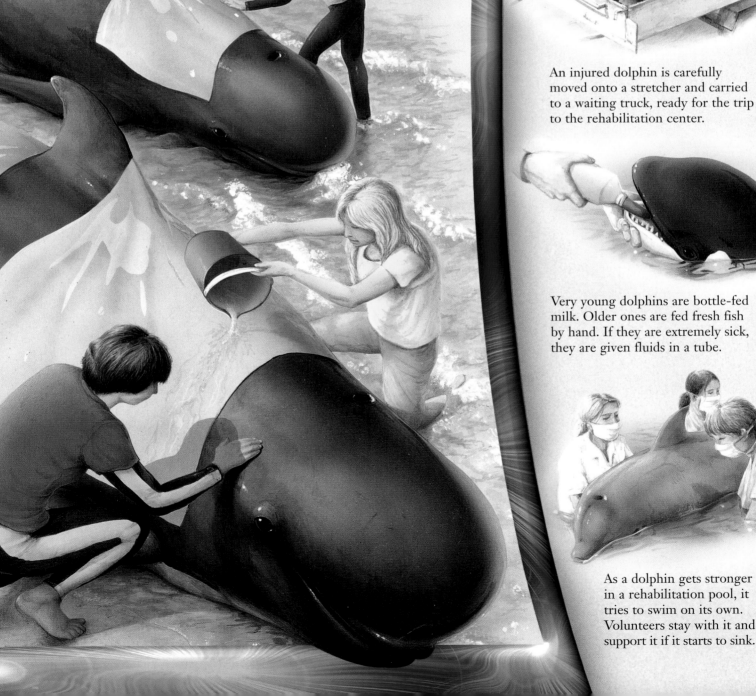

Captured Creatures

BOTTLENOSE DOLPHINS, BELUGAS, orcas, false killer whales, and finless porpoises are just some of the cetaceans that have been kept in captivity over the last 100 years. They are a favorite feature of aquariums, marine parks, and zoos, and millions of people go to see them performing tricks or simply swimming behind glass. Their homes range from large coastal enclosures, which are flushed with fresh seawater by every tide, to small, bare, concrete tanks with dirty water and no natural light.

    Some people are against keeping cetaceans in captivity. Others believe it gives us a chance to understand them. This is because ordinary people get to see cetaceans firsthand and, with the help of educational programs, come to appreciate them. And scientists have learned a great deal from studying certain species in aquariums and oceanariums.

    But cetaceans are not suited to captivity. Those that are small enough normally live in large groups, which most facilities cannot hold. And although some whales are bred in captivity, most are taken from the wild. Some adapt, but many get distressed and die young. Besides, the behavior of captive whales gives us only a limited sense of what wild and free whales are like.

NO PLACE LIKE HOME
This beluga at an aquarium in Vancouver, Canada, may be the only whale the girl will ever see. But such enclosures can never be the same as the open ocean. Many captive cetaceans circle their tanks, stop vocalizing, become aggressive, depressed, and can even hurt themselves.

CLOSE TO EXTINCTION?
The baiji, or Yangtze River dolphin, is the rarest cetacean in the world. Its only hope of surviving the heavily polluted and dammed river where it lives may be semi-captivity and a breeding program in wildlife preserves. Sadly, scientists have had trouble catching the dolphins.

INSIDE STORY

Free Keiko

Keiko is the orca that starred in the movie *Free Willy*, about a boy who helps free a captured whale. Keiko was born in the wild, near Iceland, but was captured in 1979. After the movie, he was returned to a Mexico City amusement park to perform.

    When his fans realized this, they raised money to free Keiko and in 1998, he was moved back to Iceland, to a special netted pen. Every year since then, in spring and summer, he has been encouraged to explore the wild and every year he is more accepted by wild orcas. But he always returns to his pen. After 22 years in captivity and a cost of more than $14 million, his caretakers don't know if he will ever return to the wild.

CONTACT WITH THE WILD
There are sites around the world where you can watch whales, dolphins, and porpoises in their natural habitat. At Monkey Mia and Tangalooma in Australia and Little Bahama Bank in the Bahamas, you can feed or swim with them.

Word Builders

In ancient times, an **aquarium** was a watering place for cattle. *Aqua* is Latin for "water," while *arium* means "a place for or connected with something." Today, "aquarium" has come to mean tanks, pools, or buildings with glass sides where aquatic creatures are kept.

That's Amazing!

Some aquariums fund projects to help whales in the wild. Vancouver Aquarium lets you adopt a wild orca by becoming a member of the British Columbia Wild Killer Whale Adoption Program. You get an official adoption certificate, a photo, the life story of your whale, a CD of orca sounds, and updates by newsletter. And you're helping research on orcas in the wild.

Pathfinder

• A lot of the tricks cetaceans are trained to do in captivity are based on natural behaviors like breaching. Learn more about these types of behaviors on pages 160–61.
• How do we know that cetaceans are highly intelligent animals? Go to pages 166–67 to find out.

ORCA ENCORE

Performing cetaceans in aquariums, marine parks, and zoos are extremely popular attractions. This orca's clever tricks and playful personality make it highly entertaining. It is easy to forget the distress it may be feeling when, to us, it seems to be having such fun.

FOR MY NEXT TRICK—

Bottlenose dolphins are quick learners and the tricks they are taught are similar to natural behaviors. Jumping through a flaming hoop or over a stick is a lot like breaching or making arched leaps. But the tricks don't reveal much about dolphins in the wild.

Looking for Whales

A FIRSTHAND ENCOUNTER with a whale in the wild—diving, swimming, feeding, and breaching in its own habitat—is the best way to experience these amazing creatures. Luckily, there are places where you can do just that. You can watch them from the air, land, underwater, or on the water. You can spot them yourself in kayaks, rowboats, or sailboats, or take guided trips in rubber inflatables or boats.

To be successful, you need a good pair of binoculars and plenty of patience. After all, whales spend 70 to 90 percent of their time underwater, and you'll only spot one when it surfaces to breathe—unless it's doing something spectacular like breaching or bow riding. You've also got to know the weather conditions—and, of course, where to look.

Different species are likely to be in specific areas only at certain times of the year, because they're breeding, feeding, or migrating. Some cetaceans, such as the bottlenose, dusky, and Atlantic spotted dolphins, are common close to shore. Some come so close, you can watch them from beaches, cliffs, or lookouts. But beaked whales and oceanic dolphins stay far out to sea, so you'd be lucky to ever see one of them. Whales, dolphins, and porpoises are powerful animals. So, if you do find a whale, remember to keep your distance.

BOW RIDING FUN
Sometimes, whales approach humans. Dolphins, in particular, like to bow ride in the wave at the front of a boat. They jostle and play, and may even look up at the people looking down at them.

HANDS ON
Make Your Own Logbook

It doesn't take much special equipment to watch whales, but since each sighting is memorable, you'll want to keep track of every one. Choose a notebook that easily fits into a backpack, with strong, hard covers and unlined paper (so you can make sketches). Take the notebook and a pen or pencil with you on all whale-watching trips. When you see a whale, write down when and where you saw it. Note the weather and the sea conditions. How many are there? Can you identify the whales? If not, record any identifying features—shape, color, markings, blows, fins, etc. How do they behave?

TOO CLOSE FOR COMFORT?
In the calm, sheltered waterways of Alaska, a kayaker gets a little too close to the tail-end of a whale. Whales are usually careful around small craft but if they are busy feeding they may not see you, so always keep a safe distance.

Word Builders

Gray whale mothers are highly protective—whalers used to call them "**devilfish**" because they would get so mad if separated from their calves. They'd even chase and attack whalers. These days, grays are known for their friendliness—but whale watchers never get between a mother and its baby.

That's Amazing!

Whales can hurt people. Sometimes they mean to, such as when sperm and gray whales attacked whalers and rammed their boats. Sometimes they don't mean to. Fins or tail flukes have hit people helping to rescue stranded whales and a photographer had bones broken when a southern right bumped him lightly.

Pathfinder

• Knowing where whales live can help you plan your whale watching. Find out more on pages 146–47.
• Some whales are endangered. Find out what is being done to save such whales on pages 180–81.

WHERE IN THE WORLD?

These maps show places around the world where you can see whales, dolphins, and porpoises. You can watch from the shore or take a boat trip.

A PHOTOGRAPHER'S PARADISE

From late November to March, it is possible to view humpback and minke whales in their summer feeding grounds off the Antarctic Peninsula. Tourists in small rubber inflatables get close enough to watch the whales feeding on krill near the pack ice.

ON THE LOOKOUT

During winter and spring in the Southern Hemisphere, southern right whales mate, give birth, and raise young in protected waters close to shore. People stand on clifftops in Argentina, southern Australia, and southern Africa and watch females and their calves playing just below.

Glossary

activist Someone who gets involved in direct action to support one side of a controversial issue. Whale activists worked to introduce a ban on commercial whaling.

amphipod Small crustacean.

archaic whale Ancestor of modern whales, from the Tertiary period of Earth's history.

audio image A sound picture. Dolphins use audio images to determine the shape and placement of objects.

baleen The bristly plates of keratin found in the mouths of some whales, used to strain food from seawater.

bends, the A disorder, most common among divers, caused by a rapid change in water pressure that results in nitrogen bubbles forming in the bloodstream.

blow A visible exhalation of air. A whale's blow consists of air, water vapor, seawater and mucus.

blowhole A nostril on top of the head. Baleen whales have two blowholes. Toothed whales have only one.

blubber The layer of fat beneath a whale's skin which stores energy and heat.

bow riding Riding on the wave created ahead of the bow of a boat or a large whale.

breaching Leaping far out of the water and landing back with a loud splash.

bubblenet feeding A form of hunting used by humpbacks in which they create a "net" of bubbles to surround a school of fish.

callosities Areas of bumpy, wartlike, and hardened skin on the head of some whales.

captivity Being held in a confined area. For whales, this may mean an aquarium or zoo.

cetacean The scientific order that whales belong to.

clicks A series of close-spaced, high-pitched sounds made by toothed whales when echolocating.

cold-blooded A body temperature that is influenced by the surrounding air or water. Reptiles are cold-blooded.

constellation One of the 88 official star patterns that are present in the night sky.

continental shelf The sloping, shallow area around the coast of a continent.

copepod Tiny crustacean.

courtship The complex behavior of two or more mature animals that leads to mating.

crustacean Aquatic invertebrates covered by a hard, jointed shell. Shrimps are crustaceans.

decibel A measurement of sound.

delphinidae The scientific name for the family to which dolphins belong.

DNA (deoxyribonucleic acid) Molecules of DNA are responsible for carrying genetic characteristics of an individual.

dolphin aunt Another female dolphin who helps a mother rear her young calf.

dorsal fin The fin on a whale's back which provides stability in the water.

echolocation A sound production and reception system used by whales and other animals in navigation.

ecosystem An interdependent community of organisms and their environment.

endangered species Species which are in danger of becoming extinct.

epoch A term used to describe a period of time within an era of Earth's history.

era A term used to describe a period of time in Earth's history.

extinct A species which no longer exists.

flensing knife A knife used to strip the blubber or skin from a whale.

flukes The two broad, flat, triangular lobes of a whale's tail.

fossil The buried remains of a plant or animal that has turned rock-hard over thousands of years.

gestation The time when young are carried in the mother's uterus, growing from a newly fertilized egg to a baby ready to be born.

gill The respiratory organ of many aquatic animals such as the shark.

hydrophone A microphone used to detect sound under water.

IWC (International Whaling Commission) An organization established to regulate the hunting of whales.

keratin A hard animal protein that makes up fingernails, hair, and baleen.

laminar flow The flow of water that surrounds a moving, smooth object. It travels at a different speed than the water around it.

larvae Immature invertebrates.

larynx The upper part of the throat tube that contains the vocal chord.

lobtailing Hitting the tail loudly on the surface of the water.

magnetic sensing The ability to sense Earth's magnetic field.

mammal The group of animals that feed their young milk from the breast.

melon The oil-filled forehead of some toothed whales, believed to be used in the focusing of sounds for echolocation.

migration To move regularly from one area to another for feeding or breeding.

mollusk Small invertebrate with a hard outer shell. An oyster is a mollusk.

mysticetes Baleen whales. These whales have no teeth, but have bristly baleen plates that are used for straining food from water.

myth A popular belief that has been developed over many years in an attempt to explain historical events and natural phenomena.

navigate To make one's way from one place to another.

nomad An animal that moves from place to place, usually in search of food.

odontocetes Toothed whales.

paleontologist A person who studies fossils to learn more about the distant past.

parasite An organism that lives and feeds on another organism without benefitting it.

pec-slapping Slapping the pectoral fin loudly on the surface of the water as a form of communication.

pectoral fins The flattened forelimbs of a whale that are used for steering.

phocoenidae The scientific name for the family to which porpoises belong.

pollutant An unnatural contaminant.

porpoising A style of swimming used by porpoises and dolphins at the water's surface.

predator An animal that hunts and captures other living animals for food.

prey Any animal hunted or seized for food.

puberty The period between infancy and adulthood when animals become sexually active.

radio transmitter Electronic signaling device attached to an animal and used to track it.

rehabilitation Care given to sick or injured animals until they are well enough to be returned to the wild.

rorqual An Old Norse word meaning "groove throat." It refers to the pleats under the throats of certain baleen whales.

rostrum The beaklike extension of the upper jaw present in some dolphins.

sandbar A bar of sand formed by currents and tides in a river or ocean.

school Group of animals of the same species.

scrimshaw Carvings on the bones and teeth of whales.

slip-streaming Swimming beside another whale or boat to make use of its laminar flow.

sonar A method of using sound and echo to locate objects underwater.

sonogram A visual representation of sound.

species A group of animals or plants with the same attributes.

spyhopping Raising the head vertically out of the water, usually while stationary, to see what's happening.

sternum The breastbone.

stranding When an aquatic animal is stuck on the shore, unable to return to the water.

streamlined Having a shape designed to offer the least resistance to air or water during movement.

subtropical waters The cooler waters around the edges of the tropical waters.

suckle To feed with milk from the breast.

tapering Becoming narrower at one end.

toxin A substance, produced by an animal or plant, that is poisonous to others.

tropical waters Warm waters found in regions near the equator.

ultrasound High-pitched sound beyond the human range of hearing.

ungulate A hoofed, grass-eating mammal. This group includes cows, sheep, deer, horses, and rhinoceroses.

vertebrae The series of interlocking bones that make up the backbone or spine.

vocalize To use sound to communicate.

warm-blooded The ability to maintain a body temperature independent of the surrounding air or water. Humans and other mammals are warm-blooded.

water vapor Heated water that has become a gas.

whale A water-dwelling, warm-blooded mammal, the scientific name of which is cetacean. This term is also used to describe dolphins and porpoises.

zooplankton The small animal organisms that live in the water.

Index

Acknowledgements

Birds

The publishers would like to thank the following people for their assistance in the preparation of this book: Barbara Bakowski, Renee Clark, Sidney A. Gauthreaux, Matthew Hoffman.
Our special thanks to the following children who feature in the photographs: Sienna Berney, Michelle Burk, Simon Burk, Julia Eger, Matthew Eger, Kevin Peters, Andrew Tout.

PICTURE CREDITS (t=top, b=bottom, r=right, l=left, c=center, e=extreme, f=flap, F=front, C=cover, B=back)
Ad-Libitum 5b, 14bl, 14bc, 24bl, 24bc, 27tr, 30bl, 32c, 32bl, 36c, 36tr, 44tr, 45tr, 46/47c, 46t, 54b, 58bl (M. Kaniewski). **AKG Photo London** 12tr, 20c, 20cl. **AP/Wide World Photos**, 52cl (Kathy Willens). **Aquila Wildlife Images** 13br (J. J. Brooks), 36bc (Gary Smith), 52bl (M. C. Wilkes). **ARDEA London** 57bc, 61br (D. Avon), 59br (F. Collet), 63cr (J. Daniels), 59cr (John S. Dunning), 30c (M. D. England), 17br, 46bc (Kenneth Fink), 40tr (Peter Steyn), 63tr. **Auscape** 49cr (John Cancalosi), 23tr, 51br (Jean-Paul Ferrero), 23cr (Ferrero-Labat), 40br, 47br (François Gohier), 16br (Mark Hamblin-OSF), 63br (Owen Newman-OSF). **BBC Natural History Unit** 18br (Richard Kirby), 51bl (Steve Packham), 63ebr (Tom Vezo). **Bruce Coleman Collection** 49br (Trevor Barrett), 47bl (John Cancalosi), 19b (Brian J. Coates), 41cr (Rita Meyer), 21cl, 48bl (Kim Taylor), 30bl (Gunter Ziesler). **Clemson University, SC** 42tr (C. G. Belsu). **CSIRO Australia, Division of Wildlife and Ecology** 22c (David Westcott). **Frank Lane Picture Agency** 21cr (H. D. Brandl), 36bl (Hugh Clark), 37br (F. Hartmann), 49tr (J. Hawkins), 53br (David Hosking), 38bl, 56br, 61bl (E & D Hosking), 39br (Philip Perry Kruger), 53bl (Fritz Polking), 60br (Leonard Lee Rue), 37tr, 55br, 55cr (Roger Wilsmhurst), 29br (Martin Withers). **Magnum Photos** 46bl (Erich Hartmann). **Marie Read Natural History Photography** 29tr. **Minden Pictures** 39tr (Frans Lanting). **National Geographic Society** 13bl (O. Louis Mazzatenta). **Natural History Photographic Agency** 59cr (Bill Coster). **National Museum of Natural History** 17bl (Smithsonian Institution/Chip Clark). **Oxford Scientific Films** 50bl (Mike Birkhead), 12br (David M. Dennis), 60bl (Mark Hamblin), 28l (Mark Jones), 37bl (Dr. F. Koster), 24cr (John Netherton), 34bl (James H. Robinson), 37tl (Tony Tilford), 57br (Steve Turner), 36br (Tom Ulrich). **Photo Researchers Inc.** 55ecr (Bill Dyer), 55tr (Brock May), 46/47c (Anthony Mercieca). **Jan Pierson** 40c. **Planet Earth Pictures** 17bl (Mary Clay), 24tr (Geoff du Feu), 38c (Paulo de Oliveira), 57bl (Pete Oxford). **Popperfoto** 63c. **Wendy Shattil/Bob Rozinski** 34c. **The Granger Collection** 60c. **The Photo Library, Sydney** 14bc (Eye of Science/SPL), 23br (Nick Green), 34cl (Herbert Lange). **Tom Stack and Associates** 50br (John Gerlack), 18bl (Larry Tackett). **Twin Tigers Photography** 11bl (Graeme Outerbridge). **Ullstein Bilderdienst** 35b (dpa). **University of Glasgow** 50c (Dr. Bernard Zonfrillo). **VIREO/Academy of Natural Sciences** 52br (A. Morris).

ILLUSTRATION CREDITS
Jane Beatson 4crt, 27tl, 38t, 38b, 39b, 45tl, 54/55c, 54t, 56/57c, 56t, 65tcr. **David Blundell/Wildlife Art Ltd.** 27b (Globes), 43t, 43tr, 43c (Globes). **Dan Cole/Wildlife Art Ltd.** 5c, 6tr, 8/11c, 8t, 11r, 26tr, 27b (Birds) 28/29c, 28b, 29b, 28t, 42/43b, 43br, 43cr, 42t, 43t (Birds), 64tcr. **Barry Croucher/Wildlife Art Ltd.** 4tr, 6c, 7c, 12/13c, 12t, 13cl, 13c, 13cr, 20/21c, 20t, 20cr, 20b, 21b, 65bcl, 65bcr. **Christer Eriksson** 38/39c. **Lloyd Foye** 5tl, 7t, 18/19c, 18t, 19r, 26br, 34/35c, 34t, 35r, 36/37c, 36t, 47tl, 47c, 47r, 64bcl, 64br, 64bcr. **Gino Hasler** 6cr, 14t, 14cr, 15r, 15c, 15bl, 65bl. **Rob Mancini** 5tr, 6br, 7br, 16/17c, 16t, 17c, 17b, 24/25c, 24t, 25b, 25r, 26crt, 27cr, 30/31c, 30t, 31r, 40/41c, 40t, 40b, 41b, 64tl, 64tcl, 64bl, 65tl, 65tcl, 65tr. **Stuart McVicar/Geocart** 8bl. **John Richards** 4br, 44c, 44b, 45cl, 45br, 48/49c, 48t, 50/51c, 50t, 52/53c, 52t, 60/61c, 60t. **P. Scott/Wildlife Art Ltd.** 4crb, 7cb, 22/23c, 22t, 22b, 23b, 26crb, 32t, 32r, 32b, 33b, 33c, 64tr, 65br. **Chris Stead** 45bl, 45cr, 58/59c, 58t, 62/63c, 62t. **Cliff Watt** 47tl, 47c, 47br, 47cr (Maps).

Sharks and Other Sea Creatures

The publishers would like to thank the following people for their assistance in the preparation of this book: Barbara Bakowski, Dr. Lester Cannon, Katherine Gleason, Jill Goldowski, Dr. Craig Sowden. Our special thanks to the following children who feature in the photographs: Arianna Claridge, Julia Eger, William Eger, Frederick Marks, Christopher Stirling.

PICTURE CREDITS (t=top, b=bottom, l=left, r=right, c=center, e=extreme, f=flap, F=Front, C=Cover, B=Back).
Ad-Libitum 69bc, 71c, 86cl, 93br, 104c, 105cl, 113bc (Mihal Kaniewski). **Aquarium of the Americas, New Orleans, LA** (Courtesy of John Hewitt) 97br. **Peter Arnold, Inc.** 101bl (Hanson Carroll). **Auscape International** 79bc (Doug Perrine), 114bl (Becca Saunders), 117tr (Mark Spencer). **Wayne and Karen Brown** 74t, 106tr. **Jan TenBruggencate** 100bc. **Merry Camhi** 123bc. **Bruce Coleman, Inc.** 83c (Norman Owen Tomalin), 98cl (Hans Reinhard), 78bl (Carl Roessler), 81t (Ron and Valerie Taylor). **Bob and Cathy Cranston** 87cr, 106cr (Bob Cranston). **Environmental Images** 123cr (Toby Adamson), 123c (Irene R. Lengui). **Al Giddings Images, Inc.** 101tc (Al Giddings). **Edward S. Hodgson** 94c. **Innerspace Visions** 94tl (Mark Conlin), 99br, 112tr (Bob Cranston), 115cr (Steve Drogin), 73tr (Richard Ellis), 100cl (David Fleetham), 86tr (David Hall), 81b (Howard Hall), 108cl (Richard Herrmann), 82tr (Rudie Kuiter), 72c, 73cr, 83tr, 96bc, 99tr, 103cr, 105br, 124tr (Doug Perrine), 120tr (Todd Pusser), 80bcr (Bruce Rasner), 119c (David Shen), 103tl (Marty Snyderman), 12bl (Walt Stearns), 104tr (Mark Strickland), 96cl, 102tr (James D. Watt), 77c (David Wrobel). **Michelle Jeffries/Naval Ocean Systems** 95cr. **Leighton Taylor** 80bl. **Marine Mammal Images** 85c (Tershy and Strong). **James Marks** 91cr, 104bl. **Monterey Bay Aquarium** 119bc. **Connie Lyn Morgan** 106bl. **Skip Naftel/ Ocean Surveys** 84bc. **National Geographic Society Image Collection** 113tl (Nick Caloyianis). **Ocean Earth Images** 94tc (David Hempenstall). **Pacific Stock** 79br (Darodents). **The Photo Library, Sydney** 116tr (Tony Stone Images/Aldo Brando). **Photo Resource, Hawaii** 125br (Christina Beauchamp). **Dr Andreas Rechnitzer** 120bl. **Jeff Rotman** 75tr, 94tr. **Science Photo Library** 92cl (Eye of Science), 122cl (Simon Fraser). **Tom Stack and Associates** 75br (Tom and Therisa Stack), 89bc (Patrice Ceisel). **Still Pictures** 121tc (Jeff Rotman). **The Sydney Aquarium, Darling Harbour** 117br. **Twilight Zone Photographics** 109cr (Mark Spencer). **Waterhouse** 78tr (Stephen Frink), 83cr (Chris Newbert), 124cl (Marty Snyderman). **R. Woodward** 109br. www.norbertwu.com 76tr (1999/James Watt/Mo Yung Productions), 93tr (1999/Norbert Wu).

ILLUSTRATION CREDITS Martin Camm 71tr, 80/81c, 80tl, 80tc,81tr, 81cr, 81bl, 104/105b, 104cl, 104cr, 104t, 105c, 126tr, 127tl, 127br. **Marjorie Crosby-Fairall** 68cr, 70tr, 74/75c, 74bl, 75b, 81br, 90br, 91tc, 91bc, 91br, 98/99c, 98/99b, 98tl, 108/109c, 108b, 108t, 109b, 127bc. **Marc Dando/Wildlife Art Ltd** 68tr, 82/83c, 82t, 82bl, 83bl, 83br, 86/87c, 86b, 86t, 87b, 102/103c, 102t, 103c, 103cr. **Ray Grinaway** 70cr, 71c, 76/77c, 76t, 76b, 77bl, 77tr, 77br, 85tr, 111cl, 111br, 122/123c, 122t, 123r, 124/125c, 124b, 124t, 125b, 127tc. **Gino Hasler** 90tr, 90cr, 90ecr, 92/93c, 92t, 92bl, 93b, 94/95c, 94cr, 94b, 95bl, 95br, 95cl, 96/97c, 96t, 97br, 97bl. **Ian Jackson/Wildlife Art Ltd.** 68bc, 78/79c, 78t, 79cr, 91tr, 100/101c, 100t, 101r, 110tr, 111tr, 112/113c, 112l, 112t, 113r, 120/121c, 120t, 120b, 121r, 127bl. **Roger Swainston** 68etr, 70etr, 72/73c, 72t, 72b, 73bl, 73br, 84/85c, 84tl, 85r, 91bl, 106bl, 106t, 106br, 107c, 107r, 110br, 111tl, 114/115c, 114/115b, 114t, 116/117c, 116/117b, 116t, 118/119c, 118bl, 118t, 118br, 119r, 126tc, 126bl, 126br, 127tr. **Chris Turnbull/Wildlife Art Ltd** 70br, 71br, 88/25c, 88bc, 88cl, 88bl, 88t, 25tr, 89tc, 89br, 89cr, 126tl.

Whales, Dolphins, and Porpoises

The publishers would like to thank the following people for their assistance in the preparation of this book: Peter Gill, Michael Noad, Julian Pepperrell, Professor Pat Quilty, Dr. Graham Ross, Tangalooma Dolphin Resort.
Our special thanks to the following children and adults who feature in the photographs: Charlotte Barge, Alex Hall, Cassandra Hall, Eloise Hall, Alfred Hall, Jane Liane Hall, Heide-Jo Kelly, Emily Knight, Gregory Knight, Liam Low, Nerys Low, Elizabeth Lum, Malcolm McLean, Marie McLean, Abbey Piaud, Christopher Piaud, Jules Smith-Ferguson, Pasang Tenzing.

PICTURE CREDITS (t=top, b=bottom, l=left, r=right, c=center, f=flap, F=Front, C=Cover, B=Back)
AAP Images 58br. **ABRS** 145tl (courtesy Media 24/Evening Post/Graham Ross). **Ad-Libitum** 131b, 133br, 136br, 138c, 139c, 140bl, 147c, 150bl, 151tl, 156bl, 159cr, 166t, 171tl, 175b, 181b, 186c (Mihal Kaniewski). **APL** 151c, 156br, 160tr, 162br, 163c, 176tr, 176bl, 178tr, 178cr, 178cl, 184bl, 186tr (Corbis); 156tr, 165bc (Minden/Philip Nicklin); 154bl, 161bl, 173bc. **Ardea London** 181t (Francois Gohier); 142tr. **Auscape** 184cl (Mark Carwadine), 144tr (Jeff Foott) 187tl (Colin Monteath), 149c (Stefano Niccolini), 158c (Mike Osmond), 141c (Doug Perrine), 154tr (Mark Spencer). **Brandon D. Cole** 146cl, 177b. **Bruce Coleman** 134tr. **FLPA** 146tr (Scott Sinclair/Mammal Fund Earthviews), 173bl (Marineland). **Focus New Zealand** 183c (Ingrid Visser). **Steven French** 182br. **Getty Images** 143b, 164tr, 184tr, 186cl. **Peter Gill** 135b. **Hedgehog House** 148t, 160bl (Dennis Burman), 162bl (Peter Gill), 172tr (Colin Monteath). **Innerspace Visions** 170tr (Doug Perrine). **International Dolphin Watch** 142bl, 166l (Dr. Horace Dobbs). **Marine Mammal Images** 162tr (Michael Nolan). **McCulloch/Mazzoil NMFS GA#32 30-May-00** 54l. **Newsphotos** 182cl. **Mike Noad** 164bl. **M. Osmond** 169t. photolibrary.com 140tr. **Rachel Smolker** 171cl. **Spectrogram Program by Richard Horne** 165bcr, 165br, 165tcr, 165tr (Original recording by Cornell Laboratory of Ornithology). **Tom Stack & Associates** 134cl (Randy Morse). **Tasmanian Parks & Wildlife** 178b (Rene Davidson Collection) **University of Sao Paulo** 150tr (Marcos César de Oliveira Santos, Project Atlantis). **Wildslide** 138t (S. Burnell).

ILLUSTRATION CREDITS
Anne Bowman 133bcr, 148bl, 148cr, 148t, 149bc, 149r, 152br, 160t, 161r, 175tr, 180t, 181b, 181r. **Christer Eriksson** 160/161c. **David Kirshner** 132tc, 134/135, 152tc, 153bcr, 153tcr, 153tr, 154/155, 162/163, 164/165, 168/169, 189bl. **Rob Mancini** 130tr, 131br, 132/133c, 133cl, 138/139, 146/147c, 147r, 152tr, 156/157, 184/185, 188tl, 189tl. **Chris Stead** 180/181c, 186t, 186/187c. **Kevin Stead** 130bcr, 150/151, 152/153c, 158/159, 166/167, 175cr, 188br. **Glen Vause** 174br, 178/179, 189tc. **Laurie Whiddon** 146t, 146bl, 148/149c, 187r. **Wildlife Art Ltd** 130br, 130tcr, 132br, 132cr, 133tc, 133bcr, 136/137, 140/141, 142/143, 144/145, 153bl, 153br, 170/171, 172/173, 174tr, 175cl, 176/177, 182/183, 188bl, 188/189bc, 188tr, 189br, 189tr.

Don't miss these other Pathfinders science collections:

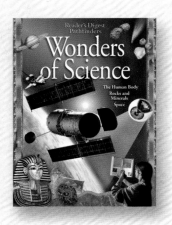

Wonders of Science

Did you know that billions of one-celled creatures live on your skin? That the planet you are standing on is actually a giant ball of rock? Or that astronauts grow slightly taller in space? You'll discover fascinating facts like these every time you open the this collection of three complete Reader's Digest Pathfinders— *The Human Body*, *Rocks and Minerals*, and *Space*.

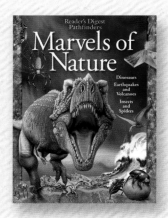

Marvels of Nature

Did you know that some dinosaurs had feathers? That a single volcanic eruption can change the weather around the world? Or that most spiders are really good guys—they eat so many insects that they are nature's pest-control experts? Facts like these are at your fingertips every time you open this collection of three complete Reader's Digest Pathfinders— *Dinosaurs*, *Earthquakes and Volcanoes*, and *Insects and Spiders*.

Pathfinders COLLECTION

Wonders of Science

Creatures of the Air and Sea

Marvels of Nature